Making and Breaking Governments offers a theoretical argument about how parliamentary democracy works. The heart of a parliamentary regime is the process by which the elected representatives choose a government, consisting of a cabinet and ministers, to serve as the executive arm of the regime. Strategic interaction among parliamentary parties creates new governments and either maintains them in office or, after a resignation or vote of no confidence, replaces them with some alternative government. The authors formulate a theoretical model of this strategic interaction, derive consequences, formulate empirical hypotheses on the basis of these, and test the hypotheses with data drawn from the postwar European experience with parliamentary democracy.

D1274917

MAKING AND BREAKING GOVERNMENTS

POLITICAL ECONOMY OF INSTITUTIONS AND DECISIONS

Editors
James E. Alt, *Harvard University*
Douglass C. North, *Washington University of St. Louis*

Other books in the series

MAKING AND BREAKING GOVERNMENTS

CABINETS AND LEGISLATURES IN PARLIAMENTARY DEMOCRACIES

MICHAEL LAVER
University of Dublin

KENNETH A. SHEPSLE
Harvard University

CAMBRIDGE
UNIVERSITY PRESS

Published by the Press Syndicate of the University of Cambridge
The Pitt Building, Trumpington Street, Cambridge CB2 1RP
40 West 20th Street, New York, NY 10011-4211, USA
10 Stamford Road, Oakleigh, Melbourne 3166, Australia

First published 1996

Printed in the United States of America

Library of Congress Cataloging-in-Publication Data
Laver, Michael, 1949–
Making and breaking governments : cabinets and legislatures in
parliamentary democracies / Michael Laver, Kenneth A. Shepsle.
    p.   cm. – (Political economy of institutions and decisions)
Includes bibliographical references and index.
ISBN 0-521-43245-6. – ISBN 0-521-43836-5 (pbk.)
1. Cabinet system.   2. Cabinet officers.   3. Representative
government and representation.   4. Comparative government.
I. Shepsle, Kenneth A.   II. Title.   III. Series.
JF331.L39   1996
821.8 – dc20   95-8757
                                                              CIP

A catalog record for this book is available from the British Library.

ISBN 0-521-43245-6 Hardback
ISBN 0-521-43836-5 Paperback

Contents

Series editors' preface

The Cambridge series on the Political Economy of Institutions and Decisions is built around attempts to answer two central questions: How do institutions evolve in response to individual incentives, strategies, and choices, and how do institutions affect the performance of political and economic systems? The scope of the series is comparative and historical rather than international or specifically American, and the focus is positive rather than normative.

Laver and Shepsle's theoretically innovative book pushes the study of government formation a big step forward. Rather than concentrating on the equilibrium collective policy that emerges from the balance and distribution of party strengths in the parliament, they treat governments as collections of ministers with individual jurisdictions and policy as a bundle of individual party-preferred policies, depending on which party receives which portfolio. Jurisdiction is the key concept, in their view. It makes a party's promises credible to its electors, for it can carry them out (only) if it receives the relevant ministry. At the same time portfolio allocation monitors party behavior, for the party receiving a portfolio has no excuse for not carrying out its preferred policy.

Their portfolio-based model of government formation is based on constitutional features carefully documented in a massive 14-country study, published in the companion volume *Cabinet Ministers and Parliamentary Government*. The model bases its predictions on a sequence of proposals from an historically determined status quo. Bargaining takes place among rationally foresighted policy-motivated parties, each with an explicit veto over every cabinet in which it could participate, in a lattice of feasible governments. Laver and Shepsle's predicted importance for "strong" parties opens up significant possibilities for comparative empirical evaluations of theirs and other contending models.

Moreover, in their model, institutions limit the number of enforceable policy outcomes, providing the possibility of equilibrium results for the government formation game where cycling would otherwise be inherent. Indeed, many other features of their model, including indivisible policies, explicit sequences, and the absence of exogenous enforcement, combined with rationally foresighted actors, also mark the work as a significant advance in the creation of theories about institutions as political solutions in situations involving politically costly transactions.

Acknowledgments

This project began in 1988 at Harvard University, where one of us (Shepsle) was a member of the faculty of the Department of Government and the other (Laver) was a visitor for the 1988–1989 academic year (on leave from University College, Galway). We taught together, played squash together, and even, from time to time, discussed research ideas together. We were especially fascinated by the fact that coalition theory – one of Laver's specialties – had lost its head of steam in American modeling circles, whereas the formal study of institutions – one of Shepsle's fields of concentration – had never really acquired a head of steam on the other side of the Atlantic. We believed that this confluence of possibilities, namely, the application of American-style institutional models to European-style coalition and governance arrangements, constituted a major opportunity, one that we investigated for the rest of that academic year. During this very fertile period, we wrote two articles (Laver and Shepsle, 1990a, 1990b) and managed to persuade the National Science Foundation to support further work (SES-8914294). At the very outset, then, we incurred a debt to University College, Galway, Harvard University, and the U.S. National Science Foundation for research leaves and financial support for which we are forever grateful.

Very early in the life of the project that culminates in this volume, we also had the good fortune to interact with three formal theorists who shared many of our interests. David Austen-Smith and Jeffrey Banks of the University of Rochester and Norman Schofield of Washington University, St. Louis, have been close friends, constructive critics, and generally have taken the time to steer us right when we've gone wrong (or at least to tell us in no uncertain terms that we had gone wrong!). Numerous others have, along the way, been sources of insight and encouragement, and we cannot name them all. But we would be remiss if we didn't acknowledge and thank Kaare Strom of the University of California, San Diego, who proved a wise sounding board, given his general sympathy for formal theory approaches and his considerable knowledge of the substance of parliamentary politics; Gary King of Harvard University for very useful advice on methodological issues; Paul Doyle of University College, Galway, for outstanding programming assistance; and Alison Alter of Harvard University for data collection and statistical assistance. We also wish to thank those who read and commented on earlier drafts of this volume. In addition to those already mentioned, these include John Aldrich, Patrick Dunleavy, Avner Greif, Paul Mitchell, Walter Petersen, Itai Sened, Steve Solnick, Paul Warwick, and Barry Weingast.

Many universities and organizations provided forums for us to develop and test out our ideas. These include the American Political Science Association (1990 meetings in San Francisco), the European Consortium for Political Research (1991 meetings in Bochum, Germany, and 1992 meetings in Limerick, Ireland), the European Public Choice Society (1993 meetings in Portrush, Northern Ireland), the European Science Foundation (1992 conference in Sesimbra, Portugal), the Office of Research and Development of the Central Intelligence Agency (which also provided support for our computer model), and political science or economics or political economics departments and programs at Duke University, the University of North Carolina, the University of Rochester, Columbia University, Princeton University, Australia National University, George Mason University, Carnegie-Mellon University, Boston University, the University of California, Berkeley, the University of California, San Diego, Stanford University, London School of Economics, University College, Dublin, 1994 Polybios Program at the Netherlands Institute of Advanced Study, Max Planck Institute, Cologne, the University of Iowa, Washington University, St. Louis, Texas A & M University, and the University of Illinois. We thank those who invited us and took our ideas seriously at all these fine institutions. We wish to single out the Rockefeller Foundation's Villa Serbelloni in Bellagio, Italy, for providing us with elegant surroundings and stimulating colleagues for a five-week period in the summer of 1992, during which time nearly all of the work for this volume was completed in its initial form; and Duke University, which provided a congenial and welcoming base for Laver in the fall of 1994 as we put the finishing touches to the manuscript. And, of course, our home universities – Harvard University, University College, Galway, and Trinity College, Dublin – provided us with research support and sabbatical leaves, and even when they expected us to work for them, they still tolerated our occasional absences to hop across the Atlantic.

Cambridge University Press has made our lives easy, not only by publishing this volume but also by publishing an earlier companion volume (Laver and Shepsle, 1994). Alex Holzman, political science editor at Cambridge, made sure that all the trains ran on time throughout the

Acknowledgments

production process. And series editors, James Alt and Douglass North, provided advice and counsel. Thanks to them all.

Finally, we thank one another and our families. Aside from the one year that we were together in Cambridge, Massachusetts, this project has been sustained mostly by e-mail, fax machine, and transatlantic travel and telephone. Blocks of time have been spent away from kith and kin and we appreciate their support, encouragement, and generosity in tolerating these absences. Those same blocks of time were spent in the household of a coauthor, so each would like to thank the other's family for fine hospitality. Finally, there is the tip of the hat from one coauthor to the other. The collaboration has also been a friendship.

Michael Laver
Dalkey, Ireland

Kenneth A. Shepsle
Wellesley, Massachusetts

PART I

The context

1

Theory, institutions, and government formation

GOVERNMENT FORMATION AND PARLIAMENTARY DEMOCRACY

This book is about the making and breaking of governments in parliamentary democracies. The essence of parliamentary democracy is the accountability of the government (or cabinet or executive or administration) to the legislature. In most working parliamentary democracies, this relationship is enshrined in a constitutional provision that the government must retain the support of a majority of legislators, tested in a legislative motion of confidence (or no confidence) in the executive. A government that loses such a vote is defeated and obliged to resign.[1] Although formal mechanisms for installing new governments differ considerably between countries, a government, however installed, is immediately exposed in the legislature to a potential vote of no confidence. It is the ability of the executive to win this vote and thus maintain the confidence of the legislature that is the universal acid test of government viability in a parliamentary democracy.

Even though the executive is responsible in this sense to the legislature, the cabinet and its ministers nevertheless retain wide-ranging power to govern the country as long as they remain in office. This power comprises both effective political control over the administrative departments of state and a firm grip on the day-to-day activities of the legislature. Apart from the opposition's ability to seek dismissal of an administration by proposing a motion of no confidence, it is difficult in most parliamentary democracies for anyone outside the executive to have a significant impact on the process of legislation. Executive control of the entire legislative

---

[1]In practice, an executive may well resign in anticipation of losing a motion of no confidence, so that we may only rarely actually see the constitutional procedure pushed to its ultimate conclusion. This does not, of course, take away from the fundamental importance of the confidence vote as one of the key institutional foundations of parliamentary democracy.

3

process, from the drafting of bills to the determination of the order of business, combined with the almost universal provision that the executive may recommend the dissolution of the legislature and the holding of new elections,[2] gives any incumbent administration considerable power over the legislature.[3]

The impact of government formation extends far beyond legislative–executive relations, however. Government formation is at the very heart of representative politics, as well as of a large part of economic and social life, in Western parliamentary democracies. If representative politics is what provides the vital connections between the preferences of ordinary individuals and the ambitions of politicians, between elections and party competition, and between legislative politics, policy making, and the governance of the country, then the formation of a government is the focal point at which all of these things come together in a parliamentary democracy. Elections have meaning for voters because they provide a choice between different packages of possible political outcomes, offered by different political parties. Parties themselves are important because they are key actors that take part in the government formation process. This means that party competition in parliamentary democracies is typically couched in terms of what different parties would and would not do if they were in government and thereby had a chance to put their ideas into practice.

After the election has been held in most parliamentary democracies, it is often the case that no party will have won an overall majority. Subsequent legislative politics is much more about building and maintaining a government than it is about legislating. Even when legislation is important, the legislative agenda in most parliamentary democracies is very much in the hands of the government.

Government formation also impinges fundamentally upon economic life. Indeed the claim that a change of government implies at least a potential change of public policy is well illustrated by the market turbulence often caused by uncertainties about the stability of a government or the outcome of an election. Good examples of this can be found in the general instability of European currency markets in the run-up to the French legislative election of 1993, given uncertainties about the impact of a change of government on official policy toward the French franc, and

[2]An important counterexample is Norway, in which the government cannot interfere with a fixed three-yearly timetable of legislative elections.
[3]Obviously, the extent to which the executive controls the business of the legislature varies from country to country with, for example, variations in the role and power of legislative committees. Nonetheless, in nearly all parliamentary democracies, the power of the executive over the legislature is very considerable. This point is made by nearly every country specialist describing the interactions between legislature and executive in the parliamentary democracies covered in Laver and Shepsle (1994).

the intense speculation against the peseta prior to the Spanish election of the same year. This turbulence arises precisely because major shifts in the partisan composition of the government can imply major changes in the rules of the economic game. And uncertainties about these rules of the game can feed back in a very volatile way onto expectations about key economic parameters, whether these relate to the money supply, the budget deficit, exchange and interest rates, or whatever.

OUR BASIC PREMISES

In what follows, therefore, we set out to explore as systematically as possible the complicated business of building and maintaining a government in a parliamentary democracy. We base our argument upon a number of premises and it is as well to be quite clear about the essential thrust of these from the very start, though we will elaborate on them in the following chapter.

The role of models

Our most fundamental premise is that it is possible to make general statements about the politics of building and maintaining a government, and that such general statements can give us valuable insights into the political processes involved. Obviously, even a casual look at parliamentary democracies around the world reveals huge diversity. Every country has a different constitution and a different historical, geographical, and cultural setting. Once we look at the formation of any individual government, the sheer welter of activity by large numbers of politicians, officials, lobbyists, interest groups, voters, and commentators in the making, running, and breaking of governments is so rich and complex as to make every particular government appear to be an utterly distinctive political entity, quite unlike any other. The purpose of our enterprise, however, is to cut through all of this variation in an attempt to see whether, at the core of it all, there are interesting and important features of government formation that are common to all parliamentary democracies.

We do this by developing a generic model of government formation in parliamentary democracies. Our model consists of a set of general statements about the process of government formation, statements that we take to be at least somewhat plausible, and a set of logical linkages between these. Our hope and intention is that systematic use of this model allows us to develop some interesting and nonobvious insights into the business of building and maintaining a government. Obviously, the model we develop can be no substitute for the careful description of any particular case. But at the same time there are on the face of things strong

5

similarities in the government formation process in parliamentary democracies at different places and times, and we do believe that our model sheds light on these. It can do this in two different ways.

First, by allowing us at least logically to hold a wide range of institutional and historical variations constant, while systematically manipulating key variables, the model may be used as a discovery tool. This allows us to enhance our understanding by attempting to answer "what if?" questions about the politics of a particular situation. What if no party wins an overall majority after the next British election? What if, after dominating every Italian government in the postwar era, the Christian Democrats suffer electoral catastrophe, as they did in March 1994? What if, after over 40 years as a major player in German governments, the Free Democrats were to fall below the 5 percent electoral threshold?

Country specialists are typically called on to answer such questions and they rarely shrink from doing so, drawing upon their detailed knowledge of a particular situation. To the extent that they can justify statements about what is likely to happen in circumstances that have not yet arisen, whether to others or merely to themselves, they must have in their minds some private model of parliamentary politics, however vague and implicit. Effectively they are saying "if we could hold these things constant and change that thing in such a way, then the outcome is likely to be this." Such statements, of course, have exactly the same form as those generated by more explicit models. We strongly believe that being more precise and explicit about models of politics can permit a scholar both to check his or her intuitions more systematically and to tease out further analysis of the problem at hand – possibly counterintuitive but nonetheless useful and even, sometimes, accurate. Explicit models of politics, therefore, are not enemies of intuition. On the contrary, they are engines of intuition.

The second important intellectual role of models of politics is as an essential prerequisite for systematic and informative empirical research. It is of course possible to collect facts about a particular situation in the belief that the situation itself is self-evidently important, that the facts speak for themselves, and that more facts are always better than fewer. Many of those who study politics unfortunately adopt this approach, either explicitly or implicitly. We believe, however, that this approach is inefficient at best and downright misleading more often than not. The essential role of empirical research, as with pure theory, is to enhance our understanding of the world. Empirical research in the social sciences does this by revealing the presence or absence of systematic patterns in actual human behavior. But there is of course a more or less infinite number of behaviors that we could study, and patterns in these that we could look for. Only a theoretical model of the situation under analysis can tell us which activities to study and what patterns to look out for.

We can put some flesh on the bones of this point by taking a political example closely related to our own work, but not a part of it. All parliamentary democracies have a constitutionally mandated maximum period between elections. In many countries, however, the government may call an election before this period has expired. In these countries, elections are in fact almost always called before the obligatory date. Since we never observe it to be a binding constraint in practice, does this mean that we could abolish the constitutionally mandated maximum period between elections with no impact on the actual frequency of elections? Most people would intuitively feel that to change the constitution in this way would make a *big* difference to electoral politics. Yet, in the absence of any democratic country that has in practice abolished the constitutional requirement that elections be held every so many years, "pure" empirical research on the calling of elections, with no model to structure it, would reveal that this constitutional provision was virtually never used. It takes a model to give shape to our intuitions. In this case it might be a model dealing with the way in which the maximum interelectoral period acts as a constraint on politicians, a constraint that they anticipate by calling early elections on dates that they expect to be more favorable to them than the ultimate constitutional deadline.[4] Without such a model, empirical research on the calling of elections is likely to be misleading.

Models are thus the essential intellectual equipment with which we both give structure to our intuition and organize our empirical understanding of the world. Of course, even the dogs in the street know that a model of a cat's brain is no substitute for the cat's brain itself. Our simple models of parliamentary democracy are mere shadows of any particular instance of the real thing. Indeed we quite consciously seek to abstract away what Milton Friedman (1953) referred to as the "attendant circumstances" of any case. To be sure one person's mere details are the heart of the matter for somebody else. This is another way of saying that what we include in a model, and what we exclude from it, are matters of choice that we must be prepared to defend.

But the reason we abstract from certain details *by design* is to allow us to formulate generalizations about a world in which we cannot conduct carefully controlled experiments. We want to find out whether things are true not only about one particular cat's brain but about the brains of other cats. In the same way we want to find out whether things tend to be true about parliamentary democracies as a whole, even if every parliamen-

---

[4]Such a model, used to make empirical estimates of the "censoring" effect on government durations of constitutionally mandated maximum interelectoral periods, has been developed by King, Alt, Burns, and Laver (1990).

tary democracy differs from every other in myriad ways. Models are not only discovery tools for use in a single country, but are also tools that can help us to highlight, and to learn from, patterns underlying politics in a range of different countries.

Rationality and the role of policy in politics

Every model of politics is based on some underlying assumption about what motivates the various actors and characterizes their decision making. The model we elaborate in this book is based on the assumption that politicians are at least implicitly rational decision makers. By this we mean that the decisions they make are in some sense (to be elaborated in the following chapter) expected to further their essential aims and aspirations. We do not assume that politicians are human calculating engines. We do assume, however, that most politicians do not behave at random but rather act as if they have some agenda, and that the political decisions they make serve to further this agenda.

For the purposes of this book we go one stage further and conceive of the agenda of individual politicians in terms of the public policies that they attempt to pursue. Thus a basic premise of this book is that policy is important for politics in general and for government formation in particular. This may seem a somewhat controversial idea, given at least one popular image of politicians as power-hungry egomaniacs concerned with nothing beyond their own personal well-being, and prepared to say and do almost anything in order to advance this. Fortunately, we do not actually need to challenge this rather depressing view of politicians when we claim that policy is important. Even if politicians *are* power-hungry egomaniacs who are not at all intrinsically interested in policy, policy seeking may nonetheless serve as their driving force. So long as policy is important for voters, activists, and other electorally relevant groups, politicians will be impelled by the incentives of party competition, operating outside the government formation process, to heed the policy priorities of voters.[5]

Of course, policy is important if politicians actually *do* care about the effects of implementing different policies but, even if they care not a whit for the substance of policy, we assume that they do care about the consequences of failing to implement their policy promises. For this reason, politicians engaged in government formation can be characterized in terms of the policy promises with which they are associated, and can be

[5]This may be, for example, because politicians compete at elections by making policy promises to voters and anticipate damage to their reelection chances if they are seen not to make an effort to implement these promises if given the chance to do so after the election.

assumed to be concerned, as agents of electoral interests, about what any prospective government will do once it has taken office. This premise, of policy-driven politics and commonly known partisan policy positions, which we elaborate in the following chapter, is a cornerstone of our analysis.

GOVERNMENT FORMATION: THE STORY SO FAR

A review of what we might think of as traditional theories of government formation can be found in Laver and Schofield (1990). Rather surprisingly, and despite the fact that this is of the essence of parliamentary democracy, political scientists have tended not to take account of the intimate interaction between legislature and executive when modeling the life and death of governments. Government formation and maintenance are typically treated as problems of legislative coalition building and many coalition theories implicitly assume that parliamentary democracies are governed directly by their legislatures. Many recent accounts of government formation, therefore, are in effect spatial models of legislative voting.

Spatial conceptualizations of politics have a long history, extending back at least as far as the seating arrangements of the French Constituent Assembly after the Revolution of 1789, in which radicals sat themselves to the left of the chair and conservatives to the right. In contemporary scholarship, the patron saints of spatial analysis are Harold Hotelling (1929), Duncan Black (1958), and Anthony Downs (1957). In their analyses, politics is conducted in terms of a set of issues that can adequately be described in terms of a single dimension of policy – this is the same left–right dimension as structured politics in postrevolutionary France. The most important result from this body of work is Black's Median Voter Theorem. Making the assumption that voters can be modeled solely in terms of their most preferred policy (ideal point) on a single dimension of policy, Black showed that the ideal point of the median voter has a vitally important property that has informed a huge body of subsequent work. *It is the only point that is preferred by some majority of voters to any other point on the policy dimension.*[6]

This result underlies the very important *centripetal* political tendencies that characterize the Hotelling-Downs-Black approach. If their approach

[6]Formally, Black's Theorem is stated for the circumstance in which preferences are "single-peaked" and the number of voters is odd. "Single peakedness" describes the shape of each voter's preference curve on the left–right dimension: The preference curve is at a maximum just over the voter's ideal point and declines from this peak for points farther away from the voter's ideal in either direction. The theorem may easily be extended to even numbers of voters. In this case, there are two median voters and the theorem says that any point in the closed interval bracketed by the ideal points of these voters has the property that no other point is preferred to it by a majority.

is applied to elections between two competing parties, each intent upon winning majority voter support, then the implication is that each party will gravitate toward the ideal policy position of the median voter. If on the other hand their approach is applied to legislative policy making, in which choices are typically made between some substantive motion and amendments to this, then the implication is that the winning version of the motion will represent the policy position most preferred by the median legislator. In either event, the final outcome of the political process is at the median of the distribution of ideal points. And this central outcome is an equilibrium in the sense that, once arrived at, there will be no movement away from it.

There are good theoretical and empirical reasons to believe that politics is not always one-dimensional, however. The natural generalization of the unidimensional approach, with its well-behaved equilibrium at the center of the distribution of policy preferences, is a multidimensional spatial model. In this, policy is characterized by as many dimensions as are necessary to capture the different world views of key political actors. Each voter's ideal political outcome may be thought of as resulting from the implementation of a bundle of ideal policies, one for each salient dimension. The famous "chaos" theorems of McKelvey (1976) and Schofield (1978) imply that, when two or more dimensions of policy are important, it is nearly certain that majority preferences between policy proposals will cycle indefinitely, with no proposal defeating all others. Any proposed bundle of policy positions will be majority-defeated by another, which in turn will be majority-defeated by another, with this process continuing until it cycles back to the original proposal and begins all over again. This suggests either that policy is in perpetual flux, with every policy proposal displaced by something else, or that the music will stop at some point and the actual proposal implemented will be selected arbitrarily from those in the cycle. Except under the most highly unusual circumstances, there is no equilibrium.

It is worth noting that, in those special circumstances in which there is an equilibrium in multidimensional majority voting games, this equilibrium is still at the center of things, in the sense that it is at the multidimensional median policy position.[7] Kadane (1972) has shown that, *when policies are selected by majority rule in a multidimensional policy space, if an equilibrium exists (and it may not) it must be the multidimensional median.*[8]

---

[7] The multidimensional median position is the position such that the median voter on each dimension gets his or her ideal policy *on that dimension.*

[8] Kadane's theorem applies when voters have preferences that are single-peaked by dimension and separable by dimension. By "single-peaked by dimension" we mean that on any specific dimension (say the jth), holding preferences on the other $n-1$

This result, of which we shall make use in Chapter 4, implies qualified centripetality. If there is a multidimensional equilibrium, then it will be central in precisely the same way that Black's Theorem yields a central result for the unidimensional case. The stark contrast between the two cases, however, rests on the issue of existence: An equilibrium always exists in the unidimensional case and very rarely does in its multidimensional counterpart.

A central feature of these results, however, is that they apply to electoral or legislative decision making on particular policy proposals and that the policies agreed upon are assumed to be implemented automatically as soon as they pass a majority vote. *The results have nothing at all to say about decision making in the political executive, or indeed about any other aspect of the actual implementation of real policy decisions.* This means that they do not apply directly to analyses of the making and breaking of political executives in parliamentary democracies.

Even the best recent work at the cutting edge of coalition theory continues to illustrate this lack of concern both for policy implementation and for the role of the executive. Very good examples are provided by Schofield (1993), working within the traditions of cooperative game theory, and Baron (1991), who proposes a noncooperative theory of government formation.[9]

dimensions fixed, the ith voter's most preferred position on this dimension is y_j^i and her preferences decline as points are considered further away from this location along the jth dimension. By "separable by dimension" we mean that i's ideal point and preferences on the jth dimension do not vary as components on the other $n-1$ dimensions are changed. In this sense dimensions may be treated as "independent" of one another. We may give Kadane's result some precision in a form that will prove useful to us in subsequent analysis. Suppose there is an n-dimensional space of policies ($n \geq 2$), and a set $V = \{1, 2, \ldots, v\}$ of voters. Let the ith voter's ideal be written $y^i = (y_1^i, y_2^i, \ldots, y_n^i)$, where, generally, y_j^i is the ith voter's ideal policy on the jth dimension. Define the *multidimensional median* as the point $m = (m_1, m_2, \ldots, m_n)$, where m_j is the median on the jth policy dimension ($m_j = \text{median}_{i \in V} y_j^i$). For convenience, we assume that the number of voters is odd so that there is a unique median on each dimension. Kadane's Theorem states that either m is an equilibrium or there is no equilibrium. Kadane's proof uses an "improvement algorithm" showing that any point not at the multidimensional median position will be beaten in a majority vote by a point that is identical in every other respect, except that it is at the median position on one additional dimension. Only for m can there be no such point (though m itself can be beaten by a point differing from it on two or more dimensions).

[9]Cooperative game theory is different from game-theoretic accounts of cooperation (see, e.g. Axelrod, 1984; Taylor, 1976, 1987). Cooperative game theory is a theory of strategic interaction in which it is assumed that any deal that is consummated is enforceable. Although no details of the enforcement mechanism are part of this theory, implicit is some exogenous mechanism or third party (like a court) that enforces deals by punishing violators with a certainty and severity sufficient to discourage reneging. Theories of cooperation, in contrast, are more interested in how individuals may secure joint advantages, even in contexts in which there is no exogenous enforcement mechanism. In these circumstances, deals struck stay stuck because they are *self-*

The context

According to Baron (1991: 138), for example, governments are formed on the basis of a legislative vote of confidence and "[i]f the motion of confidence is successful, the policy program is implemented and remains in effect until the next mandated election." Policy, once settled by the legislature, is implemented automatically and effortlessly. This is despite the fact that, in his noncooperative model, "[p]arties are unable to commit to how they will act in the future" (1991: 139). Even Baron's definition of who is in the government makes no reference to the cabinet, but only to the legislature: "[t]he term *government* will be used to refer to the parties that do not vote against a motion of confidence on a policy proposal" (1991: 138, italics in original). Supporting parties who receive no cabinet seats at all are thus counted by Baron as government members, as he in effect models a regime of "governance by legislature."

For Schofield (1993:17), the forecast policy outcome of a coalition is a unique point chosen by coalition members as a compromise between their ideal points. Implementation of this policy position is not modeled, and Schofield is silent on precisely what it means, in strategic terms, to be "in" government. As a consequence, in both these models the policy outputs of governments are determined solely by the strategic situation in the legislature, unmediated by the cabinet, the bureaucracy, or any other executive institution.

When the executive is considered at all by conventional coalition theories, it is seen not as a decision-making body in its own right, but rather as a prize to be shared out by a winning legislative coalition – a set of perks of office, the most important of which are seats at the cabinet table (Browne and Feste, 1975; Browne and Franklin, 1973; Browne and Frendreis, 1980; Budge and Keman, 1990; Gamson, 1961). Thus these latter theorists also see parliamentary government as a *legislative* process, not as a continual strategic interaction between legislature and executive. Cabinet portfolios, once allocated, are simply consumed as benefits by the legislative parties that hold them.

The conventional coalition theorists' view of governance by legislature flies in the face of the undoubtedly firm control of legislatures by the government of the day, a generalization recently reviewed and supported in a series of country studies (Laver and Shepsle, 1994). As we shall see, conceiving of the structure of policy making and implementation in a more realistic manner provides an altogether richer and more suggestive

enforcing. The study of self-enforcing strategic interaction is associated with *noncooperative* game theory. This latter class of models is appropriate for circumstances in which deal-making violations may not be subsequently adjudicated (except by nailing the SOB next time around). In general a priori terms, it might well be thought that deals among the parties of a national government are not susceptible to "external" enforcement and therefore that noncooperative game theory is the most appropriate tool for modeling them.

12

account of government formation. *A legislature makes and breaks govern-ments, to be sure, but it does not, in our view, rule the country.*

THE INSTITUTIONS OF GOVERNMENT DECISION MAKING (CABINETS, DEPARTMENTS, AND MINISTERS)

In response to what we see as a major opportunity for theoretical innova-tion in the analysis of government formation, we present an alternative approach in this book. This approach takes more explicit account of the institutional, and more specifically the departmental, structure within which policy decisions are made and implemented in the real world of parliamentary democracy.

Perhaps the most distinctive feature of our approach, therefore, is the assumption that most important policy decisions are taken by the execu-tive. Effective government decisions on a particular issue, furthermore, are assumed not to be selections of abstract positions in a continuous issue space, but rather to be choices between a very limited number of well-developed and implementable proposals for particular courses of action. Developing such proposals in the real world of public administra-tion is a major task requiring specialist skills. Taken together with the sheer volume of business that real governments must conduct, this im-plies that only the government department with jurisdiction over a par-ticular policy area is effectively equipped to develop feasible and imple-mentable policy proposals in that area and present these to the cabinet for decision. And this in turn means that the entire process of policy forma-tion on any given issue is very heavily influenced by whoever has political control over the relevant government department – the cabinet minister in charge of the department concerned.[10] In effect, the development of fully elaborated policy proposals that real governments can actually choose between is an activity strongly structured along departmental lines and heavily conditioned by the views of the political department head. Government departments and their political masters, in short, pos-sess considerable *agenda power* (Burch, 1993).

This specialization and division of labor in the development of real-world policy proposals implies that the most credible signal of government policy on a particular issue is the policy associated with the minister in charge of the department with jurisdiction over this issue. Thus a hard-line defense policy is signaled, for example, by a politician with a reputation as

---

[10]We shall, most of the time, only be concerned with the *party label* of an incumbent minister, on the hypothesis that, personal idiosyncrasies aside, politicians can be ex-pected to toe their party's line. In Chapter 12 we examine intraparty politics, at which time we entertain the possibility that different ministerial candidates from the same party may have different goals.

a hawk serving as minister for defense. A more conciliatory defense policy is signaled by replacing this defense minister with a politician, perhaps from a different party, who has a reputation as a dove.

As evidence of the plausibility of this general assumption, consider the analyses typically produced in quality newspapers when a new cabinet takes office. Much of this analysis concerns the implications for government policy of having particular individuals or parties, with particular reputations, in charge of particular government departments. Analysis by the Paris correspondent of the *Economist* (April 3, 1993, p. 29) on the appointment of a new French cabinet in early 1993 serves to illustrate this point:

Mr Balladur's new . . . government . . . is a model of fine-tuning and fairness. All of the main factions within the conservative coalition are represented. A leading anti-Maastricht campaigner, Charles Pasqua, returns to his old post at the Ministry of the Interior. But the tone of the government is strongly pro-European and pro-Maastricht, as is Mr. Balladur himself.

Alain Juppé, secretary-general of the RPR, who helped to persuade a hesitant Jacques Chirac, leader of the Gaullists, to campaign for a Yes vote in the Maastricht referendum, takes over as foreign minister. Alain Lamassoure, an ardent European, takes the European affairs portfolio. Edmond Alphandéry, another Maastricht supporter and passionate advocate of the "strong franc" policy (as is Mr. Balladur) becomes finance minister . . . . More worrying is the appointment of Senator Jean Puech, a farm lobbyist, to agriculture. This is a sensitive post, given the right's campaign promise to try to veto the GATT farm deal. Appointing a farm lobbyist bodes ill for world trade.

The new cabinet (from which the three main right-wing leaders, Mr. Chirac, Valéry Giscard d'Estaing and Raymond Barre, are all notably absent) won Mr. Mitterand's immediate approval. That was despite the appointment of François Léotard, former leader of the Parti Républicain . . . as defence minister. Mr. Mitterand is reported to have rejected Mr. Léotard's appointment to the same post in 1986. The president has promised "scrupulously to respect" the will of the people for a change of government policy.

Equivalent passages, in a wide range of sources, can be found after the appointment of almost any new cabinet in a parliamentary democracy. This reflects a strong tendency for those who need to be able to forecast government policy – and the businessmen and -women who read the *Economist* are good examples of these – to base their forecasts on the signals that are sent as a result of the allocation of cabinet portfolios between politicians with well-known positions of key issues.

Thus the logic of departmentalism in government decision making implies that the overall policy position associated with any given government is determined by the allocation of cabinet portfolios among government participants. For us, then, a *government* consists of an allocation of authority in particular policy jurisdictions to particular political parties (see note 10) with well-known policy reputations in these areas. Because there is only a handful of key policy jurisdictions and only a limited number of parties with ministerial-caliber politicians who can credibly be nominated to these, the number of different potential cabinets is also limited. Thus, government policy outputs are selected from a finite set of policy forecasts, each forecast being associated with a particular portfolio allocation. The finite nature of the set of credible potential governments means that the business of building and maintaining a government is explicable, as we shall see, in a more straightforward manner than the general spatial model suggests.

PLAN OF CAMPAIGN

The argument in this book is developed in four parts. In the remainder of this first part, we lay the foundations for a model of government formation in parliamentary democracies. We do this initially in Chapter 2, where we set out and defend our basic ideas and assumptions. In Chapter 3 we combine our ideas and assumptions into a generic model of government formation.

Part II is devoted to refining this model. In Chapter 4, we elaborate the model by using it to explore the notion of an equilibrium cabinet. One of the reasons why government formation need not be chaotic is that there is often the possibility of an equilibrium cabinet at the generalized median policy position. Another source of stability in government formation is that there may be a party in a distinctively powerful bargaining position able to dominate the progress of coalition bargaining, a theme we develop in Chapter 5.

In the third part of the analysis we use our model to structure an empirical exploration of government formation in the real world. In Chapter 6 we use the model to motivate two brief case studies of real government formation – Germany in 1987 and Ireland in 1992–1993. In Chapters 7–9 we conduct a more systematic empirical analysis, an analysis that we feel shows the value of our approach in a very convincing manner.

The fourth part of the book develops our model further, exploring a range of intriguing methodological and substantive problems associated with analyses of party competition and government formation. We beg the reader's indulgence until this point, for it is here that we entertain extensions of our model's domain and relaxations of its assumptions. In Chapter 10, we use the model to help us understand factors affecting the stability and instability of governments. We use simulations to examine the likelihood of particular cabinets being thrown into disequilibrium – a first step on the road to developing a systematic theoretical account of cabinet stability. In Chapter 11 we treat three conceptual issues that bear on our model in particular and party competition in general. These have to do with the structure of the issue space in which politics is conducted. First, we look at correlations between positions on different issue dimensions, and the ways in which higher correlations greatly enhance the prospects for and stability of equilibrium cabinets. Second, we look at what happens when preferences over public policy on one issue dimension are affected by public policy on a quite different dimension – when views about a country's foreign policy, for example, are affected by which economic policy it is pursuing.[11] Third, we look at what happens when, as is typically the case in the real world, government departments have jurisdiction over a bundle of different policy dimensions, and jurisdictions are in our sense *complex*.

In Chapter 12 are three extensions of our model to interesting substantive questions related to the making and breaking of governments. First, we look at intraparty politics, and the prospect that what we have up to this point considered as a unitary party is in fact a coalition of factions, each supporting a set of cabinet-rank politicians. Second, we look at minority cabinets, in which the cabinet comprises fewer parties than necessary to control a legislative majority, and surplus majority cabinets, from which at least one party could be expelled, while still leaving the cabinet controlling a majority. Although such cabinets appear as anomalies in many accounts of government formation, both types are not only quite common empirically, but can easily be accounted for within our general approach as well. Third, we look at administrative reform, and the prospect that alterations in the allocation of policy areas to government departments may be an integral part of what is on the table when a government is formed, rather than a rigid administrative structure that must be taken as given.

In the final chapter of the book, we review the main themes that have been highlighted by our analyses – most notably legislative–executive relations, departmentalism, and centripetal policy tendencies – and discuss the extent to which these can be reconciled with some of the received wisdom of political science. Throughout the volume we are rather catholic in our approach, combining the deductive tools of formal political theory with multivariate statistical analysis, case studies, and simulation techniques.

The single most important lesson to be learned from the discussion to follow concerns the institutional arrangements of parliamentary democ-

---

[11]Formally, what we do at this stage is to relax the assumption of separable preferences.

racy. In particular, the departmental organization of governmental decision making structures the environment in which governments are born, live, and die. The model that we develop takes this structure as its basic premise. On our account, when politicians consider the making and breaking of governments, they look ahead both to the most likely consequences of putting a particular cabinet in charge of running the country's affairs and to the most likely consequences of replacing that cabinet with some viable alternative. This leads to a theory of cabinet equilibrium. Majority-rule models that ignore the structure of government decision making often fail to identify equilibrium outcomes. Their conclusion stands in stark contrast to the real political world, where government formation appears to be more stable and is not characterized by the endless churning of alternative administrations that disequilibrium implies. A striking feature of our approach is that cabinet equilibriums are quite common and tend to be close to the center of the configuration of party policy positions.

The search for an account of equilibrium cabinets was our original motivation; its theoretical development and empirical evaluation are probably the main finished products of this volume. This search, however, proved unexpectedly fruitful. What became clear to us as we proceeded is that the making and breaking of governments is at the crux of much of what is important about parliamentary democracy. We believe the model throws light on a range of substantively important features of the political process, including government stability, minority and surplus majority government, intraparty politics, and administrative reform. We hope that even a reader initially skeptical about our general approach will agree that the model offers the opportunity to visit some interesting substantive destinations.

2

The social context of government formation

The political process that dominates our discussion in the rest of this book involves a set of politicians in a parliamentary democracy, each motivated to achieve some objective or another, competing and cooperating among themselves to form a government. The hopes and fears, aims and aspirations of each politician are fulfilled to a greater or lesser extent depending on the outcome of this process.

Before we can develop any systematic analysis of this crucial aspect of democratic politics, we must be explicit about our assumptions. In this chapter, therefore, we elaborate assumptions on a range of matters relevant to the making and breaking of governments in parliamentary democracies. These include the aims, aspirations, and rationality of key actors; the institutional process by which a government is formed; the manner in which actors forecast the likely consequences of having different governments in power; and collective decision making both between and within parties. We begin with perhaps the most fundamental assumptions of all, which have to do with the hopes and fears of politicians and the rational calculus that they use to make decisions.

THE MOTIVATIONS OF POLITICIANS

Those writing on the politics of government formation tend to assume one of two things about the fundamental motivations of politicians involved in political bargaining.[1] Some assume that politicians are concerned above all else to get into office – and that they will say and do whatever is necessary to achieve this. In their search for power, politicians may make policy promises either to each other or to the electorate but, on this interpretation, such policies are promoted for purely instrumental

[1]For a review of writings on the motivations of politicians engaged in government formation, see Laver and Schofield (1990: chap. 3).

18

reasons. If the chances of getting into power are enhanced by changing policies, then an "office-seeking" politician will see no cost in changing.

Nonetheless, to assume that a politician is an office seeker is not necessarily to imply that he or she will change policies just to suit the time of day. The need to maintain long-term credibility, both with fellow politicians and with voters, may well provide politicians with incentives to stick with a policy that in the short term has come to look like a liability. Thus even office-seeking politicians may promote distinctive policies, and the need to maintain subsequent credibility may ensure that these policies are quite stable. Indeed, once office-seeking politicians have promoted a particular policy, a strong need for credibility may even result in them behaving just as if they were sincerely trying to achieve the policy in question.

Perhaps the most influential exponent of the office-seeking assumption about the motivations of politicians has been Anthony Downs, whose position is summed up in his famous statement that "parties formulate policies in order to win elections, rather than win elections in order to formulate policies" (Downs, 1957: 28). Much of what Downs has subsequently become famous for is concerned with policy competition between parties. As his basic motivational assumption shows, however, the fundamental driving force behind such competition is the desire to get into office; policy advocacy for Downs is purely instrumental. Although Downs does have a brief discussion of multiparty politics, he was writing for the most part with a two-party system in mind. For him, "winning" an election automatically implies going into office and coalition building plays no part in government formation. He also assumed that parties behave as if they are unitary actors.

An alternative influential assumption about the fundamental motivation of key political actors is that they are intrinsically concerned above all else with public policy. De Swaan (1973: 88), for example, assumed the "considerations of policy are foremost in the minds of the actors . . . the parliamentary game is, in fact, about the determination of major government policy." This is not, of course, to deny that it may be necessary to get into power in order to enact policy. Getting into power involves both making promises to the electorate and, in coalition systems, making deals with fellow politicians. Both in elections and in government formation, it may be necessary for a party to make compromises – changing ideal policies in order to make them more acceptable to some group or another. Just as office-seeking politicians may stick to certain policies that they don't actually care about, policy-seeking politicians may change policies that they do care about. A policy-seeking politician trying to get into power in order to implement certain ideals may even behave as if he or she is a pure office seeker.

19

What all of this implies is that the "big" political game – an indefinite sequence of elections and government formations – may force office-seeking and policy-seeking politicians, who seem on the face of things to be so different, to behave in quite similar ways. Most of the pressure to do this, however, comes from part of the political process that we do not consider in this book – the interaction between politicians and voters at election time. For this reason we do not need to commit ourselves here to assuming that the politicians we are modeling are either intrinsically or instrumentally concerned with promoting particular policies.

What we do assume is that, when politicians bargain with each other in an attempt to form a government, they behave "as if" they are committed firmly to implementing their public policy positions, should they be able to do so. We remain silent on whether this is because politicians really do want to implement their published policies, or because they feel bound to do so by the need to retain credibility in the wider political game. The assumption that politicians, if given the chance, will attempt to implement the policies with which they are associated is fundamental to our approach, however. For us, the implementation of public policy is at the heart of the government formation process.

RATIONAL FORESIGHT AND PERFECT INFORMATION

In addition to making assumptions about what motivates politicians, we must also make assumptions about how, given these motivations, they decide what to do. In common with a large number of other accounts of political competition, we assume here that politicians are rational actors in the sense that they act within the best of their capacities to fulfill their fundamental aims and aspirations. This should not be taken to imply that we assume politicians approach each decision with a computer at the ready, self-consciously determined to calculate all the angles. But it does assume that politicians make important political decisions in accordance with their own best interests. In effect we assume that they operate, quite possibly unconsciously, as if they were continuously performing quite so-phisticated calculations designed to help them fulfill their basic objectives.

The continuous background of cost–benefit calculation that we as-sume to inform the strategic decision making of politicians is in many ways analogous to the continuous process of geometric calculation, most of it unconscious, that must inform physical decisions by people who are able to do no more than walk around their own homes without continu-ously crashing into things, or who can cross a busy road without being knocked over. These calculations, unconsciously performed by most of us effortlessly in real time, are far beyond our capacity to perform self-consciously in any but the most cumbersome manner. At the same time,

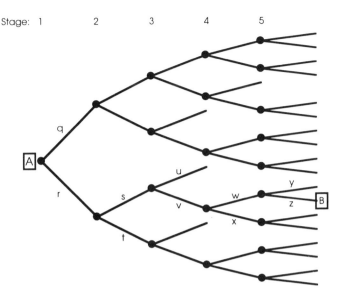

Figure 2.1. A decision tree

however, our knowledge of geometry allows an analyst explicitly, comprehensively, and realistically to model the decisions involved.

Similarly, we need not assume that rational politicians are continuously performing explicit cost–benefit calculations when they make strategic decisions designed to fulfill their basic objectives. What we do assume is that, just as people cross a crowded room as if they are performing a complex series of interlocking geometric calculations, politicians make strategic decisions as if they have the ability to perform a continuous cost–benefit calculus. And it is this calculus that we model.

An essential part of the process of making effective strategic decisions is looking ahead. Each course of action chosen leads to another set of decisions and, at any particular time, each decision maker stands at a node on a complex decision tree such as that shown in Figure 2.1.[2] For a person to get from A, where they are now, to B, where they want to be, typically involves decisions arising in a number of distinct stages. If nobody else is involved, then these decisions may all be taken by the same person. Getting from A to B in Figure 2.1 involves choosing option r over option q at Stage 1, option s over option t at Stage 2, option v over option u at Stage 3, option w over option x at Stage 4, and option z over option y

---

[2]Another way of thinking of Figure 2.1 is as the representation of an extensive form game generated by the decision process being modeled.

at Stage 5. In this way an actor navigates her way toward her objective across a decision-making landscape that may be physical, social, or psychological. Knowing an actor's preference for B over any other outcome and assuming her to be rational, one can predict her choice at any stage in the decision process. In this sense the outcome of the entire process is a foregone conclusion.

Most political decisions, of course, involve interdependent choices – outcomes depend on a sequence of choices made by a number of actors whose fates are intertwined with one another. Thus, for example, the decision tree in Figure 2.1 may involve two actors who make their choices in sequence. They could, for example, be two presidential candidates acting and reacting to each other during an election campaign. Actor 1 decides between q and r at Stage 1. Actor 2 decides between s and t at Stage 2, if Actor 1 has already chosen option r, and between other options if Actor 1 chose option q. If Actor 2 chose option s at Stage 2, then Actor 1 may choose between options u and v at Stage 3, otherwise she must choose between other options, and so on.

If the preferences of the various actors over the possible final outcomes are well known, then it is once more possible to predict the course of their interaction quite straightforwardly. This is done by working backward from each potential final outcome. To continue with the example in Figure 2.1, it will be known that, at Stage 5, if the game is at the node leading to outcome B, then Actor 1 will choose option z over option y, yielding her most-preferred outcome. Since this is the final move in the game, she will surely make such a choice if she is rational. Similarly, it is possible to predict with certainty the choice of Actor 1 at every one of the other decision nodes that might be reached in the final stage of the decision process. In effect, we can replace each decision node at Stage 5 with the outcome we surely know will be chosen by the actor with the power to do so. We can think of these outcomes as the "strategic equivalents" of the decision nodes we know will lead to them.

Having replaced every final decision node with its strategic equivalent and using the same logic, we can now predict which option Actor 2 will choose at each of the decision nodes in Stage 4 of the process. This is because, knowing what will happen at Stage 5, we know the particular final outcome generated by any choice Actor 2 makes at Stage 4. Knowing Actor 2's preferences over these outcomes, we can predict which option she would choose if she were to find herself at any of the Stage 4 decision nodes. We can therefore replace each of these decision nodes with its strategic equivalent.

In this way, we work back up the decision tree, at each stage replacing decision nodes with their strategic equivalents. Once we have determined the strategic equivalent of the very first decision node, we have in effect forecast the entire course of the game and predicted the final outcome. If the strategic equivalent of being at the first decision node of the game in Figure 2.1 is outcome B, for example, then the strategic equivalent of the entire decision process is B.

Another way of putting this is that, given sufficiently rich knowledge, everyone will have rational foresight concerning the outcome of this decision process, if it is embarked upon. One important implication of this is that, since everyone can easily forecast this outcome, it is not necessary for the actors actually to work their way through the decision process in order to find out what the outcome will be. In a world of perfect and complete information, once the actors are at A, they might as well be at B.

For the same reason it is not necessary for two chess players actually to play a particular game out to a checkmate, once both recognize that this is the inevitable outcome. Once it is clear in the final move in the game that Cassie will checkmate Seth, then Seth will resign before this. Once it is clear that Seth can do nothing to avoid allowing Cassie into this desirable penultimate position, he will resign. Once it is clear that Cassie can make an antepenultimate move that puts Seth in this vulnerable position, then he will resign. Once it is clear that Seth cannot make a move that prevents Cassie's antepenultimate strategic stroke, Seth resigns. In short, the players will work back up the game tree from the inevitable ending and anticipate it. As soon as the ending can be seen as inevitable – and the better the players, the further in advance this can be seen – the ending is assumed and the losing player resigns.

It should be clear that the logic of these examples assumes that each actor has perfect information about all aspects of the decision process, and complete information about the preferences of other actors. In the arguments that follow, we do for the most part assume that the rules of the government formation process and the preferences, expressed as policy positions, of all relevant actors are common knowledge in this sense.[3] The knowledge allows each actor to forecast the choice of every relevant decision maker at each stage in the government formation process.

Obviously, the assumption that all actors have perfect and complete information about both the rules of the government formation process and the preferences of all other relevant actors can never be realized in practice. The big wide world is much messier than this, and bargaining over the formation of real governments will in practice be much more fluid than we assume. The same problem does of course apply to any

---

[3]However, it is important to bear in mind, as we saw in the previous section, that these policies do not necessarily represent sincere preferences, but may represent published positions from which parties, for reasons originating outside the government formation process, are unwilling to diverge.

carefully specified assumption that we or anybody else might care to make about how politicians interact, and it is not an argument for not making assumptions or constructing models of the world. Notwithstanding this, the assumption that all actors' policy positions are common knowledge is probably more realistic in a model of government formation than it is in models of many other political processes. Government formation, after all, is a game played by a very limited number of elite actors who have typically interacted over a long period and therefore know each other rather well. The assumption is useful analytically because it allows us to develop a relatively parsimonious model of government formation.

POLITICS WITHIN PARTIES

In all parliamentary democracies, politicians belong to political parties that are more or less disciplined, in the sense that most members, for the most part, follow party directives on both policy and strategy. It has thus been quite common for people writing about the politics of government formation to treat political parties as if they were unitary actors. Indeed it is common in this literature for references to political parties to be heavily anthropomorphic – and in particular to treat each party as if it thinks with a single mind.

Yet parties can and do both split and fuse. It is also quite clear that vigorous and sometimes bitter debate about both policy and strategy does go on inside political parties. Internal party turmoil, such as that which resulted in the replacement of Margaret Thatcher as British Conservative leader by John Major, can lead to dramatic changes at the governmental level. So are we justified in treating parties as unitary actors when we model the making and breaking of governments?

There are sound theoretical reasons to suppose that political parties in parliamentary democracies will behave in a disciplined manner. The rationale is straightforward: If individual party politicians were permitted to pursue their own private desires at every opportunity, then their party's reputation in the wider political process would constantly be put at risk. People would not know what the party stood for, so that voters, interest groups, and others who might see the party as acting on their behalf would have nothing to rely on. As a consequence, the party would be severely hampered in its ability to attract support. Thus, the ultimate enforcers of party discipline are voters who want to know what they are voting for at election time, and who will not vote for parties if they cannot be confident that party politicians will stick to the party line after the election is over.

Empirically, the unitary actor assumption has been extensively reviewed, from the perspective of government formation, by Laver and Schofield (1990: chap. 2, app. A.). Their conclusions on the matter are based primarily on the empirical observation that it is almost always the case that parties both enter and leave cabinet coalitions as unified blocs – almost never does only part of a party enter or leave a cabinet. They take this to imply that, for the purpose of analyzing cabinet formation and maintenance over a reasonably short time scale, nearly all Western European political parties can be treated as if they are unitary actors (Laver and Schofield 1990: 28).

This evidence has recently been supplemented by a series of country studies collected by Laver and Shepsle (1994). Individual authors were not asked explicitly to comment on the unitary actor assumption. Nonetheless, many were at pains to point out that strong party discipline in the parliamentary democracies with which they were concerned means that individual cabinet members, as well as backbenchers, are not able to act independently of their party organizations. Most described politicians as agents of their party, with politicians from the same party forecast to behave in more or less the same ways when placed in the same situations. Almost none was prepared to accept that it might make a difference which politician from a given party filled a particular role. Obviously, this line of argument provides further strong support for the assumption that political parties can be treated as unitary actors, as least as far as cabinet politics are concerned.

Taking all of this into account, therefore, we assume for the bulk of the argument that follows that individual politicians behave as perfect agents of their party. Thus, while we will shortly assume that cabinet ministers have discretion within their jurisdictions, we also assume that they exercise this discretion on behalf of their party, rather than "against" their party. For the most part, this means that we treat parties as if they are unitary actors. In Chapter 12, however, we do consider intraparty politics, and explore the internal processes that might lead a party to choose one strategy rather than another in the government formation process.

PARTY POLICY

One of the most significant implications of the assumption that politicians behave as perfect agents of their parties is that each party can be treated as if it has a unique ideal policy position. As we have already seen, this ideal position may reflect the intrinsic tastes of a policy-seeking party. Alternatively, it may reflect a published position that an office-seeking party has strong incentives – derived from the wider political game – to implement if given the chance. For our purposes, what is important is that a party's ideal policy is the policy that the party is forecast to implement if given the opportunity to do so. Note that an ideal policy position in these terms is a realistic policy. It is not the policy that the party would like to see implemented in a perfect world, but rather the policy that the party would implement in the real world in which it finds itself.

It has become conventional in recent years to describe the policy positions of political actors in terms of a set of key dimensions of policy. For many people, the most familiar of these is the left–right dimension of socioeconomic policy. Those who use this dimension in effect assume a correlation between party positions on economic issues such as public spending and on social issues such as capital punishment or abortion. The left–right dimension can then be used to describe a typical European party system by placing a communist or left socialist party at the left-hand end, followed by a socialist or social democratic party, perhaps by an agrarian or center party, a Christian democratic party, a secular conservative party, and possibly a neofascist party on the extreme right. The use of a single dimension of policy to describe a party system is simple and intuitive, has a tradition stretching back at least to the French Revolution, and of course loses a lot of detailed information about the party system. Using a larger number of independent dimensions of policy – separating economic and social policy, for example – enables richer descriptions of party politics,[4] but can greatly increase analytical complexity.

This leaves us with some extremely difficult questions to answer. How many independent dimensions of policy should we use to describe adequately the ideal policy position of a given political party? Taking all parties in a given system together, how many dimensions of policy do we need for an adequate description of party competition? These are deep issues that we cannot explore fully here (for some thoughts on the matter, see Laver and Hunt, 1992). Nonetheless, since it is of the essence of our approach that party competition and government behavior are described in terms of positions on key policy dimensions, we cannot ignore them completely. The basic problem is one of deciding upon how to choose the most appropriate dimensionality of the policy space we use to describe party competition, in the knowledge that the choice of different dimensionalities can yield quite different descriptions. In concrete terms, how do we decide whether the most appropriate description of party competition in Germany, say, is in terms of one, two, three, five, ten, or even fifty key dimensions of policy?

Obviously, depending upon the level of detail we are prepared to use in collecting information on policy positions, any number of independent dimensions of policy could be detected. For example, one research project

---

[4]For example, a liberal party may now be placed toward the right of an economic policy dimension and toward the left of a social policy dimension.

has estimated party positions by content analyzing party election manifestos for a range of European party systems on a total of 54 policy dimensions. Various techniques of dimensional analysis, such as factor analysis or multidimensional scaling, were used to collapse this large number of policy dimensions into a smaller number of underlying dimensions. Ultimately, all of these data were also used to estimate positions on a single left–right dimension. Thus the same dataset could in this case be used to generate anything from a 1-dimensional to a 54-dimensional representation of policies in a given party system (Budge, Robertson, and Hearl, 1987). Furthermore, there is no single "correct" representation. Just as there is no map of a given piece of territory that is perfect for every possible purpose – we need one map for locating mountain ranges or oceans and another for finding a needle in a haystack – there is no unambiguously correct dimensionality for the policy space we use to describe party competition. Different applications call for different levels of detail in our description.

At the same time, party positions on sets of policy dimensions can be highly correlated with one another. Thus it may well be the case that party positions on the public sector borrowing dimension, for example, can be very accurately predicted from their positions on the personal taxation and/or inflation dimensions. Positions on abortion might well be highly correlated with those on divorce, and so on. This implies that a reasonably parsimonious and intuitive description of party policy positions can be given in terms of a limited number of independent underlying dimensions of policy, a matter that we consider in more detail in Chapter 11. If this is true, almost any new salient policy area that we might think of will generate a set of party positions that is highly correlated with one or more of the underlying policy dimensions. The problem now becomes one of estimating the number of underlying policy dimensions necessary to generate party positions on any salient issue in party competition.

Estimating the dimensionality of a policy space in these terms is still not a straightforward task, once it is accepted that published policy positions may in some sense be as much a product of party competition as an exogenous input to it. Normal techniques of dimensional analysis all assume that, if positions on two dimensions are perfectly correlated, then there is a single dimension underlying them both. But in the present context it may equally be the case that the correlated party positions are a strategic response to a particular circumstance of party competition. Parties could in principle choose positions on the two dimensions quite independently; in a particular set of circumstances they do not. Thus, is there one underlying dimension, or two?

We offer no magic formula for determining the most appropriate dimensionality of any given representation of party competition. We have raised the issue in the preceding discussion, however, to highlight the fact that the choice of any given spatial representation of a particular party system is no more than one among many that could have been chosen. What we offer in the following chapters, therefore, is a set of tools that can be applied to a particular spatial representation of party competition that the analyst feels happy with for reasons that are quite outside our terms of reference. We have nothing to say about which particular spatial representation might be appropriate. But we must very firmly draw attention to the fact that the choice of one spatial representation over another has fundamental consequences for the ensuing analysis. This implies that, for obvious reasons, the analyst should be very sure that he or she feels comfortable that the spatial representation to be used is valid *before* the analysis is commenced – and should resist all temptations to fiddle with the space once the analysis is under way.

As we shall see when we come in subsequent chapters actually to apply our model to particular real-world cases, however, settling upon a particular set of policy dimensions on which to base an analysis of government formation is not the open-ended problem that it might appear to be when considering the problem in purely abstract terms. One of the interesting features of our approach is that we come to most real-world cases with much of the dimensional analysis already done for us by the political system itself. This is because particular policy dimensions have been formally identified as being salient by virtue of having been designated as part of the official jurisdiction of a cabinet ministry. Indeed the formal determination of the policy responsibilities of particular cabinet portfolios, and hence the identification of the policy dimensions that are "in play," is something that we can typically take as given, even if somewhat fuzzy around the edges, at the beginning of the government formation process.[5]

THE GOVERNMENT

The government as the cabinet

People living in parliamentary democracies typically think of "the government" of their country in terms of the cabinet. Of the many arms of government – the civil service, the judiciary, publicly owned corporations, and the various tiers of local administration, for example – it is the

[5]Obviously, the allocation of policy dimensions to the jurisdiction of different cabinet portfolios may change as a result of the government formation process, a possibility to which we return in Chapter 12. Nonetheless, the set of portfolios that characterizes the outgoing government – the status quo in the government formation process – can be taken as identifying, almost in the manner of a giant living factor analysis, a particular set of policy dimensions as being salient.

cabinet that symbolizes the apex of political responsibility. It is the cabinet that is expected to guide affairs of state by making and overseeing the implementation of policy on important issues. It is the cabinet that is expected to react to and deal with major crises and emergencies. And, perhaps most significantly of all, it is the cabinet whose survival is on the line at election times. If voters in parliamentary democracies feel that they have any control over their political destinies, it is because they can pass judgment on the cabinet, albeit indirectly, when they vote in national elections. For many people, the terms *cabinet* and *government* are more or less synonymous. Although many parliamentary democracies do not explicitly use the term *cabinet*, all have a functional equivalent, whether it is called a council of ministers, an executive council, or whatever.

The typical process of forming a government in a parliamentary democracy, to which we will return in more detail, involves the selection of a prime minister, who must win a majority vote (actual or implicit) in the legislature before he or she can take office. The prime minister then nominates a cabinet of ministers, which must also be capable of winning a majority vote (actual or implicit) in the legislature. The cabinet is free to set policy on any matter, subject only to the law of the land and to the constraint that it can be dismissed on the basis of a majority vote in the legislature. In practice, as we might expect, a rational anticipation of defeat may lead a cabinet to resign in advance of losing such a vote. In this way the cabinet is held collectively responsible for government policy decisions.

In parliamentary democracies, therefore, changes in government depend on changes in the cabinet generated by changes in the balance of forces in the legislature. It is by having an effect on the balance of forces in the legislature when voting at election time that voters in parliamentary democracies can have some control over affairs of state. The fact that many voters are in effect voting for potential governments rather than for individual candidates has profound effects upon party competition, many of which are far beyond our remit here. One, at least, is very important for the government formation process, however. If voters vote for parties and not candidates, then the party label is a very valuable commodity – and being denied the party label is a very serious sanction. This sanction is a powerful weapon in the hands of the party organization, and the threat of it reduces the incentives of individual legislators to defy their party line. This in turn contributes greatly to party discipline, and the consequent ability of parties to function as if they were unitary actors. Closing the circle, it is because parties are disciplined that it makes sense for voters to vote for them at election time, since a vote for a party has some foreseeable consequence on the balance of forces in the legislature that decides the fate of the incumbent government. The effective operation of parliamentary democracy, in short, both depends upon and encourages disciplined behavior by political parties in the government formation process. And the crux of that process is voting by legislators on the future of the cabinet.

Given all of this, we assume in what follows that the government in the political process we model can be taken to be the cabinet, and that membership of the government is unambiguously defined in terms of membership of the cabinet. This explicitly excludes from our notion of government membership legislative actors who support the government in votes of confidence, but who are not members of the cabinet. In other words, we make a clear distinction between a government as such and its legislative support coalition.[6] It is this distinction that allows for the possibility of "minority" governments, comprising cabinets whose parliamentary parties do not between them control a majority of legislative seats. Despite this, a minority government must still command majority support in the legislature; otherwise it will be defeated and replaced, a matter to which we return in Chapter 12.

The departmental structure of government decision making

Although the cabinet is in theory responsible collectively for taking decisions on all significant affairs of state, the tasks involved in this are simply too massive for most government decisions in practice to be taken in cabinet. As well as being a member of the cabinet, each cabinet minister is typically the political head of a major government department, staffed for the most part by career civil servants. Each government department has formal jurisdiction – determined by the constitution, by law, or by precedent – over a particular set of policy areas.

It is clear that the pressure of work on cabinet ministers and senior civil servants is immense. Each minister faces a very heavy administrative workload, over and above the busy schedule of a full-time politician. The resources available to ministers to allow them to discharge their responsibilities are organized very much along departmental lines. Each cabinet minister can call on a considerable pool of expertise in his or her own department, expertise that is professionally focused in a very intense manner on the policy concerns of the department.[7] While cabinet minis-

[6]As we have seen in Chapter 1, for example, some analysts (e.g., Baron, 1991) include as part of the government all parties who vote for it in a confidence vote. We depart from this view.

[7]Although we can reject out of hand the *Yes, Minister* view of civil service domination of ministers, a view rejected by all country specialists in Laver and Shepsle (1994), it does need to be said that ministers need to be vigilant in dealings with their civil servants. This is for all the usual reasons concerning the possibility that civil servants have their own political agendas.

ters thereby have some hope of being able to master the affairs of their own departments, most will have very little of the time and energy needed to develop policy proposals in areas outside their jurisdiction. Not only this, but the departmental structure of the civil service means that ministers can call on very little expertise in policy areas that lie within the jurisdiction of some other department. Blondel and Müller-Rommel (1993: 13) sum up these points very elegantly:

Above all, the behavior of ministers is also likely to be affected by the belief that they will have a better chance of seeing their proposals adopted by the cabinet if they concentrate on the affairs of their department; this belief seems rather widespread. On the one hand, ministers are more likely to be left alone if they do not discuss, criticize or raise points about matters that concern other departments. On the other, even if they are or want to be "generalists," ministers are close to their departments; they are in their office throughout their working day and are members of the cabinet only episodically. It is therefore the department rather than the cabinet that is likely to be their main reference point.

All of this obviously imparts a very strongly departmental character to government decision making – government departments are the only organizations with the resources to generate fully developed policy proposals and the expertise to implement and monitor any proposal that might be selected. This pattern may well have been intensified by the increasing tendency for cabinet discussions to be extensively prepared in committees. Thiebault (1993: 96), for example, argues that "committees can be instruments legitimizing the autonomy of individual ministerial departments."

Each department has jurisdiction over a set of policy dimensions. We say that the jurisdiction is *simple* if it can be represented by a single dimension of policy. Bearing in mind our earlier discussion of the dimensionality of policy spaces, we might also think of a jurisdiction as being simple if it comprises a number of policy dimensions, but each party's position on each of these dimensions can be predicted from its position on any other. In that case we can proceed as if they are in fact a single dimension. We say that a jurisdiction is *complex* if it comprises more than one independent policy dimension. A department of foreign affairs, for example, may have jurisdiction over policy in relation to the European Community and policy in relation to the United States. It is possible to find parties that are pro-EC and pro-U.S., whereas others are anti-EC and pro-U.S., so that positions on one dimension cannot be predicted from positions on another. In this event the foreign policy jurisdiction will be complex. As we shall see in Chapter 11, the possibility of complex jurisdictions makes a considerable difference to our analysis of the government formation process.

The departmental structure of government decision making is a vital part of our model of politics in parliamentary democracies. It implies that government decision making is broken up into a series of component parts relating to particular policy areas, rather than ranging wild and free over the whole political domain. The structure that the departmental nature of cabinet life brings to government decisions creates a situation in which cabinet decision making is far less chaotic than would otherwise be the case. In this sense, government departments bring the same structure to decision making in parliamentary democracies that congressional committees bring to decision making in the United States (Shepsle, 1979).

Ministerial discretion

Given the intense pressure of work and lack of access to civil service specialists in other departments, it seems unlikely that cabinet ministers will be able successfully to poke their noses very deeply into the jurisdictions of their cabinet colleagues. This implies that members of the cabinet will have only very limited ability to shape the substance of policy emanating from the department of a ministerial colleague, an assumption that has received empirical support from a number of country specialists (Laver and Shepsle, 1994; see also Blondel and Müller-Rommel, 1993: 2; Thiebault, 1993: 95). We therefore assume in what follows that each minister has considerable discretion to act, in his or her own department, independently of other members of the cabinet. A minister may be constrained by any number of extracabinet institutions – the most consequential of which is his or her own party – but these may be taken as exogenous to cabinet decision making (and, often, more or less fixed for a government's life).

This discretion is sustained, principally but not exclusively, by the control over the policy agenda that each minister exercises in his or her own departmental jurisdiction. There seems to be common agreement among country specialists that it is difficult if not impossible for ministers to defy explicit decisions taken by the cabinet (Laver and Shepsle, 1994). Ministerial discretion thus results from the ability of a minister to use his or her position as the head of a major government department to do one or more of three things. The first is to act on matters that are not decided by the cabinet. The second is to influence which matters come to the cabinet for decision and which do not. The third is to affect the substance of specific proposals on those matters within his or her jurisdiction which do come to the cabinet for decision.

In most countries, there are either rules or strong conventions that determine which matters must be brought to cabinet, while the prime minister typically retains firm control over the cabinet agenda, taken as a whole (Burch, 1993: 112–113). The ability of individual ministers to exercise discretion over government decision making, therefore, derives from their ability to shape the substance of those proposals that do find their way onto the agenda. The prime minister can only fashion a cabinet agenda from the substantive raw material that he or she is presented with. This raw material is generated for the most part by the cabinet members with jurisdiction over the policy area in question.

Ministerial discretion, in short, results from the minister's ability to shape the agenda of collective cabinet decisions rather than to determine cabinet decisions once the agenda had been set. This in turn implies that removing the incumbent minister and putting someone with different policy preferences in charge of the department affects the shape of proposals on the cabinet agenda and, hence, the substance of eventual government policy in the jurisdiction concerned.

In the discussion to follow, we take two bites at the role of ministerial discretion in the making and breaking of governments. For most of the book we consider parties to be unitary actors and thus treat cabinet ministers as perfect agents of their parties. Thus, when we refer to ministerial discretion in this context, we are talking about a minister using discretion on behalf of his or her party vis-à-vis other political parties. Since many scholars, however, have reservations about treating parties as unitary actors, we feel that it is important to refine out model in order to take account of politics *within* parties. Hence, the second bite that we take at the role of ministerial discretion is to consider the departmental freedom of action a minister might have vis-à-vis his or her own party. A minimal departure from any conception of a party as a unitary actor, after all, involves treating party politicians as heterogeneous in their policy preferences and capable of doing something about these. If there is no diversity of tastes within the party or if the party leadership can enforce a party line on every policy decision that might be made, then the party is effectively a unitary actor.

The consequences of ministerial discretion are fundamental to our model of politics. If the policy positions of each party are well known prior to government formation, then legislators can forecast the consequences for eventual policy formulation and implementation of allocating a cabinet post to a particular party's politician. In what follows we assume that they will forecast that the minister in question will act, as far as possible, to implement party policy within his or her jurisdiction.

Finite number of governments

If there is strong party discipline, as we are assuming, so that ministers can be treated as if they are agents of their party, and if there is a strong departmental structure to government decision making, as we are assuming, then we can take two governments as effectively being the same if the same cabinet portfolios are allocated to the same parties. We can take them as being different if the same portfolios are allocated to different parties. This is because, if the same portfolios are allocated to the same parties, then key political actors will forecast, before the government is formed, that the same policy outcomes will be pursued. If the same portfolio is allocated in two prospective cabinets to two different parties, each with different policy positions, then key actors will forecast that different policy outcomes will result. They will therefore view these as effectively different governments.

This implies that, in any given government formation situation, there is only a finite number of governments that can be proposed, reflecting the number of different ways in which the fixed set of cabinet portfolios can be allocated between the fixed set of "coalitionable" parties. Indeed, if we concern ourselves only with a few key cabinet portfolios dealing with the most important political decisions, and if the number of parties is small, then there may be very few effectively different potential governments. To take almost the simplest possible example, imagine a three-party system in which all important decisions were taken either on financial policy or foreign affairs. There are only nine possible ways in which the two key portfolios of finance and foreign affairs can be allocated between three parties. In this important sense, there are thus only nine different potential governments.

We can think more systematically about the different potential governments in this simple example if we arrange them in a diagram such as that in Figure 2.2. The diagram shows two policy dimensions. The horizontal dimension represents financial policy, in the jurisdiction of the Department of Finance. The vertical dimension represents foreign policy, in the jurisdiction of the Department of Foreign Affairs. These dimensions describe a two-dimensional policy space. The ideal policies of three parties – Party A, Party B, and Party C – are shown by the black dots, labeled AA, BB, and CC respectively. These dots show the positions that we assume each party is forecast to try to implement if given control of both the finance and foreign affairs portfolios. There are six other points in the diagram, each marked with a small x. These represent a coalition government that gives one portfolio to one party and the other portfolio to another. Thus point AC represents the government in which Party A gets the (horizontal) finance portfolio and Party C gets the (vertical) foreign affairs portfolio. Note that there is another point, CA, which represents the cabinet formed when the allocation of portfolios between parties is reversed, giving foreign affairs to Party A and finance to Party C. This latter cabinet generates different forecast government policy outputs, even though it consists of the same government parties.

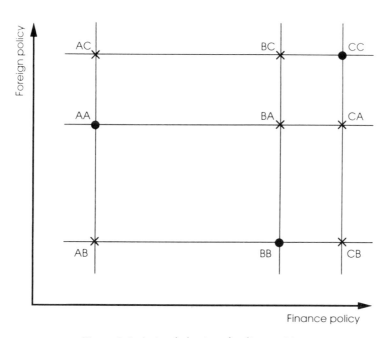

Figure 2.2. A simple lattice of policy positions

Two important technical assumptions of our model are, first, that what a party can do with one portfolio is not affected by which particular party controls some other portfolio and, second, that how people feel about what happens in one jurisdiction is not affected by what happens in another. In this particular example, these assumptions imply that what a party can do in finance is not affected by which party holds the foreign affairs portfolio, and that how people feel about decisions taken by the finance minister is not affected by the substance of decisions taken by the minister for foreign affairs.[8] This assumption is of course restrictive, but we do not believe it to be too unrealistic, given the pressures toward the departmental structuring of decision making that we discussed earlier. The effect of the assumptions is to arrange the policy forecasts associated with each portfolio allocation in the form of an orthogonal "lattice" of the type shown in Figure 2.2. If the assumptions are violated, then the lattice will be distorted – what party C, for example, will do if it holds the foreign affairs portfolio (top row of the lattice) will not lie along a horizontal line, since it will depend upon which party holds the finance portfolio. (We return in more detail to this in Chapter 11.)

[8]Technically, this amounts to an assumption that portfolio allocation effects are separable.

The context

Each point on this lattice corresponds to a potential government, defined by an appropriate portfolio allocation. Any point not on the lattice does not represent a potential government in our approach, since there is no allocation of portfolios between parties that is forecast to generate such a point as a government policy output. Such a point can be talked about, even dreamed about, but it cannot be forecast to be credibly implemented by an actual cabinet made up of living and breathing cabinet ministers, each intent upon making his or her party's preferred policies the law of the land.

Collective cabinet decisions

Most parliamentary democracies operate on the basis of a doctrine of collective cabinet responsibility – in many cases this is enshrined in the constitution. This doctrine implies that cabinet ministers are responsible as a group for every government decision. Inside the cabinet chamber, ministers may fight tooth and claw for a particular position. The cabinet may be deeply divided. In public, however, the cabinet must officially present a common front. If someone loses a fight in cabinet, then the doctrine of collective cabinet responsibility nonetheless binds the minister to observe whatever cabinet decision is finally taken, however much he or she disapproves of it. In theory, and indeed to a large extent in practice, a minister must resign or be sacked if he or she defies, or even publicly dissents from, a collective cabinet decision.

It is important to bear in mind, however, that the collective responsibility of members of the cabinet for government decisions says nothing about how those decisions are taken in the first place. The prime minister might be an absolute dictator, for example, laying down the law in cabinet and ignoring all opposition. The process of decision making in such a cabinet would not be collective at all, but ministers would still bear collective responsibility for cabinet decisions. Thus, collective cabinet responsibility is quite different from using a process of collective decision making to formulate cabinet decisions in the first place.

Collective *decision making* in cabinet is much more likely in some circumstances than in others. Most obviously, if different government departments come into direct conflict with one another, then such conflicts must be resolved if deadlock is not to result. One way to do this is by making a decision on the issue collectively. Certain policy problems – for example, urban regeneration – are intrinsically interdepartmental in character and require coordinated policy making and implementation. New issues emerge for the cabinet to make decisions on – and these may not automatically fall within the jurisdiction of an existing portfolio. In this event they must be disposed of somehow, directly by the cabinet acting outside the normal departmental structure, or indirectly by making a cabinet decision to assign jurisdiction over the problem to a particular department. For major new issues, a new department may even be created, or the existing departmental structure may be radically redesigned. Finally, and perhaps most important, the cabinet will from time to time face the need to resolve unanticipated and unavoidable political issues. These may arise unexpectedly out of the process of party competition, or hit the government like a bolt out of a clear blue sky – turmoil in international currency markets suddenly put John Major's Conservative cabinet in Britain on the spot, for example, in the autumn of 1992. Such issues, which could threaten the very life of the cabinet, may well involve collective cabinet deliberation and decision making.

The importance of collective cabinet decision making in parliamentary democracies highlights the need to be clear about the ways in which ministerial discretion has an impact on government policy. We assume in what follows that ministers make a difference, that putting a minister from one party in charge of a particular department has foreseeable consequences that are different from those of putting a minister from another party in charge. But if some, or even all, important cabinet decisions are taken collectively, how can individual ministers make a difference?

The answer is simple. A cabinet, or indeed any other decision-making body, does not make decisions in the abstract. Real-life decisions on complicated issues, such as those facing a cabinet, are choices that are made between reasonably detailed and well-elaborated programs that specify alternative courses of action. There is typically a large briefing paper for cabinet members, possibly a formal discussion document for public consumption, even detailed draft legislation. Every cabinet memoir with which we are familiar makes rueful reference to the enormous volume of paper that any minister is expected to process as part of the business of decision making. In short, the cabinet in practice does not look at a policy space in the abstract and consider proposals of the form "let's go to x." Rather, it considers whether to accept, reject, or amend a particular fully formulated policy proposal on some matter.

Such a proposal is almost always prepared by one government department or another. As Burch (1993: 109) has argued so forcefully, "the key agents for the preparation and development of policy coming to the cabinet are in the departments." A particular proposal will, of course, be located at some point in the policy space – say y. But amending such a proposal is not simply a matter of collectively deciding to go from y to x, since the amended proposal at x is not yet sufficiently well specified to be capable of implementation. If the cabinet does not like a particular proposal, therefore, it must refer it back to the originating department for detailed amendment and subsequent reconsideration. But in practice the matter of whether the amended proposal is actually "at" x is of course not transparent from the detail of the proposal itself. Each complex proposal requires interpretation before ministers can assess its implications for the broad sweep of government policy. The initial interpretation, needless to say, comes in briefing papers from the originating department. All of this gives the originating department, and in particular the minister in charge of it, considerable ability to shape the substance of the cabinet agenda, even in relation to matters that on the face of it are decided collectively. Burch (1993: 107) puts this point very clearly:

> Those within government who originate a decision proposal and who provide the information and advice attached to it are in a strong position to influence the final outcome since it is they who establish the framework of ideas and assumptions within which discussions take place; originators can therefore have a critical role. In general, this initiative is with the departments and not at the level of the cabinet system.

The collective choice is between alternatives that are departmentally conditioned. This will be known, and its effects anticipated, before the minister is appointed in the first place.

Thus even collective decision making in cabinet will, we argue, take place within the context of the departmental structuring of the agenda of choices. This is essentially because public administration is so very complex that any workable decision to be taken by the cabinet needs the expertise and resources of some government department before it can be specified in an implementable form. The person in charge of that department is clearly in the driver's seat in relation to policy areas under his or her jurisdiction. The main way to effect a major policy change in a jurisdiction is to replace the minister in charge with someone who has a different policy position.

All of this will be known in advance of the government formation process. Thus politicians will forecast that even essentially collective cabinet decisions will be heavily conditioned by their preparation (or precooking to take a term from the low countries) within existing department jurisdictions. This does not, of course, deny any role for collective decision making in cabinet; it merely emphasizes that this role will be heavily conditioned by departmental agenda power.

There is, however, an altogether different, and in our opinion more important, role for collective cabinet decision making. This concerns decisions that were *not anticipated* at the time of government formation. Departmental influence on anticipated decisions will be fully discounted at the point the government is formed and be part of the policy forecasts that underpin the government. Unanticipated events, however, cannot be impounded in expectations when the government is formed, may well not fall clearly under the jurisdiction of some particular government department, and thus may leave scope for a more collective form of cabinet decision making.

In essence, the distinction that we are making here is between routine and/or foreseeable executive decisions on the one hand, and those that are sprung upon the government unexpectedly, on the other. Unexpected decisions, by their very nature, are likely to impinge upon the government as a whole, and to represent a threat to its equilibrium. In a sense, every unexpected situation with which a government is confronted creates a new political world, and there is no guarantee that a cabinet that was in equilibrium in the world before the event in question will remain in equilibrium after it. On an extreme view, every unexpected event requires the renegotiation of the government, something that will inevitably involve the government as a whole, and thereby require collective decisions to be taken. While the prime minister typically has no line departmental responsibilities, and therefore no direct role in the process of policy implementation, a key role for the prime minister is dealing with the unexpected and managing the necessary collective responses to these unanticipated events.

At the same time, however, very much of what a government does *is* foreseeable and anticipated. Even though the crises provoked by surprises that threaten the life of governments are the things that make newspaper headlines and attract popular attention, the vast bulk of government decisions – most of the things that affect the day-to-day lives of voters and therefore affect the fates of politicians at election time – may be almost boringly predictable. Nonetheless it is these predictable but important matters that condition the negotiations that lead to the formation of a new government. And it is these decisions, we contend, that are strongly structured along departmental lines. It is simply not possible to negotiate in advance a cabinet response to every possible thunderbolt that may strike unexpectedly at the heart of a putative government. Such problems will inevitably be subject to collective responses after the event. *But by the same token they cannot, by definition, impinge upon the process of government formation that is the main concern of this book.*

Our discussion of the departmentalism inherent in government decision making is no better than a rough sketch of what happens in the real world. In reality, all sorts of complex interactions between departments are likely to condition actual decisions, and it would be silly to pretend otherwise. Once more, however, we do feel that the sketch we have drawn bears some resemblance to reality, providing a sound enough basis for the construction of a simplified model of government formation.

Legislative control of the cabinet

Obviously, the effect of the cabinet on public policy would be very limited if every detail of policy were settled by parliamentary legislation. The partisan composition of the cabinet would be irrelevant, since policy outputs would be determined by the balance of forces in the legislature. Before we can model the political role of the cabinet, therefore, we need to know how much the legislature can constrain the ability of cabinet ministers to set policy. If parliamentary action can force the hand of an unwilling cabinet minister, then the legislature can let a minister occupy a portfolio secure in the knowledge that he or she can be forced to act in particular ways should the need arise. If the legislature cannot realistically bind a minister in this way, then the minister has some discretion vis-à-vis the legislature, at least within his or her jurisdiction.

Formally, in every parliamentary democracy, parliament is sovereign. A constitutionally valid law binds an individual minister, or indeed the cabinet as a whole. In terms of practical politics, however, a cabinet in which the government parties control a majority of seats in parliament can summon up a legislative majority whenever it cares to do so, provided party discipline holds firm. Thus a majority government with disciplined parties can comprehensively dominate any legislature once it has been installed in office. This in turn means that the legislature cannot in practice pass laws constraining the government. The possibility of the legislature imposing its will on a majority executive can only arise when party discipline breaks down and dissident members of a government party join forces with the opposition to pass legislation on some particular issue. In such cases, the key political action takes place within political parties, a matter to which we return in Chapter 12.

The possibility for confrontation between legislature and executive is far more clear-cut if there is a "minority" cabinet in which the government parties do not control a parliamentary majority.[9] While a minority cabinet must retain majority legislative support in the sense that no credible alternative government is preferred to it by a legislative majority, this certainly does not mean that it can act at will. Even if a majority of legislators cannot agree on an alternative cabinet that they prefer to a particular minority administration, they can still defeat the incumbent cabinet in particular instances by passing particular pieces of legislation opposed by the cabinet.

The fact remains, however, that a minority cabinet retains the support of a majority of the legislature. If not, it would be defeated and replaced

---

[9]Minority governments in parliamentary democracies are in this sense analogous to situations of "divided government" in the United States – see Laver and Shepsle (1991).

with an alternative. If cabinet members feel strongly enough about an issue to make it a matter of overall confidence in the government, threatening to resign if they are defeated, then the minority cabinet's overall appeal to a legislative majority still puts it in a powerful strategic position vis-à-vis the legislature.

Cabinet control of the legislative agenda

One of the main ways in which the cabinet dominates the legislature in the business of making public policy has to do with the flow of legislative business. Typically in parliamentary democracies, the cabinet has a tight grip on the parliamentary timetable. By virtue of controlling the main departments of state, as we have seen, the cabinet also has a near monopoly of both the information and the drafting skills needed to prepare legislation. These factors make it very difficult for opposition parties to get significant draft statutes onto the legislative agenda and effectively prevent the legislature from imposing policies on an unwilling cabinet. Cabinet ministers thus have freedom of action relative to the legislature, subject only to the constraint that they cannot implement policies so unpopular with the legislature that a majority of legislators prefers to defeat the government as a whole. Overall, the government's opponents in the legislature can find it almost impossible to get their own proposals on to the agenda. Firm cabinet control over the flow of legislative business thus vastly reduces the opportunity for a parliament to leave a cabinet in place and yet use its legislative power to impose policy on the government on an a la carte basis. In effect, the only way for the legislature to effect a substantial change in government policy is to change the government, or at least to mount a credible threat to do so.

SUMMARY

Let us now summarize the essential features of what we take to be the social and political context of government formation, bearing in mind that in later chapters we will consider the effect of relaxing some of our more restrictive assumptions. First, we are talking about a world in which policy outputs are important – either because politicians are intrinsically concerned about policy or because they are constrained by other aspects of the larger political game to honor policy promises made to voters. We assume the preferences of politicians over the various possible policy outputs to be common knowledge, and that politicians are forecast to act so as to implement more favored policy outputs rather than less favored ones. We are talking about a parliamentary government system in which the executive is a cabinet with real power over policy outputs, responsible to the legislature in the sense that a cabinet must resign if it is defeated in a confidence vote by a legislative majority. We assume that, in considering the fate of the government, political parties behave in a disciplined manner so that politicians can be viewed, by the outside world at least, as agents of the party to which they belong.

Once a government has formed, we assume that the immense weight of decision making for which the cabinet is collectively responsible, together with the departmental organization of a civil service responsible for the detailed preparation and implementation of actual policy decisions, will give a strongly departmental structure to cabinet decision making. Specific policy proposals are brought to cabinet by the minister with relevant jurisdiction, and implemented by the same minister.

All of this results in the forecast, shared by each of those involved in building and maintaining a government, that government policy outputs in any given policy area are best predicted by looking at the position of the party in control of the portfolio with jurisdiction over the policy area concerned. It is these forecasts that inform actors' decisions during the government formation process, a process to which we now turn.

3

The government formation process

Having outlined our assumptions about how political actors view the making and breaking of governments, we now roll up our sleeves and move on to the process itself. Here we begin to assemble the raw materials out of which we will build a model. Obviously, once we get down to the nitty-gritty of how things are actually done in the real world, we find that governments are formed according to different rules and procedures in each parliamentary democracy. Any one of these differences is potentially of great importance in some particular circumstance. There are considerable broad similarities in the rules that structure government formation, however – sufficient to allow us to model a "generic" government formation procedure that can, with modest amendments, be adapted to most particular government formation situations.

First, since our rational foresight approach assumes that sophisticated political actors take account of, and adjust to, events that they can foresee in the future, we must specify what it is that triggers the government formation process in the first place. Second, we must be clear about the status quo that determines policy outputs if attempts to make a new government, or break an incumbent one, are unsuccessful. Third, we must provide a stylized description of the process that is triggered. Fourth, we must transform our stylized description into a model. Finally, we must explore implications of our model for the making and breaking of governments.

TRIGGERING THE GOVERNMENT FORMATION PROCESS

The process of government formation can be triggered in several different ways. These include an election, a government defeat in the legislature, or a government resignation.

The most straightforward way in which the government formation process is triggered happens when the legislature comes to the end of its constitutionally defined term. At this point, the legislature must be dissolved and new elections held. Obviously, if there were no fixed maximum term for the life of a parliament, a cabinet could stay in office indefinitely. Although the holding of scheduled elections is thus a very important constitutional rule, and is one of the things that makes parliamentary democracy democratic, in practice we actually observe a legislature reaching the very end of its scheduled constitutional term only in those few countries, such as Norway, in which the government has no power to dissolve the legislature and call early elections. It is far more common in practice for a government that could constitutionally continue in office to choose, of its own accord, to dissolve parliament and call an early election, thereby voluntarily triggering the government formation process.

In most parliamentary democracies the prime minister may either dissolve the legislature directly, or request a dissolution from the head of state who will, by rule or convention, accede unless the circumstances are exceptional.[1] This makes the calling of an election a very important strategic weapon in the hands of the government. Obviously, prime ministers will attempt to call elections at the times that are most favorable to them. Since the growth of widespread and accurate public opinion polling during the postwar era, prime ministers have had very good information on the likely consequences of calling an election at any particular time. Thanks in part to the efforts of political scientists, they have also gained a better understanding of cycles of government popularity, and thereby some ability to forecast future movements in public opinion.

Prime ministers are typically wary of being forced by the constitution to call an election at an inopportune time. They therefore have an incentive not to let themselves get "boxed in" to calling an election at the end of their term, with no choice as to the timing. Nonetheless, when a prime minister with a secure majority does see some benefit in calling an election before the end of the life of the legislature, this means replacing the certainty of being able to continue in office for a while longer with the lottery of an election. Though the lottery must be faced sooner or later, and though the government's odds can be improved by judicious timing, improved chances in an early election must be balanced against the possibility of losing office earlier than necessary – a difficult trade-off. All of this has the effect that a prime minister in a parliamentary democracy is liable to dissolve the legislature at what is judged to be the most favorable time during the final 12 (even 18) months of the legislature's maximum term. Empirical research on government durations confirms this pattern –

---

[1]For a summary of this in Western European parliamentary democracies, see Laver and Schofield (1990: 64).

governments tend to be terminated at a much higher rate during the final 12 months than during earlier periods of a legislature's constitutional maximum life (King, Alt, Burns, and Laver, 1990).

Thus far we have been considering the voluntary self-termination of an incumbent government that is attempting to make the best of an upcoming election. The other main trigger for the government formation process arises when a government is involuntarily terminated by its actual or impending defeat in the legislature.

As we indicated in the previous chapter, one of the key characteristics of parliamentary democracy is that an executive must resign if it loses the support of a majority of the legislature – formally tested in a motion of confidence or no confidence.[2] Governments may thus be involuntarily brought down by the legislature. Obviously, they may also resign in anticipation of such a defeat.

Every incumbent government must at some time have had the support of the legislature, in the sense that no viable alternative government was preferred by a legislative majority. Otherwise it would not have been able to gain and retain office. A government defeat in a legislative confidence vote must therefore result from some shock to the system that was not fully anticipated at the time when the government was formed. Such shocks may take many forms. There may be tough policy choices that divide the cabinet irreconcilably, but which the incoming cabinet gambled on being able to avoid. Unanticipated events may force these choices to center stage. Completely unexpected developments from within or without the system – wars, currency crises, or environmental disasters, for example – may transform the world view of key political actors. Politicians may make incorrect assumptions about the preferences or resources of their friends or enemies – they may change their strategic choices when more information on these is revealed as political developments unfold. In each case, the result may be that a government that at one time had the support of the legislature now finds that the legislature prefers some viable alternative. It therefore faces defeat.

It is by no means *necessarily* the case, however, that the defeat of a government implies the dissolution of the legislature and the holding of a new election. The situation in this regard varies considerably from country to country, though apparently more on the basis of precedent than the letter of the constitution. In some countries – Italy and Denmark, for example – it is common, after a government defeat, for the parties of the existing legislature to bargain among themselves and form a new government without an election being called. In other countries –

---

[2]Countries, such as Switzerland, in which the government is not subject to this test but can remain in office for the entire duration of the legislative term are, in this important sense, not parliamentary democracies.

Ireland, for example – a government defeat almost always involves a new election.[3]

Conversely, it is also the case that a new election does not *automatically* put an end to the life of the incumbent government. This can only happen voluntarily if the government resigns or, involuntarily, if the government is defeated. And even in this event it is entirely possible for the government formation process to fail to produce a new government, in which case the "old" government typically remains in place as a caretaker. For our purposes what is important is that a government defeat, or resignation in anticipation of such a defeat, triggers the government formation process.

In summary, the government formation process may be triggered by factors that are entirely predictable – a scheduled election, for example, or government decisions in anticipation of one. Or it may also be triggered by unanticipated shocks to the system, resulting in the midterm legislative defeat of what had previously been a stable incumbent government.

THE STATUS QUO IN GOVERNMENT FORMATION

Once the government formation process has been triggered, it is important to be clear about the policy status quo that remains in place while government formation proceeds, and which remains in place if it is not possible to form a new government. This status quo, after all, is the bottom line against which any alternative must be measured.

Both de jure and de facto in a parliamentary democracy, there is always an incumbent government. Put very crudely, somebody has to remain in office to sign the checks – someone has to have a finger on the trigger. When a particular cabinet has been installed and remains in office without resigning or being defeated, then the situation is unambiguous. The status quo is obviously the incumbent cabinet. Until this is defeated or resigns, it is free to govern at will.

In some countries, such as Germany, the requirement to defeat a government is a "constructive" vote of no confidence. In this case a no-confidence motion in the incumbent government must at the same time

---

[3]This is despite the fact that the Irish president has the explicit constitutional power to refuse a dissolution to a prime minister who has lost the support of the legislature. This power has never been used explicitly and its use would now politicize the presidency to a degree that some would consider inappropriate. The fact that the formal power does exist and might be exercised in extraordinary circumstances does, of course, condition the political game and may well explain the first ever case of a government forming without an intervening election in January 1995.

specify an alternative. In effect, one government is removed and a new one installed in a single step. In these countries, the status quo is always the incumbent government and is unambiguous.

More typically, however, a vote of no confidence in an incumbent cabinet (or a voluntary resignation in anticipation of this) is quite distinct from the investiture of a replacement. In this case, a government will technically be defeated before it is replaced by an alternative. (Obviously, those who vote to defeat the incumbent government will have some alternative in mind when they do so, but different actors may have different alternatives in mind.) Once the incumbent has been defeated or has resigned in anticipation of such a defeat, some form of administration, typically called a "caretaker" cabinet, must hold the fort pending the installation of a successor. Such a caretaker government represents the status quo during the business of government formation.

Surprisingly, there is little to read in the political science literature about caretaker cabinets, though a recent survey of the situation is reported by Laver and Shepsle (1994). With only a couple of exceptions, the position is quite uniform in the countries Laver and Shepsle surveyed. After a cabinet loses its parliamentary basis, it remains in office as a caretaker until a new cabinet is sworn in.[4] It is a strong constitutional convention that no important decisions are taken until a new fully fledged cabinet has been invested in office. The exceptions are Germany where, as we have just seen, a constructive vote-of-no-confidence procedure means that an alternative cabinet is proposed as part of the original no-confidence motion; and Ireland, where the outgoing cabinet continues with more or less undiminished powers until an alternative is sworn in.[5] In other countries, the installation of a caretaker government typically means that there can be no change from the policy status quo that was in place when the caretaker took over.[6]

Thus if a cabinet has resigned or been defeated and a caretaker cabinet has taken over, there is in effect no deviation from the policies in place

---

[4]Occasionally, as has happened in Finland, Italy, and Greece, a group of nonpartisan notables such as judges and academics forms the caretaker cabinet.

[5]In Ireland in December 1992, for example, among many other patronage appointments, a Fianna Fáil caretaker cabinet appointed a Supreme Court judge and Ireland's sole European commissioner – two public positions with the highest possible profile.

[6]This is something of an oversimplification, since there is a sense in which a caretaker cabinet represents "less" than the status quo that preceded it. For example, if some new issue arises out of the blue, an incumbent government may be widely forecast to respond to it by making some particular "new" decision. The status quo when there is a full-fledged incumbent cabinet thus incorporates forecasts about potential responses to new issues that a caretaker cabinet would be precluded from adopting. We ignore such complications here, however.

when the outgoing cabinet left office.[7] This means that we can safely assume the status quo in government formation to be the policy position of the incumbent cabinet, if it has not been defeated. If the incumbent has been defeated and a caretaker has taken over, government policy remains by default at the position of the defeated incumbent.

THE GOVERNMENT FORMATION PROCESS

We have thus far looked at government formation in terms of the actors who are trying to form a government and the nature of the governments they are trying to form. We now turn to the structure of the government formation process itself. This process has a number of key institutional features.

The executive must retain the confidence of the legislature

As we noted in Chapter 1, the essence of parliamentary democracy is that the government must retain the confidence of a majority of the legislature. Even though formal procedures for investing a new government may differ widely, every government, however it is invested in office, must immediately be able to win confidence votes in the legislature. In this sense, investiture procedures are far less important than confidence procedures. In what follows, therefore, we do not concern ourselves with potential differences in investiture procedures, and concentrate instead on the effect on government formation of procedures for voting confidence or no confidence in the government.

The procedure for initiating a legislative vote of no confidence is thus a vital part of the mechanics of parliamentary democracy, one neglected in scholarly writing. Obviously, a confidence motion cannot be debated while the parliament is not in session. (Thus parliamentary democracies are not really democracies at all during the long summer recess enjoyed by most legislatures.) Even while the legislature is in session, however, if the incumbent cabinet can block or delay a motion of no confidence, then it can prolong its own life. On the other hand if it is very easy to propose such a motion, then the legislature effectively sits as a permanent tribunal on the fate of the cabinet.

---

[7]For example, if an incumbent cabinet is defeated on its budget and resigns, then the existing budget remains in force, and may be extended on a pro rata basis into the new fiscal year, until a new full-fledged cabinet takes over. The caretaker cabinet would not be able to reintroduce the defeated budget, since this does not represent the status quo before the government resignation. The same argument applies to any other policy initiative.

The government formation process

In a review of the empirical situation in relation to no-confidence procedures, Laver and Shepsle (1994) found that

> although there are minor variations, procedures for getting no-confidence motions onto the legislative agenda are permissive in every country. The most liberal provisions of all can be found in Norway and Finland. In Norway, for example, . . . any member can . . . propose a no-confidence motion at any time, even without a seconder. In Finland, two proposers are needed, but in both cases the government has no effective means of controlling the procedure. In other countries, the number of proposers may be somewhat higher. . . . The least permissive procedure in the countries covered is in Greece, where 50 deputies must sign the motion. . . . Once more, however, the government has no effective control over the procedure. (Laver and Shepsle, 1994: 289)

The overall conclusions to be drawn are thus clear-cut. No-confidence procedures are permissive, at least in each of the countries in Western Europe considered in the Laver-Shepsle review. This has the effect that it does indeed seem to be the case that the incumbent cabinet can be defeated whenever a majority of legislators decide that they want to do so. Put another way, a cabinet remains in office as long as a majority of legislators cannot agree on a preferred alternative cabinet. We refer to this below as the *majority criterion*.

A set of cabinet portfolios must be allocated among the executive

Our general discussion in Chapter 2 of how people might forecast the effects of installing different governments concluded with the assumption that we can take the defining characteristic of a government to be the allocation of cabinet portfolios between political parties. This is illustrated by our lattice of feasible governments (see Figure 2.2). One party secures the Ministry of Finance, for example, another (or the same) party secures the Ministry for Foreign Affairs, and so on until all of the portfolios have been allocated.

In order to have at least some firm ground beneath our feet before we begin to elaborate our model, for most of this book we do take the set of cabinet portfolios in any given country to be fixed and unchanging during the government formation process. This in itself is something of an oversimplification, in that the identity and jurisdictions of government departments can be, and sometimes are, modified as a part of government formation. (We return to consider this possibility in Chapter 12.) A perfectly general model would assume that absolutely everything, including the entire administrative structure of the state, was on the negotiating table during all government formation negotiations. We do, however, have to impose restrictions on our model in order to gain some analytical purchase, and we feel the assumption that the specification of cabinet portfolios is causally prior to the government formation process is a reasonable starting point.[8]

Cabinet members can veto prospective governments

If a government can be characterized by an allocation of cabinet portfolios between political parties, then it needs to pass an additional test, over and above achieving majority support in the legislature, before it can be installed and remain in office. This test arises because political parties cannot be forced to accept cabinet positions against their will. The consequence of this is that a prospective cabinet also needs the assent of each of the parties who will control at least one portfolio. In effect, unless people can be marched into the cabinet room at gunpoint, and we assume that they cannot, every politician in the cabinet has a veto over the formation of any cabinet in which he or she participates. Since we are assuming that politicians act as agents of their parties, this means that *each party has a veto over the formation of prospective cabinets in which it participates.* As we shall shortly see, the interaction of such vetoes with the majority criterion drives much of the politics of government formation.

Rules governing the formation process

We have argued that, while the details of government formation procedures are different in each parliamentary democracy, the process of forming a government is sufficiently similar in all parliamentary democracies for it to make sense for us to suggest a generic model of government formation. As we describe it, this generic government formation process has three essential stages.

Stage I

A legislative party (call it P_i) is selected. This party proposes a particular cabinet, described in terms of a particular allocation of cabinet portfolios between parties (call this allocation x_i). If the proposal is simply a continuation of the existing cabinet status quo (call this SQ), then Stage I is repeated with some other party selected to make a proposal. If the proposal differs from the existing status quo, then the process advances to Stage II.

[8]It is worth noting in passing that the substantive structure of cabinet portfolio jurisdictions remains remarkably similar as we move from country to country. Thus every Western European country has a Department of Finance (under some name or another), a Department of Foreign Affairs, a Department of Justice, and so on. Though we do not do so in this book, it is intriguing to speculate on the reasons for this. It does, however, suggest that key cabinet portfolio jurisdictions are determined by factors other than "local" party competition over government formation.

The government formation process

Stage II

The parties allocated portfolios in the proposal (called the *participants* in the proposal) may veto it by refusing to participate in that government. If any participant exercises its veto, then the process returns to Stage I and repeats. If no participant exercises its veto, then it proceeds to Stage III.

Stage III

The proposal is put to a parliamentary vote. If the proposal receives the support of a parliamentary majority, then it replaces SQ. If the proposal fails to receive the support of a parliamentary majority, then SQ remains unchanged. In either case, the process returns to Stage I and repeats.

Figure 3.1 shows this process in diagrammatic form.[9] At each node, an individual party is called upon either to propose a cabinet or veto a proposal, or the collection of all parties is called upon to vote on a prospective government. The effect of these choices is to take the process down one of the branches emanating from the node in question. Once the process has been through all of its stages, it simply starts again from the beginning. In this sense, the making and breaking of governments is a never-ending process. Any government, whether the original status quo or a newly minted alternative, is immediately subject to the possibility of being broken by defeat in a no-confidence motion.

This bare-bones model of government formation is obviously very stylized, although we do feel that it captures the essence of the process in many parliamentary democracies. In subsequent chapters we develop some of the logical implications of the model, exploring empirical and experimental evidence that throws light on it, and relaxing some of its more restrictive assumptions. In the remainder of this chapter we restrict ourselves to discussing some of the main features of the process as we have just described it.

Selection of proposers (Stage I)

Politics in the real world is a continuous process, with no beginning, no middle, and no end. It is thus both theoretically artificial and empirically inaccurate to think of the government formation process as "starting" at some point – and, as we have seen, constitutionally, some government is *always* in place. For the purposes of exposition, however, we have to start somewhere.

We began our stylized description of government formation with the recognition of some actor who either makes an explicit proposal for a

[9]It shows an extensive-form game tree of the government formation process we model.

51

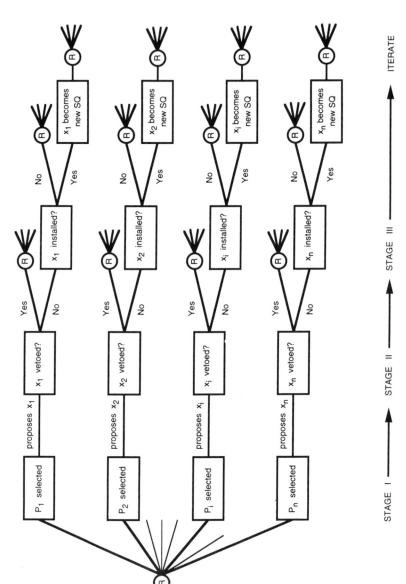

Figure 3.1. Repeat play government formation game

new cabinet or a proposal to retain the incumbent cabinet.[10] The recognition process is indicated by the encircled "R" in Figure 3.1. The actual mechanism by which an actor is recognized to make a proposal may take a range of possible forms.

In many parliamentary democracies, the recognition process entails the head of state designating someone to lead the process of government formation. This person is known to political scientists as a *formateur*. In such countries, there is typically only one *formateur* at any given time. When one *formateur* fails to form a cabinet, another is designated and the process is repeated. Obviously, the designation of a *formateur* is a very explicit political decision. In many parliamentary democracies the role of head of state is ostensibly nonpartisan, and the head of state may be insulated somewhat from politics by giving the task of finding a *formateur* to an *informateur*. An *informateur* is typically a senior, experienced (and often elderly) politician with no direct stake in the government formation process, who passes among political elites and identifies a *formateur* who is likely to be successful. The name of this person is given to the head of state who makes the formal nomination.

The head of state may have no discretion in the government formation process, however. In some parliamentary democracies – Greece, for example – the constitution specifies that the largest legislative party supplies the first *formateur*, with the second-largest party supplying the second in the event of failure, and so on. In other countries – Britain and Ireland, for example – there is a strong constitutional convention that the outgoing prime minister is the first designated *formateur*, even if this person's party is not the largest.

In our description of the government formation process, we embrace all of this potential institutional variation, without tying ourselves down to the circumstances of a particular country, by assuming that the recognition mechanism operates nonstrategically from outside the game. We may therefore think of it generically as a *common-knowledge* recognition rule. This is wholly compatible with real-world recognition procedures in which probabilities of recognition are dependent on party weights, in which parties are recognized in some fixed deterministic order, or in which particular (e.g., incumbent) parties must be recognized first. The theoretical results we report do not depend on specific features of the recognition device used,[11] though we could tease out additional results specific to particular countries, once an actual country-specific recognition device was fully specified.

It is as well to be quite clear, however, that we do assume that the

[10]The latter may be implicit in that no proposal is made at all.

[11]The only exception is that we require that every party have *some* possibility of being recognized (though the probability can be quite small).

recognition of the actors who can propose new governments is non-strategic. This implies, for example, that the head of state is not a strategic actor in the government formation process. This assumption is clearly violated in France and possibly also in Finland, but seems to us to be reasonable in many other parliamentary democracies.[12]

Veto of a proposed government by its participants (Stage II)

As we have already suggested, it seems most unreasonable to suppose that any member of a proposed cabinet can be forced into government against his or her will. Thus, if there is a proposed coalition between a Social Democratic and a Center Party in some country, for example, and the Social Democrats propose that they take the Finance Ministry while the Center Party takes the education portfolio, then the Center Party has something to say in the matter. The proposed government cannot come into being, even if every other member of the legislature votes for it, unless the Center Party agrees to accept the portfolios that it has been allocated. This gives the Center Party a veto over the proposal. Indeed, every party has a veto over every cabinet in which it participates.

Since parties cannot be forced into government against their will, the government formation process is very far from being a simple majority rule voting game, as it has often been portrayed in the literature. Indeed, our model's recognition of this basic fact of political life sets it apart from most other models of government formation.[13] It is simply not enough for a proposed government to command the support of a majority of legislators – it must also command the support of its own participants if it is to have a hope of forming.

Obviously, for those who think that government formation is simply about sharing out the short-term rewards of office, it is hard to see why any government would not be supported by all who receive the rewards. Once we take policy into account, however, it is possible that a party might prefer a government in which it does not participate to some other in which it does. This superficially paradoxical possibility can arise because a government excluding the party might nonetheless be forecast to implement policies quite close to the party's ideal policies. In contrast, a government in which the party does participate might be one that is forecast to implement policies quite far away from its ideal policies. (For

---

[12]We are aware of no scholarly treatment in the government formation literature of the role of the head of state, strategic or otherwise.

[13]The one exception of which we are aware is a version of a model proposed by Austen-Smith and Banks (1990), based on what they call the *restricted portfolio core* of the government formation game, a model that makes exactly the same assumption as we do.

example, a Social Democratic Party may prefer a minority Center Party administration to a coalition between the Social Democrats and a party of the far right, if the very disparate coalition were forecast to generate a lot of grief for the Social Democrats in policy terms.)

The possibility of participant vetoes gives a very distinctive character to the politics of government formation. Quite apart from anything else, it raises the possibility that there may be "standoffs," in which some party threatens to veto an alternative to the status quo, despite the fact that this is preferred by a legislative majority. As we shall see, the legislative majority can threaten to keep voting for the alternative, some party can threaten to keep vetoing it, and government formation can thereby be deadlocked until one side or the other backs down. Such vetoes can also give a particular strategic advantage to one particular party, arising out of its participation in, and consequent ability to veto, a wide range of popular potential governments.

Our generic model of the government formation process involves a further implicit assumption about vetoes. This is that it is not possible to veto the status quo government. This assumption is somewhat more controversial than it might seem at first sight. The matter of the unilateral resignation of one party, but not all parties, from a government raises complex and intriguing issues that have, as far as we know, been completely ignored in the government formation literature. We have already noted that constitutionally, both in theory and in practice, there must always be some government. It is just not possible for every party to abandon the government, leaving the doors of Government House swinging in the breeze and nobody running the country. As a matter of political practice, if the government parties really are determined to bail out they can do so, but a caretaker administration will be put in their place which, as we have already seen, will maintain existing government policy. Therefore the policies of the outgoing government remain in place, even after it has resigned, for the typically brief duration of the ensuing caretaker government. It is in this important sense that incumbent parties cannot veto the status quo. Even if they do resign, policy outputs under the jurisdiction of the portfolios they controlled remain essentially the same until the portfolios have been reallocated and a new de facto government has been formed.[14]

[14]The treatment of a "partial" government resignation in our generic model thus assumes that a resignation brings down the government, installs a caretaker continuing the policies of the outgoing administration, and triggers the government formation process. This is true in many countries, but in others it is possible for the incumbent government simply to reallocate the portfolios of the resigning party and to continue as if nothing had happened unless defeated in a legislative motion of no confidence. In such cases our model in effect assumes that the government formation process is implicitly triggered in the sense that the remaining parts of the incumbent government

The context

Confidence and investiture votes (Stage III)

Our generic model collapses two real-world features of the government formation process that we take to be strategically merged – the vote of no confidence and the investiture vote. As we saw earlier, one constitutional device, the constructive vote of no confidence used in Germany, does formally merge these in a requirement that a motion of no confidence in the government must designate an alternative administration as part of the motion. The constructive vote of no confidence is not common in parliamentary democracies, however, most of which have constitutionally quite separate devices for defeating one government and installing a new one.

This of course raises the possibility that an incumbent government is defeated, yet no alternative is able to pass the investiture test. In this event, as we have also seen, a caretaker administration remains in place, implementing the policies of the outgoing government. Even after a no-confidence motion has passed, therefore, the policies of the outgoing government remain in place. As far as the government formation process is concerned, therefore, the key vote is the one that installs a new government. This investiture vote is an explicit constitutional requirement in many countries. In countries without a formal investiture procedure, the implicit investiture vote occurs on the first occasion when the government faces the legislature, and exposes itself to the possibility of losing a confidence vote. Thus we feel we do not do too much violence to reality by treating the no-confidence vote and the investiture procedure as if they were part of the same strategic process, since a successful no-confidence motion changes nothing in policy terms until a new government is invested.

Our generic model of parliamentary democracy thus sees the incumbent government as being continuously vulnerable to defeat by the legislature. In effect, the government formation process is continuously iterated throughout the life of the government, though many of the actors who have the chance to propose an alternative government will in practice do nothing, implicitly proposing the continuation of the status quo.

propose a new portfolio allocation and, if this is not vetoed, the allocation is immediately subject to a legislative no-confidence motion. If this no-confidence motion is lost, a caretaker government is in place, which implements the policies of the *original* incumbent government. Thus, our model is characterizing what we feel are well established constitutional conventions in many European democracies. However, the absence of any systematic discussion of caretaker governments in the political science literature makes this point difficult to establish definitively. The government formation process, as described in the text, is then iterated.

CONCLUSION: THE DIFFERENCE BETWEEN FORMING A
GOVERNMENT AND LEGISLATING

The government formation process illustrated in Figure 3.1 and elaborated in this chapter is a stylized description of the institutional manner in
which policies are selected and implemented in parliamentary democracies. Perhaps the most important assumption underlying our approach is
that most of the business of policy making and implementation takes
place within the executive – and that actual legislation is a relatively
minor part of the policy process. Even when legislation is necessary in
order to change policy outputs, we assume that the executive retains firm
control of the resources required to develop implementable legislation, as
well as controlling the legislative timetable itself. It is thus relatively rare
in a parliamentary democracy for the legislature to succeed in imposing
detailed legislation in the face of active opposition from the executive.

According to our approach, the role of the legislature is much more
that of controlling the fate of the government than it is of implementing
policy directly. The legislature thus has the ability to choose between a
limited number of viable governments, each with different policy implications, rather than to select policy outputs directly. This distinguishes our
approach from other recent theories of government formation which
operate as if parliamentary actors engage in the direct selection of self-
implementing policies.[15] We might think of these as models of legislative
government, rather than of cabinet government, since their equilibriums
are statements about which policies a legislature would select if it had the
power to govern directly. The parameters that affect this policy selection
are simply the size and spatial policy position of all legislative parties.
Whether or not any given party is in the cabinet has no effect whatsoever
on forecast policy outputs in these theories; indeed the distinction between legislature and executive is not made at all.

In contrast our approach requires that explicit attention be given to
the identity of those who compose the government. The reason, which we
have alluded to on several occasions, has to do with the departmental
nature of policy formulation and implementation, and the inevitable ministerial agenda power that this entails. The manner in which this power
will be exercised depends on who possesses it. Thus, in our view, it is
misleading to suppress consideration of the partisan composition of the
cabinet. Since even direct legislation in parliamentary democracies tends
to be orchestrated by the government, it is also heavily conditioned by

[15]See, for example, the discussion of Baron (1991) and Schofield (1993) in Chapter 1.

departmentalism, as are the substantive outputs of implemented policies that are affected by the preferences of individual ministers.

Notwithstanding our reservations about the realism of their assumptions, there is no doubt that recent direct-legislation models of policy formation are methodologically very rigorous. The stylized process described in Figure 3.1 does, indeed, borrow heavily from one such approach, the "divide-the-dollar" model of Baron and Ferejohn (1989). In this, a group of legislators has the classic pork-barrel task of dividing a dollar, an outcome being some apportioning of the dollar among projects in legislative constituencies. As in our model, there is a recognition device by which some legislator is selected to propose a division. The proposal goes directly to a vote and, if a majority approves, the money is so divided and the game ends. If not, the recognition stage is repeated.

Though inspired by the Baron-Ferejohn direct-legislation model, our approach differs in several significant ways. First, as we have just seen, we restrict proposals in our model to the finite set of possible governments and the forecast policy outputs associated with each. Second, since we deal with actual cabinets rather than with policies in the abstract, we allow for the possibility that actors can veto cabinets (and hence policy outputs) that require their participation. Finally, since we describe the continuously repeating process of building and maintaining a government, ours is a continuous game. Baron and Ferejohn, in contrast, describe a single policy decision, leading them to specify a game that ends irrevocably once the decision in question has been taken.

Overall, therefore, the single most important thing about the process described in this chapter is that it concerns the making and breaking of governments in situations in which actors are concerned with the substantive content of government policy outputs. Governments in parliamentary democracies are created by legislators and may be destroyed by them. But, while they are in existence, governments do take on a life of their own. Legislatures have only very limited control over the precise policy outputs governments enact, and the only real sanction legislators have at their disposal is to bring the entire government crashing down around their ears. Given all of this, governments clearly have a lot of power over policy, and legislators will obviously take careful account of this when deciding which government to put in power in the first place.

PART II

The model

4

Government equilibrium

In the previous chapter we set out a stylized description of the government formation process in parliamentary democracies. This description is, in effect, a logical model of government formation. In this chapter, we begin to unfold some of the implications of our model, exploring ways in which it might increase our understanding of what it takes to make and break a government.

Since we are interested in what it takes for a government to form and stay formed, an important thread running through the rest of the argument of this book is the concept of an *equilibrium cabinet* – a notion that we hope is more or less intuitive. An equilibrium cabinet, once it is formed, stays formed because no political actor with the ability to act in such a way as to bring down the cabinet and replace it with some alternative has the incentive to do so. Conversely, no actor with the incentive to replace the cabinet with some alternative has the ability to do so. Thus we expect an equilibrium cabinet to be stable, remaining in place until a change in the external environment transforms either the incentives of some pivotal actor or the "pivotalness" of some actor already possessing the appropriate incentives.[1] (For example, an opposition party may, as a result of by-elections or defections from other parties, increase its weight and thereby the extent to which it is pivotal.) We do not expect a cabinet that is out of equilibrium to be stable, since at least one actor who has an incentive to bring down the government also has the ability to do so.

Political equilibriums can be attractive, retentive, or both. An *attractive* equilibrium cabinet is one that tends to come into being, even when it is not the original status quo. A *retentive* equilibrium cabinet remains in place if it is the original status quo, but may not come into being otherwise. For

[1]Thus, our notion of equilibrium must always be taken as relative to *anticipated* factors. Ex ante, actors choose a government in the expectation that it will remain in equilibrium. Ex post shocks to the system, unanticipated at the time of government formation, are potentially destabilizing factors.

example, a government may form in a particular strategic environment and this environment may change, perhaps because of an election result. The incumbent government may remain a retentive equilibrium, and therefore remain in office, even though, given the new election result, it would never have been able to *take* office if a different cabinet had been in power before the election.

The essential purpose of the discussion that follows, therefore, is to find ways of characterizing what it takes to form an equilibrium cabinet. This should enable us to identify those potential cabinets that are likely to be in equilibrium and those that are not, and thereby to enrich our understanding of the political factors that underpin cabinet stability. Such characterizations are based on a number of variable features of the political situation and the government formation process, and what our model does is allow us to explore each of these features in a systematic and rigorous manner. As it happens, the character of equilibrium cabinets, according to our model, is heavily conditioned by whether there exists some "strong" party that is in a particularly powerful bargaining position – in a sense to be made more precise – that allows it to dominate the making and breaking of governments.

In the remainder of this chapter we first recapitulate the basic building blocks of our model; we then characterize certain features of an equilibrium cabinet; next we discuss the role of strong parties; finally we look more generally at the distinctly centripetal tendencies implied by our model of government formation.

BUILDING BLOCKS FOR A MODEL OF GOVERNMENT FORMATION

The basic building blocks of our model are as follows:

1. There is a set of legislative parties, each with a weight and a policy position. A party's weight is measured in terms of its share of the total seats in the legislature. Each party's policy position is expressed in terms of the policy that the party is forecast to implement, if given the opportunity to do so, on each key policy dimension. This describes the political arena in which the making and breaking of governments takes place. Graphically this arena can be seen as a type of lattice, which we display in Figure 2.2 and exploit later in this chapter. The weights and policy positions of all parties are assumed in most of what follows to be common knowledge among all relevant actors.

2. There is a set of government departments, each responsible for the development and implementation of public policy in particular areas. Each department is responsible directly to a cabinet minister. While more than one department may be responsible to a single minister, no one

department may be responsible to two or more ministers at the same time.

3. There is a government formation process, set out in detail in Figure 3.1 and described in Chapter 3. Proposals for government involve the specification of which parties will hold cabinet portfolios with jurisdiction over the various key policy dimensions. A new cabinet replaces the status quo if it is proposed, receives the assent of every one of the parties participating in it, and is then supported by a majority of legislators.[2]

Winsets

The government formation process in a parliamentary democracy thus requires that, before a new government can replace the status quo, it must receive the support of each of its participants, on the one hand, plus the support of a legislative majority. The majority requirement means that one of the things of great concern to us is the set of potential cabinets preferred by a legislative majority to some cabinet that we have under consideration, which in turn depends on the policies that each potential alternative cabinet is forecast to implement if put into office. Thus, we must focus on two distinct, but related, preference relations – those over *policies* and those over *cabinets*.[3] For a policy x, the set of policies preferred by a majority to it is known as the *policy winset of x*, labeled $W^*(x)$. For a cabinet X, the set of cabinets preferred by a majority to it is known as the *lattice winset of X*, $W(X)$.[4] When we consider whether a particular cabinet might be in equilibrium, therefore, one of the first things we do is look in its lattice winset, that is, at which cabinets are majority-preferred to it.

[2]To be precise, we are assuming a legislative decision rule based on majority voting in legislatures with an odd number of legislators, or in legislatures with an even number of legislators in which there are no "blocking coalitions" – coalitions such that the coalition and its complement both control exactly 50 percent of all seats. When there is a qualified majority decision rule, requiring the support of more than a bare majority of legislators, and when there are blocking coalitions, it may well be the case that more than one party is at the "median" position on some policy dimension – a situation that could of course be modeled, but which we do not consider here.

[3]The connection between these derives, as just noted, from the common-knowledge policy forecast associated with each cabinet. By convention, we will write cabinets in uppercase letters and associated policies in lowercase letters, when it is necessary to distinguish between them. Thus cabinet X is associated with policy forecast x. Because parties in our model are policy motivated, party i prefers cabinet X to cabinet Y if and only if it prefers policy x to policy y. In this context, x and y are *vectors* of policy positions.

[4]With a slight abuse of notation, we claim that $W(X) = W^*(x) \cap L$, where L is the lattice of portfolio allocations. By this we mean that the portfolio allocations preferred to cabinet X are those represented by points on L whose forecast policies are preferred to x (i.e., cabinets whose forecast policies are elements of $W^*(x)$).

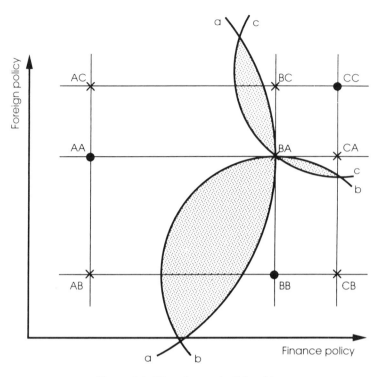

Figure 4.1. The winset of a BA cabinet

Returning to the lattice of party positions we first saw in Figure 2.2, we illustrate the policy winset of cabinet BA as the shaded area in Figure 4.1. Remember that cabinet BA gives the finance portfolio, on the horizontal axis, to Party B and the foreign affairs portfolio, on the vertical axis, to Party A. In order to arrive at this conclusion we first make the conventional political economist's assumption that the policy positions that each party prefers to the forecast policy of the BA cabinet are those that are closer than this to the party's ideal. If we also assume (once more conventionally) that closeness is denominated in the same Euclidean distances that we use in physical space, then the points that Party A prefers to BA, for example, are those inside the circle centered on Party A's policy position and passing through BA. A segment of this circle is shown in Figure 4.1, labeled aa. All points inside this circle are closer to Party A's ideal policy than is the policy forecast to be implemented by the BA government. Similarly, Party B prefers everything inside the circle centered on Party B's position and passing through BA − a segment of this is bb in Figure 4.1. The equivalent segment for Party C is cc. If the weights of the three parties are such that any two can combine to form a legislative majority, then we know that policy positions are majority-preferred to those forecast for cabinet BA (and are therefore in the policy winset of BA) if they are in the intersection of any two of the three circles just described. This area is shaded in Figure 4.1.

Thus, this winset has three segments. First, there are policy positions preferred by both Party A and Party B to BA – these must be inside circle segments aa and bb. These positions are in the lower left-hand shaded petal-shaped area in Figure 4.1. Positions preferred by both Party A and Party C to BA must be inside circle segments aa and cc. They are in the upper left-hand shaded area. Similarly, positions preferred by both Party B and Party C to BA are in the middle right-hand shaded area. The union of the three shaded areas is the policy winset of BA, which we can abbreviate to $W^*(BA)$. Every policy in $W^*(BA)$ is preferred by some legislative majority to the policy of cabinet BA.[5]

Strategic equivalents and equilibrium

The government formation process described in Figure 3.1 has no beginning and no end, but we structure our analysis by imagining some incumbent cabinet, X, and investigating what would happen if the government formation process started from a status quo of X. Our rational foresight assumption implies that all political actors will be able to figure out what will happen as a result of starting the government formation process from X – let us call this forecast outcome Y. Thus starting at X implies, for the actors, ending at Y. As we saw in Chapter 2, we can think of Y as the *strategic equivalent of X*. Once we are at X, rational behavior in the strategic context of the process depicted in Figure 3.1 yields Y.

The notion of a strategic equivalent allows us to be more precise about what we mean by an equilibrium. A status quo X is in equilibrium if the strategic equivalent of X – which we write as $SE(X)$ – is also X. An equilibrium is an X such that $SE(X) = X$. Conversely if the strategic equivalent of the status quo differs from the status quo, then the latter is not in equilibrium.

The next step in our argument is to note that, in the government formation process that we have described, the status quo can only be replaced by some alternative that is majority preferred to it. In other words, the strategic equivalent of the status quo, X, must either be X itself, or some element in the winset of X.[6] The reason for this is that

---

[5]Note that, while the policy winset $W^*(BA)$ is conspicuously nonempty, the lattice winset $W(BA)$ is empty. That is, while there are *policies* preferred to those forecast for the BA government, there is no *cabinet* (point in L) that is forecast to implement such a policy. We will pursue this interesting fact.

[6]Formally, $SE(X) \in \{X\} \cup W(X)$.

65

replacing X involved investing some alternative cabinet. This investiture must be supported by a legislative majority. If the investiture would eventually result in some alternative Z that is not majority-preferred to X, then members of the legislative majority preferring X to Z, exercising their rational foresight, would vote against it.[7]

EQUILIBRIUM CABINETS AT THE GENERALIZED MEDIAN

Figure 4.1 portrays a *simple* jurisdictional arrangement in which horizontal policy is determined by the Finance Ministry and vertical policy by the Foreign Ministry. The potential cabinet that we are investigating here – BA – has one very important strategic feature; the portfolio with jurisdiction over each policy dimension is allocated to the party with the median legislator on that dimension. Since any two parties in this three-party arrangement, by assumption, compose a majority, it follows that the "middle" party on any dimension possesses the median legislator. The advantaged party is Party B on the horizontal dimension and Party A on the vertical dimension. The forecast policy output of this cabinet, then, is the dimension-by-dimension median (DDM) in the policy space. We can think of this cabinet as the DDM cabinet. As we saw in Chapter 1, Kadane (1972) has shown that any point in a continuous policy space that is an equilibrium (i.e., a point with an empty winset) must be the DDM.[8] As we shall shortly see, this particular strategic feature of the DDM cabinet is very important in the government formation process.

The shaded areas in Figure 4.1 show quite clearly that the BA policy position under investigation does not have an empty *policy* winset. Any policy in these shaded areas is preferred by a legislative majority to the policy forecast for BA. (And Kadane's result tells us that some other point is in turn preferred by some legislative majority to any point in these shaded areas.) If BA were simply a legislative policy proposal, therefore, it could be beaten in the legislature by a wide range of alternative policies and would not be in equilibrium.

[7]Note that we assume that actors behave strategically in the sense that their decisions take account of the effects of their choices and the forecast choices of others in future stages of any game they are playing. Thus, even if the first move away from the status quo, X, is to some interim point, Y (perhaps, but not necessarily, majority-preferred to the status quo), that makes some final alternative, Z, possible, members of the legislative majority who prefer X to Z will foresee the danger of allowing Y to form in the interim, since they know that SE(Y) = Z. They can prevent Z by refusing to vote for Y, keeping X in place even if some of them prefer Y to X.

[8]Kadane's result can be extended to the situation in which the set of alternatives to the DDM is the set of lattice points, rather than the full continuous policy space. A proof is provided in the appendix to this chapter.

In our model of the government formation process, however, BA is not simply a legislative policy proposal, but rather is the cabinet (and the forecast policy output associated with it) in which the finance portfolio is allocated to Party B and foreign affairs to Party A. As we have seen there is a finite set of cabinets that can be posed as alternatives to BA, and these are represented by the other points on the lattice in Figure 4.1. These are the three cabinets identified by black dots (AA, BB, and CC), which represent giving both key portfolios to a single party, and the five other cabinets identified by an "x" (AC, BC, CA, AB, CB), each of which represents a different way of allocating the portfolios to a coalition of two parties.

We can easily see by looking at Figure 4.1 that no lattice point is in the shaded area representing the winset of BA. This means that there is no *alternative cabinet* whose forecast policy outputs are preferred by a majority to those of BA. *BA, consequently, is preferred by some legislative majority to every alternative cabinet.* For this reason, BA is an equilibrium cabinet. If the status quo is BA, then any strategic move that will result in the investiture of an alternative to BA will be blocked by the legislative majority that prefers BA to the alternative in question.

This argument generalizes to support our first proposition characterizing equilibrium cabinets in parliamentary democracies:

> *Proposition 4.1*: The DDM cabinet is an equilibrium if there is no alternative government in its winset.

Informal proof: The strategic equivalent of any point is either the point itself or an element of its winset (see note 6). Thus, if the winset of the DDM cabinet is empty, then the strategic equivalent of the DDM must be the DDM itself. This is therefore in equilibrium.[9]

Remember that Kadane's result tells us that, when there is a simple jurisdictional structure, only the DDM cabinet can have an empty winset. No other cabinet can have an empty winset. Thus the DDM cabinet will remain in place if there is no lattice point in its winset. This was the case in Figure 4.1 and, as we shall see, it is in general quite common for there to be no alternative cabinet in the winset of the DDM. The finding that there is a potential equilibrium cabinet at the generalized median position holds for policy spaces of any dimensionality.[10]

It may be the case that some alternative is preferred by a majority to

---

[9]Formally, let the DDM cabinet be written as m*. Since $SE(m^*) \in \{m^*\} \cup W(m^*)$ and $W(m^*) = \emptyset$, then $SE(m^*) = \{m^*\}$. When the DDM cabinet has an empty-lattice winset, we write it as m**.

[10]However, we will demonstrate below that the probability that the generalized median cabinet is preferred to all others decreases as the dimensionality of the policy space and the number of parties increase.

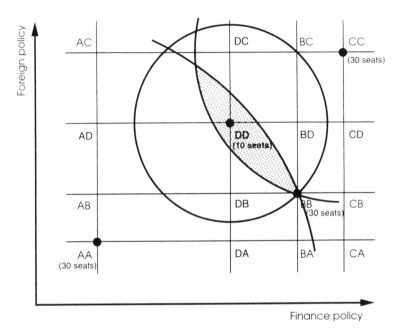

Figure 4.2. A DDM cabinet with a nonempty winset

the DDM cabinet, however, since Kadane's Theorem does not *guarantee* an empty winset for the DDM. An example of this is given in Figure 4.2. This shows a four-party system in which Parties A, B, and C control thirty seats each, and Party D controls ten seats. The DDM cabinet is BB, since Party B is at the median position on each policy dimension. The indifference curves through BB show how each of the other parties feels about BB.[11] Since Parties A and C are essential members of any winning legislative coalition that excludes Party B, while Party B obviously prefers its own ideal point to anything else, the winset of the BB cabinet is the intersection of the indifference curves centered on AA and CC and passing through BB – the shaded area in Figure 4.2. This area, however, contains an alternative cabinet, DD, preferred by both Party A and Party C (and obviously by Party D) to BB, despite the fact that BB is at the median position on both dimensions.

In this particular case, we know that both BD and DB are preferred by

[11]Recall that the points on the circle through a designated point (like BB) centered on a party's ideal are equidistant from that ideal and hence are equally preferable to the point in question (BB). Hence, the circle is called an *indifference curve*. Points inside the circle, being closer to the party ideal than is the point in question, are preferred to the latter.

a majority to DD since each of these is at the median position on just one more dimension.[12] By the same logic, BB is preferred by a majority to either BD or DB. In other words there is a cycle of potential cabinets, BB → DD → (DB or BD) → BB, with each cabinet in the cycle majority-preferred to the one preceding it. Nonetheless, as simulation results reported later in this volume confirm, most party configurations with a relatively small number of parties and salient policy dimensions do not generate cabinet cycles of this type. In these common cases, the DDM cabinet is an equilibrium, implementing policies at the generalized median of the policy space.

What is a strong party?

Although the generalized median cabinet is often an equilibrium in the government formation process, it may not be the only one. The fact that any of the members of a proposed cabinet may veto it by refusing to participate means that there may be other equilibriums. To demonstrate that this can be so, Figure 4.3 shows the same government formation situation as Figure 4.1, but now displays how the various parties feel about a cabinet in which Party B takes both key portfolios. The intersection of indifference curves aa and cc – the shaded area – is the set of policies preferred by both Party A and Party C to the policy forecast for BB. We can see quite clearly that two alternative cabinets, BA and BC, are preferred by a legislative majority (comprising Party A and Party C) to BB. Note, however, that Party B is a participant in both BA and BC, and therefore can veto these proposals. There is no alternative to BB that is preferred by a legislative majority but which Party B cannot veto. This puts Party B in a very powerful bargaining position. Once a Party B minority government is in place, for example, it may prove difficult to dislodge, since to do so requires Party B's assent.[13] For this reason we call parties that are like Party B (in ways we will shortly make more specific) strong parties. Such parties are in a position to dominate the government formation process.

We can generalize the type of situation shown in Figure 4.3 by defining Party S as *strong* if it participates in every cabinet preferred by a majority

[12]We know this from Kadane's Improvement Algorithm, on which see footnote 8 of Chapter 1 and the appendix to the present chapter.

[13]For the time being we do not worry about how Party B came to be a single-party minority government in the first place. The possibilities are not so bizarre. For example, Party B might have been a majority government before an election in which it subsequently lost its majority. Government formation would then begin with a Party B minority government as the status quo.

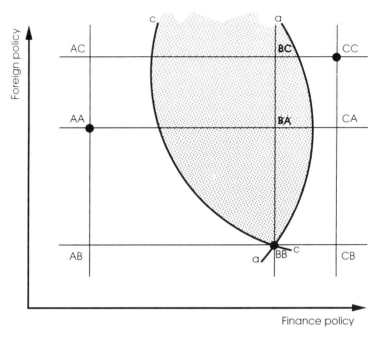

Figure 4.3. The winset of a BB cabinet

to the cabinet in which Party S takes all portfolios. In practice, there are two rather different types of situation in which this can happen. First, if no cabinet at all is preferred by any majority to some particular single-party government, then the ideal point of this particular party must have an empty winset and the party must obviously be strong. We know from Kadane's result that if a strong party has an ideal point that has an empty winset, then this is at the generalized median. In this case we designate the party as being *very strong*. Second, a party may have an ideal point with a nonempty winset, but be strong because the party participates in, and hence can veto, every cabinet in this winset. In this case, the strong party must use its power of veto in order to assert its strength. For reasons to which we will return, a particular strong party may not credibly be able to threaten such vetoes. We therefore designate a strong party whose ideal point has a nonempty winset, and whose strength derives from vetoes, as being *merely strong*.

Thus, the two different types of strong party derive their strength from different sources. The *very* strong party is strong quite simply because no majority prefers an alternative cabinet. The *merely* strong party does not find itself in this enviable position. Its strength derives from threats to veto certain alternative cabinets. While the support of a parliamentary majority is the firm foundation on which the strength of a very strong party is based, the strength of a merely strong party derives from the credibility of threats that may be firm one moment and run like sand through its fingers the next.

Strong parties have a number of properties that help us to characterize equilibriums in the government formation process. The first of these is that *there can be at most one strong party*. If there were two strong parties, say S_1 and S_2, then the ideal point of one would have to be in the winset of the other.[14] But if, for example, S_1 were in the winset of S_2, then there is a point in S_2's winset in which S_2 does not participate. This contradicts the definition of a strong party.

The fact that there can be at most one strong party means that the strong party, if one exists, will be a focal actor in the government formation process. No other actor is in a position to insist on forming a government on its own. This is because, for every other party, not only is some alternative majority-preferred to the cabinet giving the party all key portfolios, but this is an alternative that it cannot veto.

We can show by example that there may be situations in which there is no strong party. Figure 4.4 shows such an example. This is a modification of the situation shown in Figure 4.2, resulting from splitting the original Party D into two parties, D and E. Party E has an ideal point at EE. We know from Figure 4.2 that DD is preferred by a majority to BB, so Party B cannot be strong. We can see from the cc and bb indifference curves in Figure 4.4 that Parties B and C, who have a majority between them, prefer EE to DD. So Party D cannot be strong. We know from the aa indifference curve and the fact that Party B prefers BB to anything else that BB is majority-preferred to EE. So party E cannot be strong. It is also easy to see that DD is majority-preferred to both AA and CC, so Parties A and C cannot be strong. Thus there is no strong party.

In general, however, as we shall show in Chapter 6, strong parties are quite common, both in simulated and real party systems. This is important, since strong parties have a significant impact on the government formation process, as we now see.

Strong parties in government formation

Since no alternative cabinet is majority-preferred to a cabinet in which a *very* strong party takes all key portfolios, we can easily see that this cabinet is in equilibrium. This is because a very strong party must have an ideal point (written s**) at the DDM and, from Proposition 1, when the

---

[14]Assuming the majority preference relation is complete, then for any two cabinets, X and Y, either $X \in W(Y)$ or $Y \in W(X)$.

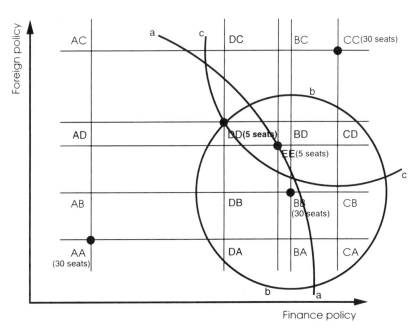

Figure 4.4. A system with no strong party

winset of the DDM is empty, the DDM cabinet is a retentive equilibrium.[15] That it is also an attractive equilibrium follows from a consideration of the government formation process described in Figure 3.1. In this, the very strong party simply waits until it is recognized and proposes its ideal point, a cabinet in which it gets all portfolios.[16] From the definition of a very strong party, this cabinet is majority-preferred to all others, including any other status quo. Since no other party participates in this cabinet, none can veto it. If some party proposes another cabinet, this proposal will lose since the strong party ideal is majority-preferred to it and no majority has any incentive to vote contrary to its preferences in this instance; this is because there is no alternative to a cabinet controlled by the very strong party that any majority could be aiming toward. So whatever the status quo might be, and however it may provisionally have been changed,[17] all parties will anticipate that the strong party ideal will

[15]Since $SE(s^{**}) \in \{s^{**}\} \cup W(s^{**})$ and $W(s^{**}) = \varnothing$, then $SE(s^{**}) = \{s^{**}\}$.

[16]Since every party has some probability of recognition, the strong party is bound to be recognized at some point.

[17]It is perfectly all right for the original status quo to be replaced by something else. Once s^{**} is proposed, it will nevertheless prevail. Consequently, with rational foresight at work, these interim changes in the status quo may never materialize (though, as noted, it won't affect our results if they do).

eventually be proposed, will not be vetoed, and will thus be invested in office. In short, a *very strong* party can form an equilibrium cabinet on its own, whether or not it controls a legislative majority.

The existence of any strong party, however, whether it is very strong or merely strong, has a major strategic impact on the government formation process. This is characterized by our second major proposition about government equilibrium in parliamentary democracies:

Proposition 4.2: When a strong party exists, it is a member of every equilibrium cabinet.

Another way of putting this proposition is that, if there is a strong party, then the equilibrium cabinet will either be the strong party ideal point, written s*, or an element in the winset of this point, W(s*), in which the strong party, by definition, participates. A precise, and slightly more general, statement of this proposition and a full formal proof are provided in the appendix to this chapter.

The crucial feature of this result is that it is not possible to form an equilibrium cabinet without the participation of an existing strong party. This in turn means that the existence and identity of a strong party is a very important strategic feature of any government formation situation. We shall have much more to say in Part III of this book about the characteristics of a strong party, but it is clear at this stage that its identity is entirely determined by the configuration of party weights and policy positions. Thus changes in weights and policy positions may forge, revise, or obliterate the identity of the strong party. Quite small changes may have quite big effects, for instance, if they move into the winset of the strong party an alternative cabinet in which it does not participate.

What this means is that not only is the role of a strong party of considerable interest in itself, but also that particular party configurations might have striking strategic discontinuities. As a result of such discontinuities, a configuration of parties can be such that small perturbations of key parameters have big effects on the government formation process, by changing the existence and identity of a strong party, for example. If a party system is close to some strategic threshold, then small changes in party weights may change the decisive structure,[18] or small changes in party policy may change the location of key indifference contours. Both types of change will affect the contents of winsets. The addi-

---

[18]In the 1992 Irish election, for example, the entire system of possible coalitions depended on the very close outcome of the final seat in one constituency. The votes in this constituency were counted over and over again for a week, with each recount changing the result and being appealed by the loser, until a final result was declared. Serious coalition bargaining could not begin until this recounting had been completed. This case is developed in more detail in Chapter 6.

tion or subtraction of points from the winset of some party ideal may well determine whether that party is strong, and hence able to dominate the making and breaking of governments. Alternatively, a configuration of parties might be quite far from a strategic threshold, so that quite large changes in the parameters, while changing the shape of the winsets in the continuous policy space, may have no effect whatsoever on the list of alternative cabinets in key winsets. In such circumstances a wide range of different election results, or quite large shifts in party policy, would sustain the same cabinet equilibrium.

Strong parties and standoffs

A strong party, and in particular a *merely* strong party, need not necessarily get everything its own way, however. Although it is a participant in every equilibrium government, a merely strong party cannot necessarily impose its ideal point as the outcome of the government formation process. Remember that a very strong party has no alternative cabinet in the winset of its ideal point, s^{**}. A merely strong party does have alternative cabinets in the winset of its ideal, s^*. It is strong by virtue of its ability in principle to veto every one of these. However, it is possible to imagine situations in which a merely strong party may be forced to lift its veto on elements of $W(s^*)$ as the result of strategic interplay with other parties. We can gain some intuition about this by revisiting the example in Figure 4.3, in which Party B is the merely strong party and the generalized median cabinet is BA. (Hold onto your hats, however; we are about to explore some quite complex strategic thinking in this deceptively simple-looking case!)

Suppose that, for some reason that need not concern us here, the status quo cabinet in Figure 4.3 is CC. We know that the strategic equivalent of CC is either CC itself or a cabinet that is majority-preferred to CC.[19] The points that are majority-preferred to CC are {AB, BA, BB, BC, CA}. From a status quo of CC, therefore, the government formation process will thus end either with an equilibrium cabinet at CC or with any of these five alternatives to CC. We also know from Proposition 2 and Figure 4.3 that, since B is a strong party, the government formation process must end with an equilibrium cabinet that is either BB or an element in its winset, $W(BB)$. Thus the equilibrium cabinet is in {BA, BB, BC}. Knowing that the status quo is CC and the strong party is B, therefore, allows us (and, far more important, the parties involved in government formation!) to concentrate on cabinets that are simultaneously in {AB, BA, BB, BC, CA} and {BA, BB, BC}, that is, on three cabinets – BA, BB, and BC.

Consider now what any of the parties can do if recognized to propose

[19]$SE(CC) \in \{CC\} \cup W(CC)$.

a new cabinet. Since it is the focal actor in the government formation process, consider first the strong party, Party B. Among the prospective replacements for CC, Party B clearly most likes its ideal point, BB. If recognized, Party B could propose this. However, BB is the point in {BA, BB, BC} least liked by Party A. Furthermore both Party A and Party C, jointly controlling a majority, prefer BA to BB. Party A could thus vote strategically against replacing CC with BB, even though it prefers BB to CC. It would do this in the anticipation of eventually being recognized and proposing BA, which is majority preferred to any other cabinet.

However, if Party A proposes BA, then Party B can strategically veto this in favor of the CC status quo, even though B prefers BA to CC. It would do this in the anticipation of eventually being recognized and proposing BB and in the further anticipation that Party A will reluctantly accept that B's veto on BA will never be lifted. If Party A does accept this, then it will vote to replace CC with BB.

This generates a potential standoff between Party A and Party B. (Party C can do no better than to vote sincerely to retain CC.) Each party prefers both BA and BB to the status quo of CC. But Party A prefers BA to BB, while Party B prefers BB to BA. This standoff is quite close to a chicken game. Party B can threaten to keep vetoing BA, thereby keeping CC in place, until Party A gives in and votes for BB (which A does prefer to CC). Party A can threaten to continue voting strategically against BB, once more keeping CC in place, until Party B gives in and lifts its veto on BA (which B does prefer to CC).

If Party A always votes strategically against BB, and always proposes BA when recognized, and if Party B forms the opinion that Party A will continue to do this, then it is rational for Party B to lift its veto over BA, vote for this as a replacement for CC, and thus allow BA to form. If, on the other hand, Party A always vetoes BA, and always proposes BB when recognized, and if Party A forms the opinion that Party B will continue to do this, then it is rational for Party A to change its strategic vote against BB, vote for BB as a replacement for CC, and thus allow BB to form.

We cannot forecast how this standoff will be resolved without making new assumptions about the opinion formation process we have just described. For the purposes of Proposition 2, however, we do not need to know precisely which of the two outcomes involved in the standoff will actually prevail, since the outcome is either the strong-party ideal or some other cabinet that is majority-preferred to this. In either case, as claimed in Proposition 2, the strong party participates in the cabinet that takes office.

Readers who want to get a flavor of the strategic logic of this argument in the context of a real-world example will find this in Chapter 6. Among other things this describes a case in which a merely strong party – in this case Fianna Fáil in Ireland in 1993 – was forced to take a coalition partner despite holding all portfolios in a minority caretaker cabinet at the beginning of the government formation process. The reason for this was because Fianna Fáil was forecast to lose key standoffs with other parties, and thus could not impose its ideal point. The party did, however, participate in the cabinet that did actually form, which was at the dimension-by-dimension median position.

The possibility of standoffs thus explains why a merely strong party is not omnipotent, and may not be able to impose its ideal point even if this is the status quo. In the example in Figure 4.3, imagine the status quo is BB, in which Party B, the strong party, gets both key portfolios. Parties A and C both prefer BA to BB. If we assume that both A and C know that Party B does not have what it takes to win a standoff, however they might conceive of "what it takes," then they can force B to lift its veto of BA, by threatening to install CC as an interim cabinet. Party B cannot prevent CC from forming. Once CC has formed, Party B will then, by assumption, lose the standoff provoked by any attempt to reimpose BB by using its veto over BA. Given rational foresight, it will not actually be necessary to install CC, since B will recognize that its inability to win standoffs undermines its ability to maintain a status quo of BB. If a strong party cannot win standoffs, therefore, it may not be as strong as all that!

This last conclusion may be qualified, however, whenever the dimension-by-dimension median cabinet has an empty winset. In this circumstance we have

> *Proposition 4.3*: When there is an empty-winset DDM, no cabinet in the winset of the strong-party ideal is in equilibrium if it is less preferred by the strong party to the DDM.[20]

A proof of this proposition is found in the appendix to this chapter. The proposition tells us that, even in those circumstances when a merely strong party does not have "what it takes" to win standoffs, the equilibrium will never be less desirable for it than a dimension-by-dimension median cabinet with an empty winset. Put another way, to the extent that a strong party can use its vetoes, it will be able to use these to impose outcomes that it likes at least as much as a DDM cabinet with an empty winset. In effect, it uses its strength to pull outcomes away from the center toward, even if not as far as, its ideal point. At the very least, it can use its vetoes to prevent the formation of cabinets it likes less than the DDM. In Figure 4.3, to continue our earlier example, BC is in the winset of the strong-party ideal and is thus in the equilibrium set identified in Proposition 4.2. BC can never be an equilibrium, however, because the strong party likes it less than BA, an empty-winset DDM. (There is no standoff between Party B and a legisla-

---

[20]Formally, no x in W(s*) for which $m^{**} >_s x$ is an equilibrium (where $>_s$ is the strong party's preference relation).

tive majority on the relative merits of BC and BA, since both Party B and a legislative majority prefer BA to BC.)

Before concluding this chapter, we note that the strong-party concept may be generalized. In the appendix to this chapter, we develop the notions of a *holdout party* and a *holdout point*, which may exist even when a strong party does not, and which specialize to the strong party and its ideal, respectively, when the latter do exist. The intuition here is that a party may not, like a strong party, be able to "hold out" for its ideal point, but nevertheless may be in a sufficiently distinguished strategic position to insist on some other portfolio allocation. Several propositions and an example on this idea are developed in the appendix.

STRONG PARTIES AND CENTRIPETAL TENDENCIES

Having specified a rather stylized generic model of the making and breaking of governments in parliamentary democracies, we have been able to identify a number of fascinating and important strategic aspects of this process.

First, one possible equilibrium cabinet is at the dimension-by-dimension median position, the DDM. Only for a cabinet at this position is it possible that no alternative cabinet is preferred by a legislative majority. If this is the case, then a cabinet at the DDM is a possible equilibrium (Proposition 4.1). This is a generalization of the strongly centripetal tendency to be found in the unidimensional spatial model of voting, with the pivotal role of the median voter. It suggests that, even when more than one dimension of policy is important, and the election does not manufacture a government by giving one party a legislative majority, the process of government formation nevertheless has strong centripetal tendencies.

Second, there may be many party configurations in which a single party is in a particularly powerful position in the government formation process. Some party may be *very* strong. Such a party has an ideal point at the dimension-by-dimension median, and no alternative cabinet is majority-preferred to it. In this case the conclusion is clear: It is very hard to see how a very strong party can be excluded from government (Proposition 4.1). In other cases a party may have an ideal point that is not at the DDM (so that there are indeed alternative cabinets that are majority-preferred to it), but may nonetheless be *merely* strong in the sense that it can veto any cabinet that is majority-preferred to its ideal point. In this event, the party clearly has an incentive to hold out for its ideal point in the government formation process although, if it is to achieve this, every pivotal actor will need to believe that the merely strong party can win strategic standoffs. Whether or not it can win standoffs, however, even a merely strong party will also be very difficult to exclude from government, either forming its ideal cabinet on its own, or participating in some cabinet that is majority-preferred to this (Proposition 4.2); in the latter case, the strong party can always ensure the formation of a cabinet that it prefers at least as much as a dimension-by-dimension median cabinet with an empty winset (Proposition 4.3).

What is striking about the role of these "stronger" parties is that they must have ideal points that are central in some sense. By definition, the very strong party is at the center of things – its ideal point *is* the DDM. In the case of a merely strong party, when the DDM cabinet is majority-preferred to all others, the merely strong party must be at the median position on at least one dimension of policy. This is because it has to be in a position to veto the DDM cabinet, which it otherwise could not prevent from forming. Thus each of these types of strong party has the intention of implementing some public policy position that is relatively central.

Finally, note how the existence of strong parties gives some structure to the government formation process, at the same time making government formation quite different from voting for bills or other items of legislative business. Strong parties are strong because of the way that their vetoes over possible cabinets can be used – and these vetoes arise precisely because parties are involved in forming a government rather than just voting on bills, and no party can be forced into government against its will. For this reason, forming a government may be more structured and less chaotic than generic policy voting in an assembly.[21]

We have nothing specific to say about government formation in those situations in which there is no strong party or when at least one alternative cabinet is majority-preferred to the dimension-by-dimension median cabinet (beyond the holdout party generalization in the appendix). In such situations, there may be cycles of cabinets – essentially of the same sort that generically plague multidimensional legislative models, that is, Cabinet B defeats Cabinet A; Cabinet C defeats Cabinet B; Cabinet A defeats Cabinet C; and so on, ad infinitum. Without making further assumptions about the government formation process, there is nothing in our model to imply anything other than a chaotic sequence of proposal and counterproposal.[22] Any cabinet that might take office would appear to be generically unstable, since some alternative must be majority-preferred to it, and this alternative cannot be prevented from forming by the vetoes of a strong party. Other things being equal, therefore (and in real life they may well not be), a party system that has no strong party and no empty-winset DDM cabinet seems likely to be more unstable than one that does.

---

[21]Furthermore, once the government has taken office, its control over the legislative agenda adds structure to other aspects of legislative decision making.

[22]Again, the generalization we offer in the appendix should be understood as a modest qualification to this assertion.

Appendix: Formal proofs and statements

TERMINOLOGY AND PRELIMINARY ARGUMENTS

Let L be the lattice of policy forecasts associated with each of the finite sets of possible portfolio allocations. For any point $x \in L$, if a point $x' \in L$ is preferred by a majority of legislators to x, we say that x' *wins* against x. The set of points on L that win against x is the *lattice winset* of x, $W(x)$ – we refer to this hereafter simply as the winset of x.[23]

We assume Euclidean preferences. Let y^i be the ideal point of party i; thus in Figure 4.1, $y^A = AA$, $y^B = BB$, $y^C = CC$. For any two arbitrary points, x and $z \in L$, party i prefers x to z, written $x\ R_i\ z$, if and only if $|y^i - x| \leq |y^i - z|$. The two sides of this inequality are, respectively, the Euclidean distance between x and party i's ideal and the distance between z and party i's ideal. Moreover, for any arbitrary point $z \in L$, we describe the set of lattice points party i prefers to it by $R_i(z) = \{w \in L: w\ R_i\ z\}$. $R_i(z)$ is i's *preferred-to-z set*.

From the assumption of Euclidean preferences, each $R_i(z)$ set will be the points on L contained in a circle in two-dimensional spaces (hypersphere in n-dimensional spaces) centered on y^i with radius equal to $|y^i - z|$. In Figure 4.1, $R_i(BA)$ for each party is indicated by the points on L inside the circle passing through BA and centered on their respective ideal points.[24] $R_i(z)$,

[23]In the appendix, lowercase letters will be used throughout to label both policies and governments. Unless otherwise specified, we shall always be referring to the *lattice* winset. If there is any possibility of confusion, we will be more explicit in distinguishing policies from governments.

[24]For preferences that weigh the dimensions according to their relative salience for i, party i's preferred-to set is, in the two-dimensional case, the set of points on L inside an ellipse (ellipsoid in the n-dimensional case). The lengths of the major and minor axes are proportional to the relative salience the party places on the various dimensions. The orientation of the ellipse relative to the dimensions of the space gives the degree to which preferences over the various dimensions are correlated. If the orientation of the ellipse yields axes parallel and perpendicular to the dimensions of the space, then preferences are said to be separable by dimension.

for each i and for any alternative $z \in L$, fully characterizes each party's preferences over alternative points on the lattice.

We may now use the preferred-to sets of individual parties to describe the preferences of majorities. To do so, recall that a party has a weight (w_i for party i) equal to its share of parliamentary seats. A collection of parties constitutes a majority if the sum of their weights exceeds one-half. Let M be the set of all majority coalitions, and let K be one such majority coalition in M.

Consider the preferences of the parties that comprise K. Specifically, for any arbitrary policy x, the $R_i(x)$ sets for i in K are the implementable policies preferred by each party in K to x. The intersection of all these sets gives the policies preferred to x by *every* party in K. Since K is in M, it follows that the intersection of the $R_i(x)$ sets, $i \in K$, contains points on the lattice that beat x in a majority rule contest with K decisive. The union of these intersections over all K in M fully describes the set of lattice points that are preferred by some majority to x. Specifically, the *winset of x*, $W(x)$, is the set of points preferred to x by all the parties in some winning coalition.[25]

A party, S, may be such that it participates in every point in the winset of its ideal point, s^*. We call such a party a *strong party*. The median position on any policy dimension is defined in the normal way. The multidimensional median position is labeled m^*. If all portfolio jurisdictions are simple (unidimensional), then $m^* \in L$.[26]

If all jurisdictions are simple, then an extension of a result by Kadane (1972) shows that, if any point has an empty winset, it must be m^*. Kadane's proof uses an "improvement algorithm" whereby any point x that is not m^* is beaten in a majority vote by some other point x' that is identical to x in every respect save that there is some dimension for which x is not at the median position and x' is at the median position. Iterative application of the algorithm until $x' = m^*$ yields the proof: Either m^* has an empty winset or it is part of a majority cycle. (Note that, if at least one jurisdiction is complex and $m^* \notin L$, then it can be shown by example that it is possible for a point that is not m^* to have any empty winset.) Thus, when all jurisdictions are simple, at most one point can have an empty winset; if such a point exists, we designate it as m^{**}.

[25]For K a majority coalition, the set of points on L preferred by all its members to x may be written $\cap_{i \in K} R_i(x)$. We may now write the winset of x as:
$$W(x) = \cup_{K \in M} [\cap_{i \in K} R_i(x)].$$
[26]If at least one jurisdiction is complex (multidimensional), then m^* may not be an element of L, because the same party may not be at the median position on all dimensions within a given jurisdiction. In this appendix we restrict attention to simple jurisdictions; complex jurisdictions will be taken up in Chapter 11.

Appendix to Chapter 4

KADANE AND THE LATTICE

In Figure 4.1, notice that W(BA) is empty. The set of policies preferred by any majority coalition does not intersect L. There are clearly *policies* that majorities prefer to those that the BA government would implement. But there is no *cabinet* (i.e., lattice point) preferred to BA.[27]

Notice also that BA is the *multidimensional median*, m^*: Party B is median on the horizontal dimension, while party A is median on the vertical dimension. In fact, this is a special case of a more general proposition, an extension of Kadane's Theorem to the lattice:

> *Kadane's Theorem on the Lattice*: In a multidimensional, majority-rule, spatial model restricted to the lattice and simple jurisdictions, where parties have preferences that are single peaked and separable by dimension, either m^* has an empty winset or no point does.

Proof: To establish the result we must show that $W(x) \neq \varnothing$ for any lattice point $x \neq m^*$. Let $x = (x_1, x_2, \ldots, x_n)$ and $m^* = (m_1, m_2, \ldots, m_n)$, with $x_i \neq m_i$ for one or more index values by hypothesis. Specifically, assume $x_j \neq m_j$. Consider $z = (x_1, x_2, \ldots, x_{j-1}, m_j, x_{j+1}, \ldots, x_n)$ — z is simply x with the jth component replaced with m_j. Since x and m^* are elements of L, then so is z. Next consider the hyperplane, H, through z and m^* (see Figure 4.5). From the definition of m^*, H partitions the space into two subspaces. For each subspace, the ideal points in it or on its boundary (H) have weights summing to one-half or more. Consider now the hyperplane H', the perpendicular bisector of the line from x to z. A fortiori, the set of ideals on H' or in the subspace containing z sum to one-half or more. Hence a majority prefers z to x, that is, $z \in W(x)$. Since x is any arbitrary lattice point other than m^*, the theorem is established.

STRONG PARTIES

In this section we establish Propositions 4.2 and 4.3. The statement below of Proposition 4.2 is more precise and slightly stronger than the version in the text. We write the strong party as S and its ideal point as s^*.

> *Proposition 4.2*: When S exists, the stationary subgame perfect equilibrium of the government formation game is in $\{s^*\} \cup W(s^*)$. Specifically, (i) if the status quo (SQ) is not an element of $W(s^*)$, then the equilibrium is s^* if S wins standoffs and an element of $W(s^*)$ otherwise; (ii) if SQ is an element of $W(s^*)$, then so is the equilibrium.

[27]If we write the conventional spatial modeling winset as $W^*(x)$ – this is the set of points in the full space (not restricted to L) preferred by a majority to x – in which case $W(x) = W^*(x) \cap L$, then W(BA) is empty, whereas $W^*(BA)$ is not.

81

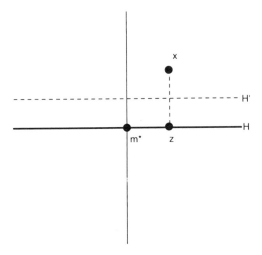

Figure 4.5. The Kadane Theorem and the lattice of credible points

We establish Proposition 4.2 by examining four mutually exclusive cases that between them exhaust all possibilities. These are defined according to whether the status quo is an element of $W(s^*)$ and on whether the resolution of the various standoffs favors S in the sense that it will prevail (written: "S favored"). Thus, we do not explicitly model beliefs about relative bargaining skill ("intestinal fortitude" or "resolve"); we take this as exogenously given and commonly known ex ante.[28] We derive four statements, set out schematically in Table 4.1, that jointly establish the proposition. The logic supporting each statement then follows.

Statement A: If S is favored and SQ $\notin W(s^*)$, then $SE(SQ) = s^*$.

Partition the actors into $\{S\}$, P_1, and P_2. P_1 is the set of actors (other than S) who prefer s^* to SQ, while actors in P_2 prefer SQ to s^*. Stationary subgame perfect strategies for actors in each group yield s^* as the equilibrium. Party S is in the driver's seat. Since it is common knowledge that S is favored, no other actor will propose a $y \in W(s^*)$, because he anticipates S's certain veto that cannot be undermined by strategic threats (this is what "S favored" means). Thus, the only conceivable proposals are s^* itself or some $y \notin W(s^*)$. For every such y from this latter set, there is a majority preferring s^*. Thus, for no y (other than s^*) is it true that $SE(y) = y$. Why? Because, if y becomes SQ, party S (or some member of P_1) will at some point be recognized, propose s^*, and it will pass.

---

[28]So long as the common-knowledge condition is met, the precise outcome of standoffs is of no consequence for the validity of the proposition.

Table 4.1. *Statements establishing Proposition 4.2*

	$SQ \notin W(s^*)$	$SQ \in W(s^*)$
S favored	Statement A: $SE(SQ) = s^*$	Statement B: $SE(SQ) \in W(s^*)$
S not favored	Statement C: $SE(SQ) \in W(s^*)$	Statement D: $SE(SQ) \in W(s^*)$

Statement B: If S is favored and $SQ \in W(s^*)$, then $SE(SQ) \in W(s^*)$.

This follows directly from Statement A. If the path from SQ were to pass through a $y \notin W(s^*)$, then $SE(SQ) = SE(y)$ and $SE(y) = \{s^*\}$ from Statement A. But because a majority prefers SQ to s^* by construction, and $SE(y)$ is s^*, this majority would never permit a path through a $y \notin W(s^*)$. The equilibrium path from SQ, therefore, must remain in $W(s^*)$.

Statement C: If S is not favored and $SQ \notin W(s^*)$, then $SE(SQ) \in W(s^*)$.

In this situation, SQ involves a standoff between S and members of a majority who (i) prefer some $y \in W(s^*)$ to s^*, and (ii) prefer s^* to SQ. Part (i) follows since, if there were no such y for any majority, then S would be very strong with ideal point s^{**}, in which case Proposition 4.1 would apply. Part (ii) follows since the premise of the statement is that $SQ \notin W(s^*)$. This set of actors (a generic member of which is Alf) can vote strategically against s^*, if this is proposed, retaining SQ in the expectation of y being proposed. We know from the definitions of strategic equivalents and equilibriums that $SE(SQ) \in \{SQ\} \cup W(SQ)$. If S is forecast not to be favored in the ensuing standoff, then Alf must expect to realize a portfolio allocation y that is in both $W(s^*)$ and $W(SQ)$. Recall that Alf's preferences are $y >_\alpha s^* >_\alpha SQ$. If $SE(SQ) \notin W(s^*)$ and yet there were a standoff from SQ, then this would require Alf to be voting strategically for SQ over s^*, even though he preferred s^* to SQ and had no hope of getting anything better in $W(s^*)$, clearly contradictory behavior. This establishes that, when party S is not favored and $SQ \notin W(s^*)$, then $SE(SQ) \in W(s^*)$.

Statement D: If S is not favored and $SQ \in W(s^*)$, then $SE(SQ) \in W(s^*)$.

This follows directly from Statement C. If the equilibrium path from SQ to $SE(SQ)$ passes through a y, then $SE(SQ) = SE(y)$. If $y \notin W(s^*)$ then

SE(y) $\in$ W(s*), since, by assumption, S is not favored (Statement C). Thus SE(SQ) $\in$ W(s*) as well. Otherwise, the equilibrium path from SQ remains within W(s*).

This concludes the proof of Proposition 4.2. It is worth noting that the *only* circumstance in which a strong party forms a single-party minority government is when SQ $\notin$ W(s*) (SQ can be s*, itself). And even here, S may be denied some of the portfolios if it cannot discourage standoffs. Consequently, the existence of a strong party is *not* equivalent to an assertion that it will uniquely form the government; the proposition only claims that S will always be a member of the government.

We assume that the bargaining skill of S is common knowledge, so that all actors know the row of Table 4.1 that applies. Of course, the common-knowledge assumption about preferences means they know the column as well. These common-knowledge conditions affect which government forms from the equilibrium set identified in Proposition 4.2. Party S nevertheless has some influence independent of bargaining skill. This effect is identified in the next proposition (although only for the case where an empty-winset DDM, m**, exists).

Proposition 4.3: No x $\in$ W(s*) for which m** $>_S$ x is an equilibrium.

Assume, contrary to the proposition, that an x inferior to m** for S is an equilibrium. Since S is strong, s* is the unique holdout point (see text and next section of appendix); there are no other holdout points. Thus, no participant in m**, other than S, can credibly veto a move to m**. Reason: Any policy outcome they might seek by this move would then be their holdout point – contradiction. This means that, in accord with the government formation game of Figure 3.1, any player preferring m** to x may move m**, no non-S participant in m** will credibly veto that motion, and a legislative majority prefers m** to any other point. Consequently, the only ways in which m** will not be the equilibrium are (1) if S vetoes m** or (2) if some member(s) of the majority preferring m** vote strategically. The first will occur only if S can obtain a y $\in$ {s*} $\cup$ W(s*) that it prefers to m**; in this case x is not an equilibrium and an outcome satisfying the proposition obtains. The second cannot occur: A majority, by construction, prefers m** to any policy objective a potentially strategic voter might pursue and will block it; hence m** will result, again consistent with the proposition. Thus, the assumed x, contrary to the proposition, cannot constitute an equilibrium.

Appendix to Chapter 4

HOLDOUT POINTS

We have just seen that a strong party can be in a position to have a considerable impact on the government formation process. Even when there is no strong party, however, one particular party may be in a stronger bargaining position than the others. It may be in a position to "hold out" for a cabinet that, while not its ideal point, is closer to its ideal cabinet than the generalized median.

This situation can arise for the following reasons. When there is no strong party there is, by definition, no party that participates in every cabinet that is majority-preferred to its ideal cabinet. However there may still be a party, H, that can find some cabinet, h (not necessarily Party H's ideal point, h*), such that Party H both prefers h to every cabinet that is majority-preferred to h, and participates in every one of these cabinets. In this event, Party H, the *holdout party*, has an incentive to hold out in the government formation process for cabinet h, the *holdout point*, in just the same way as a strong party has an incentive to hold out for its ideal cabinet.

Formally, h is a *holdout point* and H is a *holdout party* iff:

1. H participates in every y in $W(h)$;
2. H prefers h to every y in $W(h)$;
3. other participants in h prefer it to every y in $W(h)$; and
4. H prefers h to every other point satisfying conditions (1)–(3).

Throughout this development, we make use of an assumption that requires a modicum of preference diversity among party ideals:

Preference Diversity Assumption (PD): On each policy dimension a location is occupied by at most one party.

We are now able to establish a number of interesting properties for holdout points, properties we use subsequently to establish several theoretical propositions.

Property 1: The holdout point for party H is H's ideal point, h*, if and only if H is strong.

Sufficiency follows by a direct application of the definition of a holdout point. Condition (1) of the definition is satisfied since H is strong and hence participates in every point in $W(h^*)$. Condition (2) is satisfied since h* is H's ideal. Condition (3) is satisfied trivially. Condition (4) follows again because h* is H's ideal. To establish necessity, suppose h* were a holdout point, but H were not strong. But by condition (1), H must be strong. This contradiction establishes necessity.

Property 2: When there is no strong party, every holdout point must be at a median position on at least one dimension.

Consider a lattice point x at a median position on *no* dimension. Consider all the lattice points that result from projecting x onto median hyperplanes one dimension at a time. Call these projections $x^1, x^{2,} \ldots, x^n$ (where n is the dimensionality of the space). The point x^i is identical to x except that it is at the median position on the ith dimension. From Kadane's Improvement Algorithm, we know that every such x^i is in W(x). For x to be the holdout point of some party, H, that party must participate in every point in W(x), and thus, by construction, in every one of the projections, x^i. This is possible only if x is H's ideal. But this means, from Property 1, that H is a strong party, contrary to hypothesis. Thus, when there is no strong party, every holdout point must be median on at least one dimension, and the statement is confirmed.

Property 3: There is no holdout point for any party not participating in m*.

Assume Party R, with ideal point r*, is a nonmedian party (it does not participate in m*), and its holdout point is h. Thus, h must be nonmedian on at least one dimension. Consider the projection of h onto the point x that differs from h only in that x is median on exactly one additional dimension (this is possible since h is not m*). There is, from the PD assumption, a unique party P that is median on this dimension. Thus, P participates in x. By the Pythagoras Theorem, $x >_p h$, and by the Kadane Improvement Algorithm, x is in the winset of h. Thus, party P is a participant in x, a point in the winset of the alleged holdout point, h, and prefers x to h. This contradicts part (3) of the definition of a holdout point. This implies that an h (distinct from m*) cannot be a holdout point for any party not participating in m*.

Property 4: There can be no more than one non-m* holdout point.

Since there is no holdout point for parties not participating in m* (Property 3), we may focus on median-participating parties, P and Q. Assume h_p and h_q are holdout points for P and Q, respectively, and that these points are distinct both from m* and from one another. From the completeness of the majority rule relation (putting ties to one side), without further loss of generality, let h_p be in the winset of h_q. This implies that Q participates in h_p from Condition (1) of the definition of holdout point applied to h_q.

The alleged holdout point, h_p, is nonmedian on at least one dimension (otherwise it would be indistinct from m*). On at least one of these dimensions, Q's ideal, q*, is median (since Q is a participant in m* and the PD assumption assures us that Q is the unique median participant on each of these dimensions). Project h_p onto a point, x, so that x differs from h_p on exactly one of the dimensions on which Q is median. By the Kadane Improvement Algorithm, x is in the winset of h_p. By the Pythagoras Theorem, $x >_Q h_p$. Since Q participates in h_p, the latter is in violation of Condition (3) of the definition of a holdout point. Thus, h_p either cannot be distinct from m^* or is identical to h_q.

> *Proposition 4.4*: The holdout party is a participant in every equilibrium cabinet. The equilibrium cabinet is either the holdout point or an element of its winset. That is, the equilibrium cabinet is an element of $\{h^*\} \cup W(h^*)$.

Since there is at most one non-m^* holdout point, h_q, the logic used to prove Proposition 4.2 (where party Q replaces party S and h_q is substituted for s^*) can be used to show that $SE(SQ) \in \{h_q\} \cup W(h_q)$ for any SQ.

Paralleling the treatment of strong parties, a further generalization suggests that a holdout party influences the final equilibrium, whether it possesses the intestinal fortitude to win standoffs or not. We state this, without proof, as

> *Proposition 4.5*: When there is an empty winset DDM, no cabinet in the winset of the holdout point is in equilibrium if it is less preferred by the holdout party to the DDM. That is, no $x \in W(h)$ for which $m^{**} >_H x$ is an equilibrium.

In sum, a holdout party is strong if there is a strong party, but a holdout party may exist even when there is no strong party. A nonstrong holdout party, like a strong party, has an advantage in government formation bargaining, and indeed should be a member of every equilibrium cabinet (Propositions 4.4 and 4.5).

The intuition concerning a holdout party works as follows. Suppose a party tried to hold out for its ideal point in the government formation process. That is, suppose its strategic purpose was to have itself installed as the sole party of government, taking all the key portfolios. If it were strong, it might be able to pull this off. Depending on the status quo and the beliefs of other parties about the intestinal fortitude of the party in question, the final government equilibrium will either be the strong party's ideal or a cabinet in its winset (Proposition 4.2). A nonstrong holdout party cannot hold out for its ideal (otherwise it would be strong). But it can hold out for some other cabinet. Specifically, on one of the dimensions on which it is median,[29] the holdout party can find a cabinet which it likes less than its ideal, but more than other feasible alternatives. An example will illustrate this.

[29]See Property 3 of holdout parties.

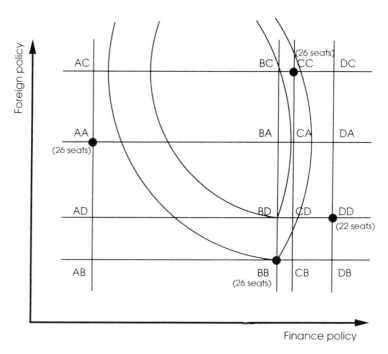

Figure 4.6. A system in which Party B can hold out for BD

Figure 4.6 shows a 100-seat parliament with two portfolios, finance and foreign affairs. Parties A, B, and C each have 26 seats, so that any pair of these have sufficient votes between them to install a government; Party D, with 22 seats, is a dummy. It is clear from the indifference curves through BB of Parties A and C that Party B is not strong, since there are lattice points in the winset of BB in which Party B does not participate. It may similarly be shown that none of the other parties is strong.

Since BA is the multidimensional median with Parties A and B its participants, these two parties are the only candidates for holdout party.[30] The only candidates for holdout point are lattice points lying on the median lines of the two median participants.[31] The best Party A can do is to hold out for BA itself; as shown in Figure 4.6, there is no non-DDM holdout point for A lying between AA and BA. So we turn our attention to Party B. The only holdout point candidates for B must lie on the dimension on which B is median,[32] and by inspection the only possibil-

[30]See Property 3 of holdout parties.
[31]See Property 2 of holdout parties.
[32]See Property 2 of holdout parties.

ity is BD. In fact, BD *is* a holdout point: (1) Party B participates in every lattice point in W(BD); (2) Party B prefers BD to each of these points; (3) Party D, the other participant, prefers BD to each of these points; and (4) Party B cannot hold out for anything it likes better.

This example suggests a general search procedure when looking for holdout points. First, look for a strong party. If no party is strong, then identify the median-participating parties as candidates for being a holdout party. Lattice points lying on the lines[33] containing both party ideals and the multidimensional median are holdout point candidates. At most, one of them can be a holdout point.[34] Our example establishes that a holdout party and holdout point can exist when a strong party does not. Thus, it does constitute a genuine generalization of the strong party concept.[35] However, we tend to find strong parties far more frequently than holdout parties in real data, so that the generalization may well turn out to be of greater theoretical than practical interest.

[33]Hyperplanes in more dimensions.

[34]See Property 4 of holdout parties.

[35]It is somewhat deflating to rely on a made-up example to illustrate holdout points. In fact, as the empirical analysis in Part III demonstrates, real instances of holdout points do arise in the data (but any of these would take some time to elaborate, so we relied for the purposes of exposition on a fictional case).

5

Strong parties

One of the key conclusions of the previous chapter – and indeed of our entire analysis – had to do with the role of strong parties in the making and breaking of governments. In a nutshell, if a party is *very* strong, then the cabinet giving that party all portfolios is preferred by some legislative majority to any alternative cabinet. A party may also be *merely* strong, however, if it participates in every cabinet that is preferred by a legislative majority to the cabinet in which it controls all portfolios. In the previous chapter we show that there can be at most one strong party. Our central result, stated in Proposition 4.2, is that a strong party can dominate the business of government formation and guarantee itself a place at the cabinet table. This result has fundamental implications, both for the analysis of particular cases and for our general understanding of the making and breaking of governments in parliamentary democracies.

If we want to analyze a particular government formation situation using our model, one of the first things we need to know is which party (if any) is the strong party. If we want to understand the process of government formation more generally, then we need to know about the conditions under which a configuration of legislative parties generates a strong party. Thus in this chapter we take a closer look at strong parties and the party configurations that sustain them.

We do this in several ways. First, we briefly discuss how to squeeze as much juice as we can out of our model by focusing on necessary and sufficient conditions for the existence of a strong party. Second, since this formal analysis does not give us much intuition about the existence of strong parties in actual party systems, we switch to an alternative mode of analysis, using simulation experiments to provide us with a feel for the circumstances in which a strong party might exist. We conclude the chapter by comparing our notion of a strong party to distinguished parties identified by other authors; in particular, we look at van Roosendaal's *central party* and Schofield's *core party*.

Strong parties

Our model bases its strategic account of government formation on three types of information. The first is the jurisdictional structure of government decision making. This is seen in terms of the allocation of key policy dimensions to the jurisdiction of particular cabinet portfolios. The second is the decisive structure of the legislature. This is generated by the set of legislative parties, their weights, and a decision rule. The decisive structure describes the combinations of parties whose joint weight exceeds a threshold defined in the decision rule. Such combinations of parties are said to be decisive and, in this context, determine whether a government constitutionally retains the support of the legislature. In this book we take the decision rule to be majority voting, but there is absolutely no reason why our model should not be modified to work with other decision rules. The third type of information we use concerns the policy positions of legislative parties on key policy dimensions. With information on each of these three matters, we can implement our model to perform a strategic analysis of a particular case to determine the existence and identity of empty-winset DDMs and strong parties, and thereby identify potential equilibrium cabinets. In almost all of what follows, we assume a simple jurisdictional structure in which each cabinet portfolio has jurisdiction over a single key policy dimension (or at least over a very highly correlated set of key policy dimensions – we return to explore such matters in Chapters 11 and 12). What we will be concerned with in this chapter, therefore, are the ways in which particular configurations of party weights and policy positions sustain the existence of strong parties.

We have elsewhere conducted a formal analysis of the conditions for the existence of a strong party (Laver and Shepsle, 1993). Part of this analysis does offer us some intuition in the very simple special case in which there are two policy dimensions and three parties, any two of which are needed to support a government in a vote of confidence. Formal conditions for the existence of a strong party in the three-party case with two simple jurisdictions are derived in the appendix to this chapter. We can summarize these briefly in the following terms. Generically, the policy positions of three parties in two dimensions will form a triangle.[1] The longest side of this triangle will be the distance between the two parties who are farthest apart. Neither of these parties can be the strong party.[2] Thus only the third – "more central" – party

---

[1] If the three parties are precisely arranged on some line in the two-dimensional space, the analysis in this section collapses to one dimension in which the "central" party will always be strong

[2] By construction, each of these parties prefers the ideal point of the third party to the ideal point of the other. The third party prefers its ideal point to anything. Thus the

can be strong.[3] The formal results in the appendix to this chapter (to which the technical reader may wish to repair at this point) show that it usually is strong, but that it is not always strong.[4] (The simulation results to be reported provide more precise estimates of frequencies.) Thus the findings in this simple case reinforce the conclusion of the previous chapter that strong parties tend to be central, because they typically need to be participants in (so as to be able to veto) the dimension-by-dimension median cabinet. This implies that, while the power of strong parties may be used to pull cabinet policy away from the dead center of the party system, it will not be used to impose extreme policy positions, since parties in extreme positions cannot be strong in our sense.

We have also generalized our conditions for the existence of a strong party in more complex cases (Laver and Shepsle, 1993: 441–443). Unfortunately, while these conditions are not difficult to write down, they are not easy to relate intuitively to actual party configurations. They are thus not very useful – although they do teach us the general lesson that, even though strong parties are quite common in practice, the conditions for the existence of a strong party are subtle and complex. In practice this has the important implication that, while we can simply look at a particular party configuration and make guesses as to the existence and identity of a strong party, these guesses will not always be right, and a comprehensive strategic analysis can yield surprising results.

Paradoxically, therefore, the complexity of the formal conditions identifying a strong party is actually rather encouraging – the strong-party concept is not simply restating something obvious. Nonetheless the "ugliness" of these expressions indicates diminishing marginal returns from formal analysis and suggests that there is probably little to be learned from further mathematical manipulation. In order to deepen our intuitions, therefore, we offer a somewhat different perspective on strong parties – one gleaned from large-scale simulation experiments.

third-party ideal will be in the winset of the ideals of the two parties who are farthest apart, a point neither can veto. Thus, they cannot be strong.

[3]This party is more central in the sense that its ideal is closer to the ideals of the other two parties than the other two party ideals are to each other – a generalization of the notion of the central party of three parties arranged on a line.

[4]The "central" party will not be strong if the cabinet giving one portfolio to each of the other parties is in the winset of the central party's ideal – an unlikely but possible circumstance. To construct such an example, place the three parties in a triangle that is almost (but not quite) equilateral, identify the central party (not the two who are furthest apart) and rotate the triangle in relation to the lattice until the central party is median on neither policy dimension.

SIMULATED PARLIAMENTS

We have just seen that the conditions specifying the existence and identity of the strong party in a given party system depend on complex interactions between key variables. These interactions can be written down as mathematical expressions, but these expressions do not give us much intuition about the practical circumstances in which we are likely to encounter strong parties. We can of course begin to answer this question by looking at government formation in the real world, and we do this in Part III, where we provide an empirical evaluation of our model. However, strange as it may seem at first sight, the real world may not be the best laboratory for a full exploration of the possibilities for equilibrium in the government formation process we model. The reason is simple. When we study government formations we are studying important, but rather rare, events. In each of the countries we study, few governments actually form, while many variables change both between countries and between the formation of two consecutive governments in the same country. The real world simply does not provide us with the range of variation in key parameters that would allow us to conduct a full exploration of the equilibrium characteristics of our model.

Our attempts to elaborate the full implications of our model are thus constrained in two directions. Formal theoretical analysis (such as is found in Laver and Shepsle, 1993) yields expressions that, while rigorously derived, do not give us much intuition about what is likely to happen in particular real-world cases. Yet there are too few real-world cases to generate a rich empirical universe in which we can systematically explore our approach. Furthermore, one of the most valuable benefits of any model, including ours, is to allow us to address counterfactual – "what if?" – questions about situations that have not yet arisen in the real world. One solution to such problems is to use our model to conduct experiments in a simulated world. Although it is still rather rare in political science, the simulation approach has a number of advantages. We can generate as many cases as we like, and we can control as many variables as we like, carefully exploring the effect of manipulating our variables in a very systematic manner. We can thereby derive generalizations that are in many ways analogous to those derived from a formal deductive analysis, but which are much more closely related to things that we can observe in the real-world processes we are studying. Simulations are not a substitute for the real world that we analyze in Part III, and they certainly do not "test" our model in the way that we can with real-world data. Rather they are a theoretical development tool. In a complex theoretical environment, they allow us to develop generalizations that are useful surrogates

93

for the type of abstract theoretical proposition we have just found so unhelpful when trying to determine conditions for the existence of a strong party.

For our present purposes, the use of simulation experiments allows us to generate a large number of hypothetical government formation settings in order to study their equilibrium properties. This allows us to explore systematically the ways in which particular characteristics of the government formation setting affect the existence and identity of a strong party.

For example, we can investigate systems with five equally weighted parties embedded in a policy space in which two dimensions of policy are important. We can use a computer to generate one, two, ten thousand, or ten million cases of such systems, in each of which the parties have different policy positions while everything else remains exactly the same. (This is the kind of dataset that it would take longer than the expected life of the universe for the real world to generate!) For each of these simulated parliaments, we can use our model to identify the strong party, if one exists. Taking the dataset as a whole, we can then explore the configurations of party policy positions that tend to sustain a strong party.

We can then repeat the analysis for different five-party decisive structures, for example, one with five parties in which one party can form a winning coalition with any of the other four, while all of the other four must combine to exclude the "dominant" party. We can explore three-, four-, six-, seven-, and eight-party systems, with various decisive structures. We can look at three-, four-, and five-dimensional policy spaces, and so on. In short, only the practical limits of our endurance and our computer firepower constrain our ability to create simulated worlds that allow us to explore relationships between variables that are too complex to characterize analytically, at least in an intuitively useful manner.

An analogy might give a better feel than a sermon for the role of simulation experiments such as these. Imagine that we want to find out some interesting things about a dart board – say, the area of the bull's eye. Calculating this area is a straightforward application of elementary geometry. Suppose, however, that you replaced the bull's eye with a picture of the face of your worst enemy. It is impossible, analytically, to calculate the precise area of this irregular and unpleasant object, but all is not lost. You can conduct an experiment to estimate very easily the ratio of this area to the area of the board as a whole. And, since you can easily calculate the area of the dart board, you can then estimate the area of your enemy's face. Pin your enemy's effigy to the bull's eye. Put on a blindfold and throw a thousand darts at random in the direction of the board, as hard as you like. If you have not been cheating and if the darts have really been thrown randomly, then the ratio of the number of darts hitting your enemy's face to the number hitting the board gives the area of that face relative to the area of the whole board. The dart throwing experiment enables you to estimate something that you could not calculate analytically. Improving the precision of the estimate is simple, and might even be fun in this case. Just throw more darts, but don't peek till you're done! Note that you derive an estimate of the size of your enemy's face, not a precise calculation of its area; if the experiment was repeated, a different, but not very different, number of darts would hit the face.

The situation in which a strong party can exist, like the face of your worst enemy, is one of those ugly objects that defies analytical manipulation. We are able to give a precise characterization in the simplest of cases (as we do in the appendix to this chapter), but the analysis fails to provide insight as we complicate things, considering party systems with more than three parties, governments consisting of more than two portfolios, jurisdictions consisting of more than one dimension, and so on. Indeed, as we mention in the preceding few paragraphs (and demonstrate explicitly in Laver and Shepsle, 1993), the analytical conditions for the existence of a strong party in these more complex circumstances imply irregularly shaped regions of the policy space within which a strong party position might be located (generalizations of Figure 5.4 in the appendix to this chapter). Rather like throwing random darts at a board, however, we can generate random configurations of party positions for particular controlled sets of parameters and estimate the proportion of these in which a strong party exists. We can thereby get an idea of the relative size of the area in the policy space within which a party will be strong, relative to the area defined by the range of possible party positions. Repeating these experiments for different parameter settings allows us to identify the way in which changing particular parameters changes the likelihood of a strong party. We can do this even if we cannot provide a closed-form solution to the ugly set of conditions defining this area analytically.

Obviously, our simulated world will differ from the real world in many important respects, the most significant of which is that real party positions are not random. Rather, they are the result of complicated strategic interactions in larger political struggles of which government formation is but a part. An important consequence of this fact is that, even if a particular party configuration is extremely unlikely in random data, rational and strategic parties might home in on it with great frequency, making this configuration not at all atypical of the real world. Two Downsian parties in a unidimensional spatial world, for example, will home in on the ideal point of the median voter, even though randomly generated locations for these parties would render such a configuration very improbable.

This highlights the very important point that we do not present these simulation results as a test of our model in any sense whatsoever.[5] Rather, we emphasize that we are using simulations to get a feel for the way in which particular conditions, such as the decisive structure, the number of parties, or the dimensionality of the policy space, have an impact on the existence and identity of a strong party.

In subsequent chapters, notably Chapters 6 and 10, we go beyond this basic use of simulation technology and apply it to an enterprise to which it is ideally and uniquely suited. We use simulations to conduct "sensitivity" analyses on equilibriums in particular cases. Two quite different types of sensitivity analysis can be used to add considerably to our account of the making and breaking of governments. The first, which we will encounter in Chapter 6, allows us to estimate the potential impact of unreliable empirical data. The second, which we will encounter in Chapter 10, relates to cabinet stability. We briefly preview each of these analyses in the next two paragraphs.

In our empirical work in Part III of this book we rely on an expert survey of party policy positions in particular countries (described further in Chapter 7). We treat the mean expert opinion of a party's policy position as an estimate of where a particular party is *really* located. For particular countries, the number of experts can be small and the variance in their opinions can be large. As in any empirical research, there is inevitably some error in our data, therefore. Using our simulation technology, however, we can estimate the sensitivity of our findings on particular equilibrium cabinets to measurement error by simulating the error process. We do this by taking a particular "base case" in which we are interested, and generating a large number of simulated cases in each of which party policy positions are scattered randomly around our point estimates of the "real" party position. Each simulated party position is our base-case estimate of this plus an error term, the error term varying according to a variance estimated from observed variations in actual expert opinions in this case. We have less statistical confidence in the equilibrium forecasts of our analysis when our sensitivity analysis reveals that these are not robust to the variance in the experts' collective wisdom.

Perhaps the most important application of our simulation technology, however, is developed in Chapter 10 and has to do with the stability of cabinet equilibriums. Our model of Chapters 3 and 4 describes an environment in which there are major strategic discontinuities. In certain

---

[5]We do not after all want the suspicious reader to form the impression that we are setting out to test our model on data we have made up ourselves!

circumstances, for example, big changes in party positions may make no difference at all to the existence and identity of a strong party. Other circumstances may be much more delicately balanced, with very small changes in party positions making big differences as to whether some party is strong.[6] The more delicately balanced equilibrium is obviously far more susceptible to shocks to the system that could not have been anticipated at the time of government formation. In that sense, it is less stable. In Chapter 10, therefore, we use our simulation technology to conduct a different type of sensitivity analysis, estimating the sensitivity of particular cabinet equilibriums to random shocks, and thereby deriving estimates of the relative stability of cabinets.

In the next section, however, we use simulation as an exploratory tool to get a general sense of which factors affect the existence and identity of a strong party. While we can use pencil-and-paper techniques to apply our model to the strategic analysis of simple two-dimensional cases of government formation, if we add more dimensions, complex jurisdictions, and many parties, we quickly find that manual analysis is tedious and error-prone at best, impossibly time-consuming for even a single example at worst. However, the arithmetic of calculating the set of cabinets that are closer to some party ideal point than the particular cabinet under investigation – the arithmetic underlying the calculation of winsets – is essentially straightforward, if incredibly boring. In other words it is just the job for a computer, and we have designed a computer program, WINSET, that does the job for us.[7] This program can in principle take any number of differently weighted parties, each with positions in any number of dimensions, which may be allocated to a set of jurisdictions, and calculate the lattice winsets of any points in which we might be interested. The program can also identify empty-winset DDMs, search for the strong party if one exists, identify holdout points (the generalization developed in the appendix to Chapter 4), generate thousands of random party systems in a very carefully programmed manner to allow us to conduct controlled simulation experiments, and bake bread.

[6]Some party ideal may be very close to a crucial indifference curve defining the winset of the strong party ideal, for example. In this case, a small movement in party positions may easily undermine the strong party. In another case, no party ideal may be anywhere near a crucial indifference curve, so that huge changes in party positions are necessary before the status of the strong party changes.

[7]The WINSET program, which runs under DOS, is freely available for personal research and teaching use via Internet. The program itself, program manuals, and sample data files can be downloaded by connecting to FTP.TCD.IE, logging on as user "anonymous," and supplying a complete e-mail address as a password. The latest release versions of all files are located in the directory /PUB/POLITICS, which contains a README file describing what is available.

The model

In what follows we use WINSET to create large numbers of datasets, each comprising 1,000 randomly generated parliaments. In each dataset we explore a particular type of party system, holding constant the dimensionality of the policy space, the number of parties in the system, and the decisive structure of the legislature – what we allow to vary randomly are the positions of each party on each policy dimension. We calculate the proportion of all such cases for which strong and very strong parties exist. We then repeat this experiment for different configurations of party system. We vary the number of parties, the decisive structure of the legislature, and the dimensionality of the policy space. Each time we generate a 1,000-case random dataset for a particular configuration of party system, with each of the 1,000 cases having all parameters constant except for randomly varying party positions. As a result of exploring the impact of the variation of various parameters on the identity and existence of strong parties, we gain some insight into the types of party configuration that can sustain a strong party.

Table 5.1 reports the results of a number of such simulation experiments. Each row represents a run of 1,000 experiments under specified conditions. Columns 1 and 2 describe those conditions. Columns 3 and 4 report the frequencies of all strong parties, then just of very strong parties, out of 1,000 different spatial party configurations. Each party policy position on each dimension in each configuration was an independent random draw from the uniform probability distribution on the [0,1] interval. The number of dimensions varies between two and four.

In column 1 we identify party systems ranging in size from three to seven for which we examine specific decisive structures. In all cases we restrict attention to nondictatorial structures – those in which no party's weight exceeds one-half. It is worth noting that there are far fewer different decisive structures for a given number of parties than there are different allocations of seats between parties. In the three-party case, for example, it does not matter what weights we assign parties, so long as none exceeds one-half. In the four-party case we examine the two "generic" decisive structures. The first involves a large party that can win with any coalition partner and three small parties that can only win without the large party if all join together; hereafter we refer to this as a *dominated decisive structure*. The second consists of three strategically equal parties plus a dummy (the latter a party that contributes essential weight to no winning coalition).[8] Of the many five-party decisive structures, we focus

[8]There are two other four-party structures, both involving blocking coalitions. One gives some party exactly half of the weight. The other makes any set of three parties

Table 5.1. *Simulation experiments: frequency of strong and very strong parties under various dimensionalities and decisive structures.*

Decisive structure	Number of dims	Frequency of	
		Strong party	Very strong party
Three party			
(.33, .33, .33)			
	2	907	327
	3	734	102
	4	536	36
Four party			
(.40, .20, .20, .20)	2	791	331
	3	554	131
	4	370	43
(.30, .30, .30, .10)	2	803	339
	3	578	103
	4	383	31
Five party			
(.40, .15, .15, .15, .15)	2	766	411
	3	516	201
	4	326	106
(.20, .20, .20, .20, .20)	2	622	201
	3	311	35
	4	150	1
Six party			
(.40, .12, .12, .12, .12, .12)			
	2	730	428
	3	477	240
	4	316	117
(.18, .18, .18, .18, .18, .10)			
	2	551	175
	3	236	27
	4	92	4
Seven party			
(.46, .09, .09, .09, .09, .09, .09)			
	2	740	471
	3	504	261
	4	333	133
(.14, .14, .14, .14, .14, .14, .14)			
	2	455	131
	3	130	9
	4	37	1

on two – one in which a large party can win with any partner and another in which any three of the five parties is winning. Similarly, in the six-party case, we focus on two decisive structures – one in which a large party can win with any partner and another in which any three of five specific parties constitute a winning coalition while the sixth party is a dummy.[9] Finally, we examine two seven-party structures. The first involves a dominant party that wins with any partner. The second is such that any four of the seven parties are winning.

In each of the party systems in Table 5.1, the two generic decisive structures we consider represent extremes among decisive structures. One is the most egalitarian, making all parties (or nearly all) equal. The other concentrates the most bargaining power possible on one party, without making it a dictator. Other experiments, not reported here, suggest that results for other decisive structures lie between these extremes.

Column 3 gives the number of times per 1,000 runs that a strong party emerges in different random party systems. We may summarize this set of results quite straightforwardly. There is almost always a strong party in low-dimensional three-party systems; there is almost never one in high-dimensional, strategically equal, seven-party systems. The frequency of strong parties decreases monotonically as either the size of the party system or the dimensionality of the policy space increases, and is affected by the decisive structure. *All other things equal, strong parties are more likely in party systems with fewer parties, fewer policy dimensions, and dominated decisive structures* (and these variables interact with one another).

The impact of a dominated decisive structure on the frequency of strong parties is particularly striking in large party systems of high dimensionality. A strong party is nine times as likely in the seven-party, four-dimensional case with a dominant party (333 of 1,000) than in the same case with equal-sized parties (37 of 1,000). In contrast, the decisive structure matters much less in four- and five-party systems. In all but the most extreme circumstances (six or seven roughly equal-sized parties), strong parties are common. The equilibrium concept on which our propositions of Chapter 4 are based is not a rare and esoteric idea that depends rigidly on very specific parameter settings.

Very strong parties – parties that are strong because there is no

winning. The first can only arise in an even-seat parliament in which one party wins precisely half the seats. The other only arises in a parliament in which the seat total is divisible by four with each party winning precisely the same number of seats. These decisive structures are considered pathological rather than generic and, for the sake of parsimonious presentation, are not investigated further. Of course, if such a decisive structure proved of interest, our simulation technology would be perfectly applicable.

[9] To enable all six parties to be strategically identical, it is necessary for the parliament to consist of a seat total divisible by six with each party possessing an identical number of seats. This is regarded as nongeneric.

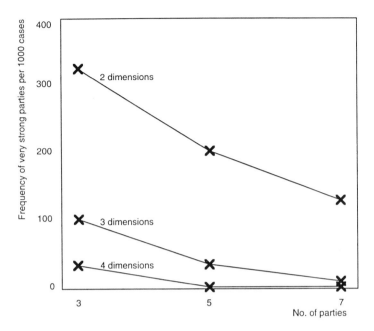

Figure 5.1. Frequency of very strong parties in "egalitarian" party systems of different sizes and dimensionalities

lattice point in the winset of their ideal – arise much less frequently than strong parties, as shown in column 4 of Table 5.1. Their frequency varies with both the size of the party system and the dimensionality of the policy space. This is exhibited in Figure 5.1, where the frequency per 1,000 of very strong parties in the most egalitarian decisive structure is displayed. Moreover, their frequency is quite sensitive to the decisive structure. In five-, six-, and seven-party systems with four policy dimensions, for instance, very strong parties are roughly 100 times more frequent in systems with a dominant party than in those without one.

Overall, the lessons from Table 5.1 and Figure 5.1 are quite clear. The existence of very strong parties is highly sensitive to the configuration of the party system. They become much less likely as the dimensionality of the party system increases and the decisive structure becomes more egalitarian. Strong parties in general are more likely, other things being equal, in small low-dimensional party systems with unequal distributions of bargaining weight, and much less likely in large high-dimensional systems with equal distributions of bargaining weight.

101

Table 5.2. *Frequency of strong parties in random five-party, two-dimensional party systems with different decisive structures*

Decisive structure	Frequency of strong party (per 1,000)	Identity of strong party				
		1	2	3	4	5
Weight of party *(1, 2, 3, 4, 5)*						
A (40, 15, 15, 15, 15)	766	559	51	58	44	54
B (40, 17, 17, 17, 9)	712	407	87	104	102	12
C (44, 24, 24, 4, 4)	671	297	131	149	49	45
D (26, 26, 26, 11, 11)	683	223	226	211	9	14
E (26, 26, 16, 16, 16)	644	188	207	71	81	97
F (20, 20, 20, 20, 20)	622	133	142	121	105	121

Table 5.3. *Frequency of very strong parties in random five-party, two-dimensional party systems with different decisive structures*

Decisive structure	Frequency of very strong party (per 1,000)	Identity of very strong party				
		1	2	3	4	5
Weight of party *(1, 2, 3, 4, 5)*						
A (40, 15, 15, 15, 15)	411	373	6	6	14	12
B (40, 17, 17, 17, 9)	306	241	15	23	27	0
C (44, 24, 24, 4, 4)	268	160	43	58	4	3
D (26, 26, 26, 11, 11)	284	94	95	95	0	0
E (26, 26, 16, 16, 16)	191	77	64	10	15	25
F (20, 20, 20, 20, 20)	201	38	41	40	36	46

SIZE AND STRENGTH

Table 5.1 gives us a general picture of the relationship between the existence of a strong party and some overall features of the party system, but it still does not answer the question of what it takes for a party to be strong. Specifically, given the parameters that determine the out-

Table 5.4. *Frequency of merely strong parties in random five-party, two-dimensional party systems with different decisive structures*

Decisive structure	Frequency of merely strong party (per 1,000)	Identity of merely strong party				
		1	2	3	4	5
Weight of party *(1, 2, 3, 4, 5)*						
A (40, 15, 15, 15, 15)	355	186	45	52	30	42
B (40, 17, 17, 17, 9)	406	166	72	81	75	12
C (44, 24, 24, 4, 4)	403	137	88	91	45	42
D (26, 26, 26, 11, 11)	399	129	131	116	9	14
E (26, 26, 16, 16, 16)	453	111	143	61	66	72
F (20, 20, 20, 20, 20)	421	95	101	81	69	75

put of our model, how is strength affected by a party's position in the decisive structure? And how is it affected by a party's policy position? We begin to answer these questions by building on the simulation experiments of Table 5.1 to explore the relationship between a party's position in the decisive structure and its likelihood of being strong. To do so we intensively analyze all nondictatorial decisive structures of a five-party parliament with two policy dimensions, each constituting a simple jurisdiction. We report a five-party legislature for this analysis because it is rich enough to allow a wide range of variation in strategic parameters, while still remaining tractable. Unreported experiments in other types of party systems suggest similar results. Again we use our computer program, WINSET, to generate simulated parliaments. For each decisive structure a dataset consists of 1,000 cases in which five parties are assigned policy positions in a two-dimensional space, their positions on each dimension drawn independently from a uniform distribution over the [0,1] interval.

An analysis of these simulations is presented in Tables 5.2, 5.3, and 5.4. The rows present data on each of the six generic decisive structures for the five-party case.[10] Column 2 of Table 5.2 gives for each decisive structure the frequency of strong parties per 1,000 runs of our simulated parliament, and the final panel of columns identifies which of the five parties is

[10]For details on these decisive structures, see Laver and Shepsle (1992).

strong.[11] Tables 5.3 and 5.4 partition these data according to whether we are dealing with *very* strong parties or *merely* strong parties.[12]

Table 5.2 presents a fairly clear picture of the impact of a party's position in the decisive structure on whether it is strong. In decisive structures A and B, Party 1 is dominant in the intuitive sense that it may win in coalition with any other party in decisive structure A and with any other nondummy party in decisive structure B.[13] In each of these cases a strong party is very likely to exist. If a strong party does exist in such circumstances, it is typically the dominant party. The remaining non-dummy parties in decisive structures A and B are about equally likely to be strong and, perhaps surprisingly, even a dummy party may be strong by virtue of its position in the policy configuration of parties. Party 5 in decisive structure B is a dummy in the sense that it is an essential member of no winning coalition. Any coalition that is winning with it is also winning without it. Yet it is a strong party in 12 trials out of 1,000.[14]

Among the remaining four, more egalitarian, decisive structures, a strong party also exists quite frequently. Nonetheless, the final panel of columns shows that a party's position in any decisive structure has a great bearing on its likelihood of being strong. When a party is in a more powerful position in the decisive structure, it is much more likely to be strong. This can be seen very clearly in decisive structure C, where Party 1 is in a more powerful position (in the sense of being a pivotal member of more winning coalitions) than Parties 2 and 3, which are in turn more powerful than Parties 4 and 5. The likelihood of each party being strong is strongly related to its position in the decisive structure.

Tables 5.3 and 5.4 disaggregate Table 5.2 and contrast what it takes to be very strong with what it takes to be merely strong. Between them they show that decisive structures with a dominant party (such as decisive structures A and B) are much more likely to generate *very* strong parties. Table 5.3 shows that the likelihood of a very strong party is crucially affected by the decisive structure, declining rapidly as the decisive structure becomes less dominated. As might be expected, the very strong party is almost invariably the dominant party. This is because a dominant player cannot be excluded from a winning parliamentary coalition unless (nearly) all the other parties gang up on it. In the simulation experiments

[11]Thus, for each row the entries in panel (3) sum to the entry in column (2).

[12]Thus common cell entries in Table 5.3 and 5.4 sum to the corresponding cell entry in Table 5.2.

[13]This is nearly identical to the formal definition of *dominant player* given in Peleg (1981).

[14]Parties 4 and 5 in the decisive structure D are also dummies; jointly, they are strong in about 4 percent of the instances in which there is a strong party. A strong dummy party is illustrated in Figure 4.2 for a four-party, two-dimensional setting; in that figure, Party D is strong.

with random party systems, it is quite unusual for those other parties to have spatial locations that provide incentives for all of them simultaneously to want to gang up in this way.

Put differently, a very strong party, by definition, has an ideal point with an empty winset. We know from our adaptation of the Kadane Theorem in Chapter 4 that, in the simple jurisdictional structure we investigate here, this ideal must be at the median on each policy dimension. This is much more likely to happen for a dominant party than for any other party.[15] It may be noted, moreover, that a dummy party can *never* be at the median on any dimension and thus can never satisfy this necessary condition for being very strong. In confirmation, Table 5.3 reveals that Party 5 in the decisive structure B and Parties 4 and 5 in decisive structure D – all dummy parties – are never very strong.

In contrast to the results for a very strong party, Table 5.4 shows that the existence of a merely strong party is much less a product of the decisive structure. Merely strong parties are more or less equally likely in each of the five-party decisive structures. The probability of a party being merely strong is still distinctly related to its position in the decisive structure but much less strikingly so than the likelihood of a party being very strong. Parties with a weaker position in the decisive structure may nonetheless be strong. But they are far more likely to be merely strong, and hence to have to rely on vetoes, than to be very strong – having only to rely on majority support for their ideal point in the legislature.

Thus a powerful position in the decisive structure enhances a party's control over the making and breaking of governments in two ways. First, a more dominant position in the decisive structure is far more likely to make a party strong, and hence an essential member of any government. Second, while even parties with weaker positions in the decisive structure can be strong if they occupy the right position in the configuration of party positions, dominant parties are far more likely than these to be very strong, and thus not to have to rely on their ability to win standoffs. Parties less well placed in the decisive structure are far more likely, if they

[15]The likelihood that a party located randomly will be at the multidimensional median is a probability that may be calculated a priori. In decisive structure F of Tables 5.2–5.4, the probability that a specific party is at the median on *one* dimension is .20. The probability that this party is at the median on *both* dimensions, given independent random draws, is .20 × .20 = .04. In contrast, in decisive structure A, Party 1 has a probability of .60 of being median on one dimension – this is the chance that it is neither the left-most nor right-most party on this dimension – and thus a probability of .6 × .6 = .36 of being located at the multidimensional median, a probability *nine* times larger than in the equal-size structure. This is borne out in the simulation results of Table 5.3, where the strong party in the equal-size structure is very strong, on average, 40 times per 1,000, whereas the dominant party in the first structure is very strong 373 times per 1,000.

are strong, to be merely strong, and thus to have to be able to win standoffs with other parties if they are to exploit their strength to the full.

POLICY AND STRENGTH

Having examined the connection between party size and the likelihood it is strong, we now turn to the relationship between a party's position in the policy space and that likelihood. We continue with our intensive investigation of five-party, two-dimensional party systems, considering all nondictatorial decisive structures. Characterizing a party's position in two-dimensional policy space relative to the positions of other parties, is not a straightforward matter, however, especially when the number of parties moves beyond three.[16] As the number of dimensions moves beyond two, the problem becomes even more complex. One important feature of a party's policy position, however, and one that is of great significance to our approach, concerns whether a party is at the median position on one or more policy dimensions. If a party is at the median on any key policy dimension, it is a participant in the dimension-by-dimension median cabinet – a cabinet that is often one potential equilibrium. In addition, as we saw in Chapter 4, the strong party is typically a participant in the DDM cabinet – thus the strong party is typically at the median on at least one policy dimension.[17] A very strong party, as we have seen, must have an ideal at the median position on *all* policy dimensions.[18] In what follows, therefore, we use a party's occupation of median positions on key policy dimensions as an indicator of its policy position relative to other parties.

In Tables 5.5, 5.6, and 5.7, we investigate all five-party, two-dimensional, decisive structures. For each decisive structure, we compute the frequency per 1,000 trials that a party is strong, given that it is median on no, one, or two policy dimension(s). The results for when a party is at the median on no policy dimension are reported first, in Table 5.5. Each cell reports two pieces of information. The first number is the proportion of trials in which Party X is strong given that it is at no median. The second number gives the number of times per 1,000 trials that Party X is indeed median on no policy dimension.[19]

---

[16]Note our characterization of a generalized "center" party and two "extreme" parties in the three-party, two-dimensional case.

[17]If the DDM cabinet has a nonempty winset, however, the strong party can in theory be nonmedian on every dimension.

[18]Assuming, as we have here, a simple jurisdictional structure.

[19]This proportion can be computed a priori. In the case of the largest party in the most dominated structure, it is nonmedian on a dimension if and only if it is first or fifth in the ordering of the parties. This occurs with probability .40. Thus, the probability that it is median on neither dimension is .40 × .40 = .16, so we should expect it to be nonmedian on both dimensions approximately 160 times per 1,000 simulations.

Table 5.5. *Relative frequency of strong parties among parties occupying no median position*

Decisive structure	Party				
	1	2	3	4	5
Weight of party (1, 2, 3, 4, 5)					
A (40, 15, 15, 15, 15)	0.0 (161)	0.0 (809)	0.0 (809)	0.0 (834)	0.0 (811)
B (40, 17, 17, 17, 9)	0.00 (242)	0.01 (707)	0.01 (698)	0.00 (671)	0.01 (1000)
C (44, 24, 24, 4, 4)	0.00 (345)	0.00 (585)	0.01 (578)	0.01 (881)	0.02 (892)
D (26, 26, 26, 11, 11)	0.00 (425)	0.00 (418)	0.00 (463)	0.01 (1000)	0.01 (1000)
E (26, 26, 16, 16, 16)	0.01 (497)	0.01 (492)	0.01 (738)	0.01 (751)	0.02 (730)
F (20, 20, 20, 20, 20)	0.02 (649)	0.01 (622)	0.01 (638)	0.02 (644)	0.01 (661)

Note: Cell entries give the proportion of trials for which a party is strong if it is at no median. In parenthesis is the number of trials (per 1,000) for which the party was in fact at no median.

The results of Table 5.5 provide startling evidence of the strategic importance for the making and breaking of governments for a party to be at the center of things. If a party is at no median position, it has almost no chance of being strong. This is clearly true for dummy parties (Party 5 of decisive structure B and Parties 4 and 5 of decisive structure D), who by definition are never median. But it is even true for the largest party in the most dominated decisive structure. Party 1 in decisive structure A is at no median in 161 of the 1,000 simulated cases; in no instance is it strong.

Table 5.6. *Relative frequency of strong parties among parties at m**

| Decisive structure | Party |||||
	1	2	3	4	5
Weight of party *(1, 2, 3, 4, 5)*					
A (40, 15, 15, 15, 15)	0.96 (386)	1.00 (6)	1.00 (5)	1.00 (14)	0.92 (13)
B (40, 17, 17, 17, 9)	0.97 (246)	0.94 (16)	0.85 (27)	0.93 (29)	– (0)
C (44, 24, 24, 4, 4)	0.95 (167)	0.90 (48)	0.97 (59)	1.00 (4)	1.00 (3)
D (26, 26, 26, 11, 11)	0.90 (101)	0.89 (102)	0.92 (103)	– (0)	– (0)
E (26, 26, 16, 16, 16)	0.91 (82)	0.91 (69)	0.77 (13)	0.79 (19)	1.00 (25)
F (20, 20, 20, 20, 20)	0.95 (40)	0.93 (43)	0.91 (44)	0.85 (41)	1.00 (46)

Note: Cell entries give the proportion of trials for which a party is strong if it is at m*.
In parenthesis is the number of trials (per 1,000) for which the party was in fact at m*.

The results of Table 5.5 suggest unequivocally that, *almost without regard to the position of a party in the decisive structure, if a party is at the median on no policy dimension, then it will almost never be strong.* We have of course shown analytically in Chapter 4 that, in the simple jurisdictional structure, a strong party must be at the median on at least one policy dimension if the DDM cabinet has an empty winset (so as to be able to veto this). In theory, a strong party can be median on no dimension when the DDM has a nonempty winset. Table 5.5 adds considerably to our understanding of this, however, by showing that a strong

Table 5.7. *Relative frequency of strong parties among parties at median on only one dimension*

Decisive structure	Party				
	1	2	3	4	5
Weight of party *(1, 2, 3, 4, 5)*					
A (40, 15, 15, 15, 15)	0.41	0.23	0.24	0.18	0.22
	(453)	(185)	(186)	(152)	(176)
B (40, 17, 17, 17, 9)	0.33	0.25	0.28	0.25	–
	(512)	(277)	(275)	(300)	(0)
C (44, 24, 24, 4, 4)	0.28	0.23	0.25	0.30	0.25
	(488)	(367)	(363)	(115)	(105)
D (26, 26, 26, 11, 11)	0.28	0.28	0.27	–	–
	(474)	(480)	(434)	(0)	(0)
E (26, 26, 16, 16, 16)	0.26	0.32	0.20	0.24	0.24
	(421)	(439)	(249)	(230)	(245)
F (20, 20, 20, 20, 20)	0.27	0.28	0.23	0.18	0.23
	(311)	(335)	(318)	(315)	(293)

Note: Cell entries give the proportion of trials for which a party is strong if it is at the median on one dimension. In parenthesis the number of trials (per 1,000) for which the party was in fact at the median on one dimension.

party can be nonmedian, regardless of the winset of the DDM, only in very particular circumstances.[20]

By way of dramatic contrast, consider now the frequency with which a party is strong if it is median on both dimensions. These results are given

[20]This is an appropriate point to repeat our caveat about the relationship between simulations and the real world. When party positions and weights are strategic rather than random, and information is perfect and complete, it is possible that actual outcomes may home in relentlessly on those very particular party configurations.

in Table 5.6. Each cell gives the proportion of times that Party X is strong if it is located at the dimension-by-dimension median (the DDM) and the frequency per 1,000 that Party X is at the DDM. As Table 5.6 reveals, parties at the DDM are nearly always strong, quite regardless of their position in the decisive structure (though the latter very significantly affects the frequency of being median on both dimensions).

Our simulation experiments once more add considerably to our understanding by suggesting that, *whatever its weight, and whatever the decisive structure, a party at the dimension-by-dimension median is nearly certain of being strong, and therefore of being a party of government.*

Tables 5.5 and 5.6 thus present refreshingly clear-cut findings. If a party is at no median it has almost no chance of being strong. If it is at both medians it is almost certain to be strong. In each case the finding holds almost regardless of the weights and positions of other parties. What, however, if a party is at the median position on only one of the two policy dimensions? The results of our simulations for such are displayed in Table 5.7.

The results are again quite intriguing. As in the previous tables, the two bits of information provided for each party in each decisive structure are the proportion of times that Party X is strong given that it occupies the median position on precisely one dimension, and the frequency per 1,000 that it occupies precisely one median position. Not surprisingly, the dominant party in a decisive structure is much more likely than other parties in that structure to occupy one median (compare the second bit of information for Party 1 in decisive structures A and B to that for all the other parties in those structures). More surprising is that the largest party(ies) occupies one median with approximately the same frequency in all but the equal-size decisive structure. Most surprising of all is that, with the exception of the dominant party in the most dominated decisive structures, the proportion of times a party is strong if it occupies precisely one median is about 0.25, and is independent of party size or decisive structure. Even the very tiny parties in the third decisive structure are strong about 25 percent of the time when they are at the median position on one key policy dimension.

The conclusions we can draw from the simulation experiments reported in Tables 5.5, 5.6, and 5.7 can be summarized quite succinctly. If a party is at no median, then it is almost certain not to be strong. If a party is at both medians, a situation that is much more likely if the party is the largest in a dominated decisive structure, then it is almost certain to be strong (thereby guaranteeing itself a place in government). If a party is at one of the two medians, then it has about a 25 percent chance of being strong. With very few qualifications, then, the likelihood that a party is strong depends on whether it is at two, one, or no median positions. Once

110

this is determined – and of course larger parties are more likely to be at the median on some dimension, other things being equal, than smaller parties – then the prospect of a party being strong does not vary much either with party size or decisive structure. These results clearly suggest that being in median policy positions – being at the center of things in this sense – gives a party considerable hold over the making and breaking of governments.

CONCLUSION: STRONG PARTIES AND OTHER "DISTINGUISHED" PARTIES

We have covered a great deal of ground in this chapter. We displayed the logic undergirding the existence of a strong party in the simplest of settings – that of two unidimensional jurisdictions and three parties. Formal conditions for the general case are "uglier" and, in our judgment, not particularly pregnant with further insights.

We thus turned to simulation experiments in order to explore conditions affecting the existence and identity of strong parties. The conclusions we drew from these are quite compelling. Strong parties exist with great regularity, especially in lower-dimensional policy spaces, in small(ish) party systems, and in decisive structures with a dominant player. Moreover, and quite consistent with casual intuition, both a party's position in the decisive structure and its position relative to others on key policy dimensions have a profound influence on whether it is strong. In Part III of this book, we examine the making and breaking of real cabinets in a range of postwar European parliamentary democracies. As we shall then see, the empirical case for the importance of strong parties is quite compelling. Strong parties exist with great frequency in real party systems (and very strong parties exist in a surprisingly large proportion of these cases). Such parties are indeed much more likely to get into government.

The final task for this theoretical chapter, therefore, is to locate our concept of a strong party in the now well-established literature on coalition theory. This is harder than one might imagine, both because the search for distinguished policies, parties, and coalitions has been an odyssey with a long history in game theory and coalition modeling, and because our own theory is a rather radical departure from this theoretical tradition.

In Chapter 4 we argued that the making and breaking of governments, a process involving several parties in a multidimensional issue space, nevertheless may possess some Archimedean points. We say "nevertheless" because spatial modelers and coalition theorists have for some time been frustrated by the apparent (theoretical) chaos associated with majority rule processes (including those by which governments are formed). We

111

provided the prospect of ducking between the horns of this dilemma by formulating a specific sequential model of government formation and wedding it to a novel interpretation of the "space" of alternatives (namely, the lattice of feasible governments). Governments that form in our model, moreover, are subjected to an especially stern test. Since we endow our actors with rational foresight, the government they form must not only prevail over the existing status quo, but also must be expected to survive subsequent confidence motions.

Thus, the salient features of our model of government formation consist of:

- policy-motivated parties;
- a lattice of feasible governments;
- a status quo government;
- a sequential process by which the status quo government may be replaced;
- common knowledge permitting each actor to exercise rational foresight; and
- no exogenous enforcement of deals between parties.

Nearly every one of these features departs from conventional models of coalition formation in general and government formation in particular.

First, early coalition models, of which Riker (1962) is the exemplar and pioneer, assumed that parties were *office* seeking, not policy motivated; over the 30 years of coalition studies, this is probably the modeling convention that has been relaxed the most.

Second, all coalition theories based on an assumption of *policy*-seeking politicians were imbedded in a spatial model that assumed that any point in the policy space was a feasible basis around which a winning coalition could assemble. Our lattice is a major departure, emphasizing as it does the fact that in practice it is not policy agreements that come into being, but governments, each government comprising a set of cabinet ministers. Every actual or potential government is a discrete entity with a particular forecast policy output. Our argument is that the only really effective way for legislators to control a government is to (threaten credibly to) replace it with another government, which is another discrete entity, also with a particular forecast policy output.

Third, with some exceptions (Brams and Riker, 1973, and Austen-Smith and Banks, 1988, 1990), formal models of government formation processes have been timeless and ahistorical. Ours, by contrast, commences from a historically determined status quo, on the one hand, and unfolds in a constitutionally established sequential form, on the other (the latter inspired by the work of Baron and Ferejohn, 1989).

Fourth, and closely tied to the sequential nature of our model, our

112

political actors are not myopic. Put differently, they are strategic in their thinking and thus capable of seeing beyond their noses. In proposing portfolio allocations, in deciding whether to consent to cabinets in which they participate, and in determining whether to support particular investiture and/or confidence motions, they think ahead. This constitutes a stiffer test for equilibrium concepts than those based on the myopic behavior explicitly or implicitly assumed by many earlier theories.

Fifth, nearly all of the early game-theoretic approaches to the subject of government formation took a cooperative approach. The major departures from this convention, and our own model departs in the same way, were displayed in the work of Baron and Ferejohn, as well as of Austen-Smith and Banks. These noncooperative approaches of course accept that parties engage in "cooperative" ventures such as coalitions. They claim, however, that any cooperation that does transpire – for example, in forming coalitions, making policy compromises, and allocating portfolios – does so because it is in all cooperators' interests to stick to the deal they have negotiated. Their cooperation, that is, depends only on *self-enforcement;* it does not require or assume some unmodeled exogenous enforcement agent.[21]

Given the variety of ways in which our model departs from so many of its predecessors, it exceeds our own capabilities to compare and contrast these alternative approaches in a systematic manner. Instead, we focus on a few recent approaches that may contain a familial resemblance to our own. Specifically, we briefly examine van Roozendaal's central party and Schofield's core party, though even here we can hardly be thorough.

In a number of recent papers, van Roozendaal (1990, 1992, 1993) has emphasized the centripetal tendencies of government formation. He defines a *central party* as the weighted-voting analogue to the median voter in simple voting models.[22] This concept is tied expressly to a unidimensional ordering of parties, so it is spatially much less complex than our own approach. Through any of a number of different empirical means – expert surveys of leaders or voters, factor analyses of party manifestos or other campaign statements, parliamentary voting analyses – the parties of a po-

[21]Cooperative game theory *does* assume exogenous enforcement, so that once parties to an agreement sign on the dotted line, the agreement is implemented without a hitch. There is no reneging, no ex post departures from ex ante commitments. The early inspiration for this modeling convention was economic exchange in which it was not implausible on its face to assume an exogenous umpire or court system that costlessly and perfectly enforced contracts between traders. Even in economics, however, with its more modern attention to incomplete contracts and enforcement problems, cooperative game theory conventions have been called into question. See, for example, Williamson (1985).

[22]In related work, van Deemen (1989) defines a *dominant party* that is "centripetal" in terms of weight, not spatial policy location (van Roozendaal works with this concept as well). Because it is a nonspatial concept, we do not pursue it further here.

litical system are ordered on a single underlying dimension of policy, usually the conventional left–right continuum. Let R_p be the sum of weights of all parties at or to the right of Party P. Define L_p in a symmetrical fashion for parties to the left of P. Then, for a given set of parliamentary weights, the central party is that party for which $R_p \geq \frac{1}{2}$ and $L_p \geq \frac{1}{2}$. It is the median of the weighted party ordering on the underlying dimension. In one dimension a central party always exists and, except for rare configurations of weights, is unique. The central party is pivotal to everything that happens in the parliament that requires majority support – it "controls the political game," as van Roozendaal (1993: 40) puts it. Consequently, "it follows that the central party will not be left out of the cabinet"; van Roozendaal predicts that, "when a central party is present, it will be included in all cabinets that are formed" (van Roozendaal, 1993: 41). He does not provide a theoretical rationale for this prediction in the form of an explicitly modeled government formation process, though in the unidimensional case it is compatible with numerous theoretical formulations.

The central party is subsumed by our model of government formation. In the one-dimensional special case of our model, the weighted median party is very strong. In other words, in this special case, van Roozendaal's central party is also a very strong party. Consequently, the strategic outcome of the government formation process as we model it explicitly is for this party to become the government. Hence, our one-dimensional forecast subsumes van Roozendaal's. In more than one dimension (something on which van Roozendaal is silent) the natural generalization is the dimension-by-dimension weighted median (DDM). If the DDM is a party ideal point, then, in the spirit of van Roozendaal, that party is *very central*. But it need not be very strong (it is so only if its winset is empty).

The most comprehensive theoretical alternative to our own notion of a strong party, however, is that of the core party, invented by Norman Schofield, a grizzled veteran of the coalition theory wars. In a series of papers authored singly (an important subset of which is Schofield, 1978, 1986, 1987, 1992, 1993) and collaboratively (McKelvey and Schofield, 1986, 1987), he provides theoretical conditions for the existence of spatial equilibrium points in a weighted majority-rule setting analogous to voting in legislatures. This generalizes well-known results for a majority rule equilibrium in a one-person–one-vote committee (Plott, 1967).

In the pure, unweighted, majority-rule setting – a legislature with no parties in which every legislator voted on his or her own initiative, for example – a majority-rule equilibrium, or *majority core*, is a very rare bird indeed. In an odd-numbered committee, such a point exists if $n-1$ of the voters may be paired up in a manner so that the respective contract loci of each pair (in two dimensions the lines joining their ideal points) intersect at the ideal point of the remaining voter. That voter's ideal is the majority core. Small perturbations in the location of one or more of these voters destroys the radial symmetry that defines the majority core – hence this is, in Schofield's terms, *structurally unstable.*

However, since one of Schofield's main interests, like ours, is in government formation in legislatures with political parties of various sizes, he is interested in a majority core in circumstances in which each "voter" (party) may not have the same number of votes. Moreover, he is decidedly more interested in majority cores that are robust to small perturbations – in his terms, these are *structurally stable majority cores.*

Schofield establishes a necessary and sufficient condition for the existence of a core point. He begins with a multidimensional policy space in which party ideal points are located. For any minimum winning coalition of parties[23] there is a Pareto set – the set of policy points from which departure to any other point harms at least one of the coalition parties. For policy spaces based on Euclidean distance, this is simply the convex hull of coalition party ideals – the points contained in the geometric body created by the lines connecting party ideal points. Schofield also refers to this as the coalition's *compromise set.* A policy point is a core point if and only if it lies in the compromise set of every minimum winning coalition. If the intersection of these compromise sets is empty, then there is no core. Moreover, if, for a particular core point, small changes in party ideals still leave it in the compromise set of every minimum winning coalition, then that core point is structurally stable.

A *core party* is a party whose ideal policy is a core point. Schofield suggests that when such a party exists, the government formation game is likely to conclude in a minority government in which the core-party ideal becomes government policy (Schofield, 1993: 8).

When a core party does not exist, as is often the case, Schofield shifts attention to the region of the space within which cycles among coalitions and policies are likely to be located. He calls the latter the *cycle set.* The union of the cycle set and the core is known as the *heart.* Schofield establishes that the heart always exists – either there will be a core point or a cycle set (not both and not neither).

The cycle set can be shown in a partially made-up example. We reproduce figure 3 of Schofield (1993) as Figure 5.2. Five Dutch parties, holding 90 seats of the 100 seats of the Tweede Kamer, are the principals of the government formation game after the June 1952 election. The threshold is 51, and the remaining 10 seats are held by Communists and independents who are assumed to sit on the sidelines during this process. The Labor Party (PvdA) and the Catholic People's Party (KVP)

---

[23]This is defined conventionally, namely that the weight of parties in the coalition exceeds one-half and that the removal of any party reduces the coalition's weight to less than one-half.

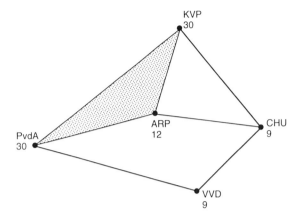

Figure 5.2. An empty core and nonempty cycle set (taken from Schofield, 1993)

each hold 30 seats, the Anti-Revolutionary Party (ARP) 12, and the Christian Historical Union (CHU) and Liberals (VVD) hold 9 seats each. The parties are given spatial locations hypothetically. The three lines, respectively connecting [PvdA,KVP], {KVP,ARP], and [PvdA,ARP] are known as *median lines*. Each line has the property that either on or to one side of the line can be found parties that between them compose a legislative majority. Thus, to take the [PvdA,ARP] line, parties holding 72 seats lie on or above the line, while parties holding 60 seats lie on or below the line. The same holds for each of the other two median lines. If there were a core point, all median lines would intersect at it, clearly not the case here.

The shaded area bounded by the median lines is identified by Schofield as the cycle set. For any point outside this region, majority voting will pull policy toward it. Thus if, for example, a policy to the east of the shaded region were proposed, say by CHU, the majority on or to the west of the [KVP,ARP] median line – KVP, ARP, and PvdA – would pull policy in a westerly direction. On the other hand, if particular policies are proposed that are inside the cycle set, then there will be pulls and tugs, but these will never take the process outside the boundaries of the cycle set.

The implications of Schofield's theory can be divided according to whether a core party exists or not. We should emphasize, however, that he does not explicitly model the government formation process or the actual allocation of portfolios, but rather concentrates on the equilibrium policy that emerges given the constellation of forces in the parliament.[24]

---

[24]This focus on *policy* rather than on *portfolio allocation* is what makes comparisons between the two theories so speculative.

Strong parties

First, suppose a core party exists. Schofield's theory implies that policy will reflect the core party's ideal point. It may form a single-party minority government or form a coalition with other parties. The assignment of portfolios does not matter to Schofield's parties, since they care only about policy (like parties in our model) and policy deals can be struck without the policing mechanism of portfolio allocation (unlike our model). Schofield's is a cooperative game-theoretic account, so that he assumes any deals are exogenously enforced – deals that have been struck, stay stuck!

It may be shown that the winset of the ideal of a core party is empty – no policy is preferred by a parliamentary majority to it. Schofield's core party is, by our lights, *very strong*, though our very strong party need not be a core party.[25] Thus the core party is a special case of a very strong party. According to Proposition 4.2, the equilibrium will be the ideal point of a very strong party, if one exists. So, it would appear that the predictions of the two theories are compatible in this event.

If no core party exists, Schofield's theory predicts an outcome in the cycle set. In the partially made-up example of Figure 5.2, he speculates (Schofield, 1993: 11) that either the "surplus" cycle set coalition {PvdA,ARP,KVP], the minimum winning coalition {PvdA,KVP}, or one of the two minority coalitions {PvdA,ARP} or {KVP,ARP} will form. A specific claim that he makes is that CHU and VVD are weak players – "we might expect them not to be formal members of government" (Schofield, 1993: 11).[26]

Our theory comes to a potentially different conclusion. Just for the fun of it, we took seat distributions and party positions exactly as Schofield gave them in Figure 5.2,[27] superimposed our lattice on his spatial representation (Figure 5.3), and input these data into WINSET.

We have maintained Schofield's convention of treating Communists and small religious parties as voting against all proposed cabinets; thus the decision rule requires 51 of the 90 votes controlled by the "coali-

[25]Why? Because our very strong party has the property that its ideal is preferred by a majority to every other *lattice* point, not to every point in the space.

[26]This claim by Schofield, though intuitively plausible, is entirely speculative since his theory has *nothing* to say about portfolio allocations.

[27]This yielded the following configuration, rescaling positions to lie on the [0, 1] interval. The threshold is 51 seats. This in effect makes the conservative assumption that Communists and fundamentalist religious parties are liable to vote against any proposed government.

Party	Seats	Policy position
PvdA	30	0.000, 0.313
ARP	12	0.589, 0.500
VVD	9	0.714, 0.000
KVP	30	0.700, 1.000
CHU	9	1.000, 0.438

117

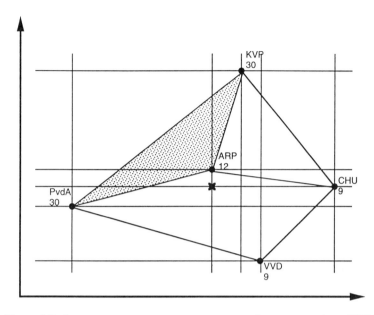

Figure 5.3. An empty core, a very strong party, and an empty-winset DDM

tionable" parties. In Figure 5.3, both the ARP ideal and the (ARP, CHU) coalition cabinet – marked with an "x" – are equilibriums, according to Propositions 4.1 and 4.2.[28] Indeed, the ARP is a very strong party. This leads to three implications. First, the ARP is very strong on our account, without being a core party, according to Schofield. Second, our account produces a set of potential equilibriums (the ARP ideal and the point marked with an "x" in Figure 5.3) that only partially overlaps the equilibrium set of Schofield's account (shaded in Figure 5.3). Finally, we note that CHU is not a "weak" player – as it is according to Schofield.

Which theory is right? It's hard to say, since these data are made up. But it does suggest that the two theories can be compared in principle. tverall, however, the comparison between the two approaches is quite striking in one important regard. Schofield's approach, which does not consider the government formation process at all and concentrates instead on voting in legislatures, identifies a core party as an important equilibrium concept. Our approach subsumes this in the notion of a very strong party. But note that a very strong party has an empty lattice

[28]Because there is a restricted set of coalitionable parties, the effective decision rule requires more than simple majorities (51 votes out of 90 available) among the parties in Figures 5.2 and 5.3. We note as a consequence that there can be – and, in this instance, are – multiple empty-winset points.

winset. In an important sense, its position also depends only on voting in legislatures, since the very strong party does not need to exercise its vetoes. Our notion of a merely strong party (and holdout party, for that matter) has no analogue in Schofield's work or indeed in any other approach to government formation of which we are aware. The reason is simple. A merely strong party is strong because it is in a position to veto cabinets that are majority-preferred to its own ideal cabinet (in which it gets all portfolios). These vetoes arise because parties cannot be forced into cabinets against their will, and it is only by modeling cabinet formation, as opposed to voting in legislatures, that the logic of this process, and the rationale for strong parties, becomes apparent.

Appendix: Formal conditions for the existence of a strong party with three parties and two jurisdictions[29]

Consider three parties, I, J, and K. Each has weight, w_I, w_J, and w_K, respectively, and a spatial position, i, j, and k, respectively.[30] If some party controls more than half of the weight, then it is very strong by definition. We exclude that case in what follows and assume no party's weight exceeds one-half; that is, we assume a *nondictatorial* decisive structure. This means that any pair of parties can form a parliamentary majority. Finally, let $d_t(uv)$ be the Euclidean distance between party T's ideal point, t, and the government in which the horizontal portfolio is given to party U and the vertical portfolio to party V (where T, U, and V are each elements, not necessarily different, of {I,J,K}). This government implements the policy uv – a horizontal-dimension policy given by U's ideal, u, and a vertical-dimension policy given by V's ideal, v. We now state the conditions under which party I is strong.

Strong Party Characterization Proposition: Party I is a strong party in a three-party, two-jurisdiction setting if and only if

$$d_j(jk) < d_j(i) \rightarrow d_k(jk) > d_k(i). \tag{1}$$
$$d_j(kj) < d_j(i) \rightarrow d_k(kj) > d_k(i). \tag{2}$$
$$d_k(i) < d_k(j). \tag{3}$$
$$d_j(i) < d_j(k). \tag{4}$$

Conditions 1–4 lay out the circumstances in which no policy of a government (no lattice point) that excludes party I is majority-preferred to party I's ideal. Condition 1 states that if a JK government is preferred by party J to a government in which party I controls all portfolios (because the JK government policy, jk, is closer in Euclidean distance to party J's ideal, j, than i, the policy that an exclusively party I government would pursue), then this JK government is not preferred by party K. (The converse is

[29]This development is drawn from Laver and Shepsle (1993).
[30]Spatial positions are vectors in the two-dimensional policy space.

implied by this statement as well, namely, if party K prefers the JK government, then party J does not.) Condition 2 requires the same for a KJ government. Finally, conditions 3 and 4 require that no other single-party government is preferred to a government in which party I gets all portfolios. The only remaining governments are those in which party I is a participant, so we thus may validly claim that conditions 1–4 are *sufficient* for party I to be strong. Conversely, if any of these conditions is violated, then there exists a lattice point in the winset of the putative strong party in which the latter does not participate. This establishes the *necessity* of conditions 1–4.

Figure 4.1 in the previous chapter shows these conditions at work. Party B is strong because:

1. Although party A prefers an AC government to one comprising only party B, party C does not.
2. Although party C prefers a CA government to one comprising only party B, party A does not.
3. Party A prefers a government comprising only party B to one comprising only party C.
4. Party C prefers a government comprising only party B to one comprising only party A.

Having established the conditions for the existence of a strong party in the three-party, two-jurisdiction case, we may now determine when, in fact, these conditions will be realized. We arbitrarily locate parties K and J in the two-dimensional policy space displayed in Figure 5.4. This determines the lattice points of the JK and KJ governments, as well as of the governments in which either party J or party K gets all portfolios. Now we seek to determine the set of locations for party I that simultaneously satisfies conditions 1–4 of the Strong Party Characterization Proposition. Condition 3 requires that I be located inside a circle centered on K through J. Condition 4 requires that I be located inside a circle centered on J through K. Arcs of these circles running through J and K are displayed in Figure 5.4. Condition 1 requires that I either be inside the circle centered on J through JK or inside the circle centered on K through JK. Condition 2 requires that I either be inside the circle centered on J through KJ or inside the circle centered on K through KJ. The shaded area in the figure comprises the locus of points simultaneously satisfying these requirements. Given the fixed locations for parties J and K, if party I's position is in the shaded area, then I is strong.

To this region we may add, though we do not display it in the figure, the locus of policy positions for party I that render either party J or party K strong. The area of the union of these three regions, relative to the area of the two-dimensional space, gives a measure of how "difficult" it is to

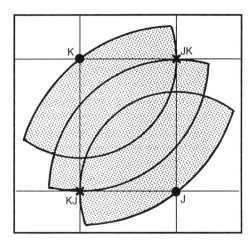

Figure 5.4. Locating a strong party in a three-party two-dimensional system

satisfy the conditions of the Strong Party Characterization Proposition. As our simulation experiments reported in the body of the this chapter reveal, this irregularly shaped region comprises approximately 90 percent of the area of the policy space in which parties are able to locate. That is, in the three-party, two-jurisdiction case, a very high proportion of all possible spatial party configurations supports the existence of a strong party.

PART III

Empirical investigations

6

Two cases: Germany, 1987; Ireland, 1992–1993

In Part I we described the background to the making and breaking of governments in parliamentary democracies. In Part II we developed and elaborated a theoretical model of this process. We move on in Part III to apply our model in a systematic way to the real world of government formation. In Chapters 7, 8, and 9 we describe an extensive empirical investigation of the model in a wide range of government formation situations in postwar Western Europe. Before we do this, however, in order to get a feel for what is going on and to understand what we need to do before we can apply the model to the real world, we look here at two particular cases from our dataset in some detail – Germany in 1987, and Ireland in 1992–1993. We make no claim that these examples are typical of government formation in parliamentary democracies. We have chosen them for purely didactic purposes: Each case allows us to elaborate a number of key features of our model in a relatively simple context. A more systematic empirical analysis of the universe of such cases appears in subsequent chapters.

GERMANY 1987

Our model of cabinet government uses information about a number of features of the party system to determine whether there are equilibrium allocations of cabinet portfolios between parties, and to identify these if they exist. The basic pieces of information that are needed are the number of legislative seats controlled by each party and the number of legislative votes needed to pass a motion of no confidence (between them these determine the decisive structure); the policy positions of each party on each salient dimension of policy; and the cabinet portfolio with jurisdiction over this policy dimension. Given this information, our model identifies potential equilibrium portfolio allocations.

Four parties were represented in the 497-seat West German national parliament (the Bundestag) after the 1987 election, the results of which can be found in the top panel of Table 6.1. Largest were the Christian Democrats, an alliance of the Christian Democratic Union (CDU) and the Bavarian Christian Social Union (CSU) that we treat as a single party in this analysis, and refer to henceforth as CD. Then came the Social Democrats (SPD), the Free Democrats (FDP), and the Greens (G). A total of 249 votes was needed for an absolute majority in the legislature, meaning that no party could control the Bundestag on its own.[1] Any government facing a vote of no confidence would need the support of a *legislative* coalition of at least two parties to be able to stay in office.[2] The *executive* itself might be a single-party minority cabinet, but a majority legislative coalition would be needed to ensure that this could win potential confidence votes to remain in office.

Actually, it is not necessary to know the precise seat totals won by each party in this or any other government formation situation. What is important for the making and breaking of governments is the set of combinations of parties that are able to win majority votes in the Bundestag. The set of party combinations that could win majority votes after the 1987 Bundestag election is listed in the bottom panel of Table 6.1. The essential pattern is quite simple. The CD could form a legislative majority with any one of the other three parties. The same cannot be said for the next largest party, the SPD. This could form a majority legislative coalition with the CD; otherwise it needed both of the other two parties. Indeed, in this respect, the SPD is in precisely the same position as the FDP and the Greens. We can summarize the set of majority legislative coalitions quite

---

[1]The German constructive vote of no confidence unambiguously requires any motion of no confidence in the incumbent government to specify a successor, effectively collapsing confidence and investiture procedures. The 5 percent vote threshold for representation under German electoral law denies representation to minor parties and results in there being only a small number of parties in the legislature. Elsewhere, minor parties surprisingly often prove to be pivotal in government formation, yet it can be difficult to assemble information on their positions on all key policy dimensions.

[2]Note that abstentions in legislative votes are treated as votes for or against a proposal, depending on the strategic context. Thus, in the German case, if there were a minority CD government in office and the Greens proposed a motion of no confidence, an absolute majority of the Bundestag would be needed to defeat the government. If the FDP committed themselves to voting against the government, then an SPD abstention on this motion would be the strategic equivalent of a vote for the government. The government remains in office as a result of the SPD abstention, when a vote against by the SPD, in the knowledge that the other parties would vote against, would have brought the government down. In the wider political game – in terms of the story told to the public, for example – an abstention may have different implications from those of a vote for the government. But in terms of the government formation game both votes amount to the same thing. In the same way, if a new government is proposed and some party abstains on the investiture vote with the effect that the proposal fails when a vote in favor would have carried it, then the abstention is in effect a vote against the proposal.

Table 6.1. *Decisive structure after the Bundestag election of 1987*

	Seats
Individual parties	
Christian Democratic Union/ Christian Social Union (CD)	223
Social Democratic Party (SPD)	186
Free Democrats (FDP)	46
Greens (G)	42
Total	497
Majority threshold	249
Winning coalitions	
CD + SPD	409
CD + FDP	269
CD + G	265
SPD + FDP + G	274
CD + SPD + FDP	455
CD + SPD + G	451
CD + G + FDP	311
CD + SPD + FDP + G	497

simply, therefore. It comprises coalitions of the CD with any other party, the coalition of the three other parties, and any superset of the aforementioned coalitions formed by adding some other party – the grand coalition of all parties, for example, or of all parties bar the Greens, the SPD, or the FDP.

This set of winning coalitions is the *decisive structure* of the legislature.[3] The key impact of election results on the making and breaking of governments is to determine the decisive structure of the new legislature, rather than to generate the precise distribution of seats between parties.

[3] In the terms of the previous chapter, the CD thus dominates this decisive structure.

Thus, if the SPD had lost 20 more seats to the Greens in 1987, for example, it would have made no difference to the decisive structure of the government formation process in Germany. It would still have been the case that the CD could have formed a majority coalition with any other party, but a combination of all other parties would have been needed to defeat the CD. If on the other hand the Greens had won 20 fewer seats and the SPD 20 more, then the Greens would have been an essential member of no winning coalition (they would have been a dummy party) and they would have been in a much weaker position in a quite different decisive structure. This would have had a big strategic effect on the making and breaking of German governments.

Having identified the set of winning legislative coalitions, the next step is to identify the positions of the parties on those dimensions of policy that we assume motivate them when bargaining over government formation. As we indicated in Chapter 2, there is no unambiguously "right" way to identify the set of key policy dimensions. Analyzing this particular case, therefore, we proceed incrementally, beginning with what we take to be the most important dimensions of policy, then adding another, and another, building an account of government formation in stages.[4]

Few would argue with the assertion that, in almost every modern parliamentary democracy, the management of the economy is today considered to be the government's most important policy concern. Certainly, if we are forced to select only one dimension of policy with which to reflect the concerns of German parties, a left–right economic policy dimension would be an obvious choice.

The next task is to estimate the policy position, or ideal point, of each legislative party on the left–right economic dimension. There are a number of ways to do this, reviewed in Laver and Hunt (1992: 31–34). These include: content analysis of party policy documents; analysis of mass survey data (relating either to the policy positions of party supporters, or to respondents' perceptions of party ideal policies); and surveys of expert commentators on politics in the country in question. The most comprehensive set of expert estimates of party positions on a range of policy dimensions is based on a survey conducted by Laver and Hunt (1992). In this, 1,228 experts on the politics of 25 democracies were asked to place all parties in their respective countries on eight common policy dimensions, as well as any "local" dimensions that they felt appropriate. We use

[4]In practice, the lack of comprehensive data on party positions on every relevant policy dimension, the massive computer firepower needed to solve high-dimensional cases and the real-world correlations between party positions on different dimensions that we discuss in Chapter 11 combine to mean that we will only ever need (or be able) to analyze the allocation of the subset of "key" cabinet portfolios.

Table 6.2. Positions of German parties on two economic policy dimensions

	Mean position (standard error)			
Party	Increase taxes (1) vs. cut services (20)		Promote public ownership (1) vs. oppose pub. ownership (20)	
Greens	5.2	(0.65)	7.1	(0.58)
SPD	6.5	(0.44)	8.1	(0.52)
CDU/CSU	13.5	(0.54)	13.6	(0.40)
FDP	15.7	(0.61)	17.4	(0.39)

Source: Laver and Hunt, 1992: 197
Note: Estimates are based on 19 expert responses.

estimates of party positions based on these data in most of the empirical analyses that follow. These estimates can be supplemented for most parties in a number of countries with the results of a content analysis of party and coalition policy documents, conducted by the Manifesto Research Group of the European Consortium for Political Research (Budge et al., 1987; Laver and Budge, 1992).

Positions of the German parties on the economic left–right policy dimension can be derived from both sources. Two of the specific scales used in the Laver-Hunt expert survey relate to this policy dimension. The first scale contrasts raising taxes in order to increase public services, on the left, with cutting public services in order to cut taxes, on the right. The second scale contrasts promoting maximum public ownership of business and industry, on the left, with opposing all public ownership of business and industry, on the right. The "increase services versus cut taxes" dimension was rated by country specialists to be the more salient of the two in most countries, and we take this as our yardstick of economic policy. In many cases including that of Germany, either dimension would yield the same results. Table 6.2 shows party positions on the two dimensions in Germany in 1989, the time of the expert survey, estimated on a 20-point scale that ranges from 1 on the far left to 20 on the far right.

Whichever dimension is used, it is clear that the median legislator on the economic policy dimension in Germany belongs to the CD. This judgment is confirmed by the Manifesto Research Group's content analyses of party policy documents for 1987. The CD was at the median on both of the main economic policy dimensions coded, reflecting "capitalist economics" and "state intervention" (Klingemann and Volkens, 1992:

129

209). It was also at the median on all but one of the left–right scales collated from the existing literature by Laver and Schofield (1990).

As we saw in the theoretical discussion in Chapter 4, and in our treatment of van Roozendaal's model in Chapter 5, when only one dimension of policy is salient, then the portfolio allocation model is very simple to implement. The ideal point of the party with the median legislator will always have an empty winset, making the median party very strong. The portfolio allocation model thus characterizes the median party as an essential member of every government if only one dimension of policy is important in government formation. If only the economic left–right policy dimension were important in West German government formation in 1987, therefore, then the CD would be a very strong party and the portfolio allocation model forecasts that it would occupy the all-important finance portfolio. In fact, the CD was in government after the 1987 election and did occupy the finance portfolio.

Many would of course consider a one-dimensional representation of politics such as this to be a gross oversimplification of the complex reality of government formation in Germany. Our model allows us to consider any number of additional policy dimensions, provided that we can both identify these and derive reliable estimates of party positions on them.

Which additional policy dimensions should we consider for Germany in 1987? Laver and Hunt set out to answer this type of question in the specific context of the government formation game by asking experts to list the key cabinet portfolios that must be filled as part of the process of forming a government, ranking these in order of importance. They derived mean rankings for the 10 most important German cabinet portfolios, shown in Table 6.3.

The two most important portfolios are foreign affairs and finance. There is no statistically significant difference in the expert rankings of these portfolios, but each is ranked significantly higher than the next portfolio, interior. Interior, in turn, has a significantly higher ranking than the next three most important portfolios – defense, labor and social affairs, and economics. These latter three are effectively ranked equally. On this basis, the next dimension of policy that we should consider in the German case is clearly foreign affairs. By implication, the foreign affairs portfolio and that of finance are the two most important cabinet positions to be filled. If we want to add a third policy dimension, it should clearly be related to social policy, over which the Ministry of the Interior has jurisdiction.

Laver and Hunt's estimates of the positions of the German parties on the foreign affairs portfolio in early 1989 (before the tearing down of the Berlin Wall) were based on attitudes toward what was then still the Soviet

Table 6.3. Rankings of German cabinet portfolios

Portfolio	Mean ranking of portfolio	Standard error
Foreign affairs	1.8	0.29
Finance	2.1	0.27
Interior	3.3	0.29
Defense	4.6	0.46
Labor and social affairs	4.7	0.38
Economics	4.9	0.42
Justice	6.3	0.35
Youth, family, women, and health	7.3	0.58
Food, agriculture, and forestry	8.8	0.29
Environment	8.8	0.84

Source: Laver and Hunt, 1992: 196
Note: Estimates are based on 19 expert responses.

Table 6.4. Positions of German parties on foreign policy dimension

Party	Mean position (standard error): Pro (1) vs. anti (20) USSR	
Greens	4.0	(0.48)
SPD	4.6	(0.35)
FDP	6.6	(0.47)
CDU/CSU	9.8	(0.68)

Source: Laver and Hunt, 1992: 197
Note: Estimates are based on 19 expert responses.

Union. They estimated the various parties to have the positions on this dimension shown in Table 6.4.[5]

Implementing the portfolio allocation model when more than one dimension of policy is important is rather more complex. However when the number of parties is small and only two policy dimensions are impor-

[5]The Klingemann-Volkens manifesto analysis did not estimate party positions on a foreign policy dimension, and we can find no other estimates of German party positions on this dimension.

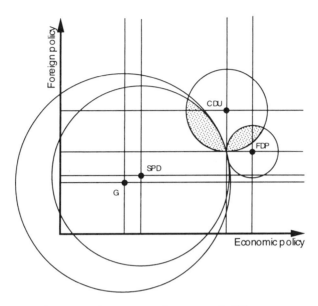

Figure 6.1. Two-dimensional German policy space: Indifference curves relating to CD-FDP cabinet

tant, each allocated to a single jurisdiction – we earlier called this a *simple* jurisdictional structure – it is still possible to draw the relevant policy space and implement the portfolio allocation model "by hand." The policy space generated by the economic and foreign policy dimensions in Germany in 1987 is shown in Figure 6.1. The economic policy dimension, under the jurisdiction of the finance portfolio, is the horizontal axis, and the foreign policy dimension, under the jurisdiction of the foreign affairs portfolio, is the vertical axis. The ideal policies of the four legislative parties are each marked with a black dot. The 16 possible allocations of the two portfolios between the four parties are given by the intersecting lines of the lattice shown in the figure. In this figure, an indifference curve for each party is traced through the portfolio allocation giving the CD control over the finance portfolio (and allowing it to implement CD economic policy on the horizontal dimension) and the FDP the foreign affairs portfolio (allowing it to implement FDP policy on the vertical dimension).

What those indifference curves show in this particular example is how the various parties feel about a potential government that gives finance to the CD and foreign affairs to the FDP. The circle centered on the CD shows how the CD feels about this. Everything inside the indifference

132

curve is closer to the CD's ideal policy position than this potential government. Thus everything inside the circle is preferred by the CD to the government in question. We note that, obviously, the CD prefers a government in which it gets both key portfolios – represented by the dot at its ideal policy position. We see that the CD also prefers a government in which it gets the foreign affairs portfolio, leaving finance to the FDP – this is the lattice point immediately to the right of the CD position. Each of the other circles represents an indifference curve with the same type of interpretation. Thus the indifference curve centered on the SPD shows which potential cabinets are preferred by the SPD to the cabinet with CD in finance and FDP in foreign affairs, and so on.

When two or more circles through the same cabinet intersect each other, we see policy outputs that *groups* of parties prefer to the cabinet in question. Thus the area inside the intersection of the CD and SPD indifference curves contains policies that *both* of these parties prefer to the CD-FDP cabinet. Note that no lattice point is inside this area – thus there is no cabinet that both CD and SPD prefer to the CD-FDP government.

We have concentrated in Figure 6.1 on the cabinet giving the CD the finance portfolio and the FDP foreign affairs because it is the dimension-by-dimension (DDM) median portfolio allocation. We know from Chapter 4 that only this allocation can have an empty winset. We can see from Figure 6.1 that the DDM allocation in Germany in 1987 does indeed have an empty winset. We do this by considering in turn each of the winning legislative coalitions, as determined by the decisive structure (listed in Table 6.1). We inspect the intersection of the indifference curves through the DDM of each of the parties involved in the winning coalition. This intersection shows us which cabinets are preferred by this winning coalition to the DDM. In this case, we have already seen that no cabinet is preferred to the DDM by the winning coalition of CD and SPD. Likewise, the intersection of the indifference curves centered on the CD and FDP shows that no cabinet is preferred by this winning coalition to the DDM. Finally, the same is true for the CD-Green winning coalition, and for the coalition of Greens, SPD, and FDP (this area is tiny and located to the southeast of the intersection of the circles).

Thus no alternative cabinet is preferred by a winning coalition to the DDM. The DDM – a cabinet giving finance to the CD and foreign affairs to the FDP – has an empty winset. If this cabinet were the status quo at the beginning of the government formation process, as it was in Germany in 1987, then our model predicts that it would remain in equilibrium. This is because any proposal to replace this status quo with an alternative, if made and not vetoed by some participant, would have been blocked by some legislative majority that preferred the CD-FDP cabinet at the multidimensional median position to the alternative in question. There is no proposal

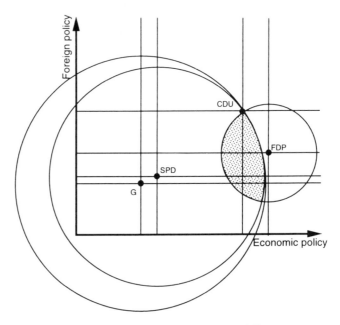

Figure 6.2. Two-dimensional German policy space: Indifference curves relating to CD ideal point

that could have been made that would not have been blocked. As a matter of fact, starting from a status quo CD-FDP cabinet a new CD-FDP cabinet did actually form in Germany after the 1987 election.

Figure 6.2 shows how the parties feel about another point in the space, the ideal point of the CD. From this we can see that the CD was a strong party after the 1987 election. In this particular case, the only decisive coalition we need to consider is the one in which all other parties coalesce against the CD. The lens-shaped shaded area under the ideal point of the CD shows the intersection of these other parties' indifference curves through the CD ideal. It shows that there are indeed other cabinets preferred by a winning coalition to the cabinet giving both portfolios to the CD, but that these all involve the participation of the CD. They are thus susceptible to a veto by the CD. This implies, if we assume only these two dimensions of policy to be important, that there were certain circumstances in which the CD would have been able to sustain themselves as a minority government. This is because the CD's three opponents were unable to agree on an alternative government, excluding the CD, that they all preferred to the CD minority government. Because the CD faced

Table 6.5. *Positions of German parties on decentralization of decision making*

Party	Mean position (standard error): Pro (1) vs. anti (20) decentralization of decision making	
Greens	5.3	(1.18)
SPD	11.1	(0.67)
FDP	11.1	(0.62)
CDU/CSU	9.9	(0.62)

Source: Laver and Hunt, 1992: 197
Note: Estimates are based on 19 expert responses.

an opposition divided among themselves in this way, our model implies that they could, in the right circumstances, have governed alone.

Note, however, that our model would not have predicted a CD minority government in Germany in 1987, starting the government formation process from the status quo of a CD-FDP coalition cabinet. As we have already seen, some legislative majority would have been able to block any proposal to move away from the status quo at the multidimensional median. Given the particular status quo, the CD was thus not in a position to impose a minority government comprising only itself. If, on the other hand, the status quo had been something else, for example, a coalition between SPD and the FDP, then it is possible that the CD would have been able to use its position as a strong party to impose a CD minority government.[6]

Table 6.3 clearly shows that, if we wish to add a third dimension of policy to our analysis, then it should relate to the jurisdiction of the Ministry of the Interior. A number of policy dimensions might fall within the jurisdiction of this portfolio. One of the most obvious to include in a federal state such as Germany, and on which information was collected by Laver and Hunt, is a "decentralization of decision making" dimension that has to do with the devolution of powers to regional and local government. Estimated party positions in Germany on this dimension are given in Table 6.5.

Obviously, it is not easy to draw the three-dimensional German policy space that we are now dealing with, or the spherical indifference contours that describe how each of the parties feels about each potential cabinet.

[6]In fact, the case of Germany 1987 illustrates in all respects the content of Proposition 4.2 as stated precisely in the appendix to Chapter 4.

However, WINSET, the computer program we described in Chapter 5, does the job for us. If we investigate a three-dimensional, three-jurisdiction representation of the government formation process in Germany after the 1987 election, we can see from Tables 6.2, 6.4, and 6.5 that the dimension-by-dimension median cabinet gives finance to the CD, foreign affairs to the FDP, and the Interior Ministry to the CD. This was not the status quo at the outset of the government formation process, however, since the FDP controlled the interior portfolio. Using the WINSET computer program we can see that this status quo cabinet does not have an empty winset, but that it is, however, in the winset of the strong party ideal. Thus Proposition 4.2 of our model would have predicted that the incumbent CD-FDP-FDP cabinet would remain a potential equilibrium in the new government formation situation. As a matter of fact, this is the cabinet that did actually form in Germany in 1987. WINSET also tells us that the CD remained a strong party in the three-dimensional German representation, albeit not very strong since there were nine governments, including the status quo, in the winset of the CD's ideal point. We also note that the strong party did go into the government in Germany in 1987.

Thus each of the one-, two-, and three-dimensional implementations of our model for government formation in Germany after the 1987 election generates a plausible account of what happened in practice. Since the data on which these implementations are based are derived from expert judgments, however, and since even experts are not only fallible but frequently disagree with one another, we should consider the extent to which our results are subject to measurement error. We could in principle use the standard errors reported in the tables to calculate confidence limits for the positions of the ideal points on which the winset analyses are based. We could then draw a set of lattices and a series of indifference curves for each party based on a set of party ideal point estimates within this range and investigate the myriad different winsets that this generated, but this would be an extremely cumbersome procedure.

An alternative method is to simulate the process of measurement error, and this can be done using the WINSET computer program. Rather than calculating results on a single case, based on the point estimates of party positions, we can calculate results for a large set of cases. Each case is a simulated party configuration. Each has the same party weights as those in Germany after the 1987 election. Party ideal points in each case, however, are based on the point estimates derived from the Laver-Hunt expert judgments, but vary randomly around these in the same way that we assume the measurement error to arise. Specifically, in each case, we calculate each party's position on each dimension as the mean expert judgment of that position, plus a normally distributed random error with a mean of zero and a standard deviation equal to the standard error of the

Table 6.6. *Distribution of strong parties and empty-winset DDMs, given variation in estimates of party ideal positions on economic and foreign policy dimensions*

	Cases / 1,000
DDM with empty winset *Finance-foreign affairs*	
CD-FDP	996
FDP-FDP	4
All other points	0
DDM with non-empty winset	0
Strong party	
CD	710
FDP	216
SPD	0
Greens	0
None	74

estimate of the mean in the expert data, as reported in Tables 6.2, 6.4, and 6.5.[7] In other words, each case represents a set of expert judgments that we could have derived, the probability of deriving which is based on the actual variation in the expert judgments that Laver and Hunt observed when they collected their data.[8]

Table 6.6 reports the results of an analysis investigating the susceptibility of the two-dimensional German analysis to measurement error of this sort. It shows key features of the results of the investigation of 1,000 hypothetical party systems, with party policy positions generated as speci-

[7]With Laver and Hunt's finite sample of experts on German politics, the position of, for example, the CD on the economic policy dimension is calculated for each case, using the parameters reported in Table 6.2, as $13.5 +$ normal $(0, 0.54)$, where normal $(0, 0.54)$ is a number randomly selected from a distribution with a mean of 0 and a standard deviation of 0.54.

[8]Note that this interpretation of the standard errors of the estimated positions assumes that there is a single "true" position on each dimension, and that the variation in expert judgments represents measurement error. This is consistent with our assumption that all policy positions are common knowledge. It does, however, preclude the possibility that the variation in judgments has some substantive meaning as a parameter in the government formation process – for example, being an estimate of the fuzziness of particular policy positions.

Table 6.7. Decisive structure after the 1992 Dáil election

	Seats
Individual parties	
Fianna Fáil (FF)	68
Fine Gael (FG)	45
Labour (Lab)	33
Progressive Democrats (PD)	10
Democratic Left (DL)	4
Others	5
Total	165
Chair	1
Majority threshold	83
Winning coalitions	
FF+FG	113
FF+Lab	101
FG+Lab+PD	88
FF+FG+Lab	146
FF+FG+PD	123
FF+FG+DL	117
FF+Lab+PD	111
FF+Lab+DL	105
FG+Lab+PD+DL	92
FF+FG+Lab+PD	156
FF+FG+Lab+DL	150
FF+FG+PD+DL	127
FF+Lab+PD+DL	115
FF+FG+Lab+PD+DL	160

fied in the previous paragraph. The results are quite striking, and show the two-dimensional German example we have been discussing to be quite robust to the level of measurement error we are likely to have encountered in the expert data. As we have already seen, given that the CD-FDP cabinet was the status quo, the model (accurately) predicts the continuation of the status quo in 1987. Of the 1,000 simulated cases we generated, 996 were such that the CD-FDP cabinet was at the DDM and had an empty winset; in all of these cases the correct forecast would have been made (in only 4 of the 1,000 cases would the model's forecast have been incorrect). The analysis reported in Table 6.6 thus strongly suggests that this prediction is not sensitive to potential measurement error in estimates of the party ideal points.

Table 6.6 also shows that the identification of the strong party in the 1,000 hypothetical "German" cases is, however, much more susceptible to measurement error. The reasons for this can be seen clearly from Figure 6.1. The CD and FDP are almost equidistant from both SPD and Greens. Whichever of the two is estimated to be the closer is likely to be the strong party,[9] and small perturbations in their ideal points are likely to make one or the other strong. However, given the status quo of a CD-FDP coalition, the prediction that the strong party, if one exists, will be in government does not depend on whether it is CD or FDP that is strong. What is particularly striking about Table 6.6 is that neither the SPD nor the Greens is identified as being strong in any of the 1,000 simulated cases, and neither, of course, was in government.

Overall, therefore, we can be quite confident that our analysis of the German two-dimensional case is not sensitive to likely levels of measurement error. Our model thus does seem to provide both a plausible and a robust account of government formation in Germany in 1987.

IRELAND 1992–1993

Party strengths in the 166-seat Irish legislature (the Dáil) after the general election of November 1992 are shown in the top panel of Table 6.7. Five parties were represented – the "others" listed were all independents whom we may regard for the sake of simplicity (and realistically enough in this case) as effective votes against any government.[10] With five parties in Ireland in 1992 instead of four in Germany in 1987, there are quite a

---

[9]This is because the location of the SPD and Green indifference curves are such that, if the CDs are closer to the SPD and Greens than is the FDP, then the CD ideal will be in the winset of the FDP ideal, and the FDP therefore cannot be strong. If the FDP is closer than the CD to the SPD and the Greens, then the converse holds.

[10]One "independent" was in fact a member of the Green Party. A further complication is introduced as a result of the role of the chair. The outgoing chair is a deputy who is reelected unopposed to the subsequent Dáil. The election of a new chair is the first business of the new Dáil and, given a close election result, can if contested have a considerable bearing on government formation. The outgoing chair in 1992 was an independent who it was presumed would continue, thus the effective size of the Dáil is taken as 165 and the threshold is taken as 83. The following analysis would not change if the choice of chair were treated as a part of the government formation process, the effective size of the Dáil were taken as 166, and the threshold were raised to 84 seats.

Table 6.8. Positions of Irish parties on two key policy dimensions

	Mean position (standard error)			
Party	Increase taxes (1) vs. cut services (20)		Pro (1) vs. Anti (20) British presence in N. Ireland	
Fianna Fáil	12.05	(0.37)	16.27	(0.31)
Fine Gael	14.23	(0.42)	10.60	(0.59)
Labour	7.45	(0.39)	12.07	(0.54)
Prog. Dems	16.97	(0.42)	10.07	(0.61)
Dem. Left	4.77	(0.74)	8.66	(0.86)

Source: Laver, 1994.

few more possible winning coalitions – 14 as opposed to 8. This more complex decisive structure is listed in the bottom panel of Table 6.7.

As an aside it is worth noting that the decisive structure is incredibly finely balanced in this particular case. Indeed a single closely contested seat, in the Dublin South Central constituency, determined the entire decisive structure. Originally the seat was awarded to the Democratic Left (DL), which would have given the DL 5 seats and Fianna Fáil (FF) 67. The result of this would have been to have given an additional anti–Fianna Fáil coalition (Fine Gael-Labour-DL) a majority. A recount was demanded, and in this and subsequent recounts over a period of a week after the original result was declared, the seat changed hands several times between Fianna Fáil and DL, with the decisive structure flip-flopping at the same time. After ever closer scrutiny of spoilt ballots, a decisive number of which were write-in votes for Dustin, a puppet turkey on a popular children's television show, the seat was decided in the end by five votes, and awarded to Fianna Fáil. Only after this did serious government formation negotiations commence. The delicately poised decisive structure that constrained these was quite possibly shaped by a handful of voters (and a puppet turkey!) in a single constituency.

Turning now to party policy positions, the Laver-Hunt survey was repeated on a panel of 32 Irish politics experts during the 1992 election campaign.[11] Estimated party policy positions on the key policy dimensions, for 1992, are given in Table 6.8. Figures 6.3 and 6.4 give two-dimensional plots of these positions. Using these data in the same way as

[11]A detailed report of this survey can be found in Laver (1994).

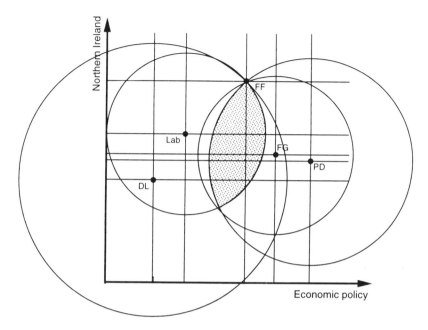

Figure 6.3. Two-dimensional Irish policy space: Indifference curves relating to FF ideal point

we did for Germany in 1987, the most appropriate two-dimensional representation of party policy positions in Ireland makes economic policy the most important dimension and Northern Ireland policy the next most important dimension. Overwhelmingly the most important economic policy portfolio was the Department of Finance, ranked first among cabinet portfolios by each of the 32 expert respondents. Northern Ireland policy was the responsibility of the very highly ranked Department of Foreign Affairs[12] (which deals with Britain on the matter and is largely responsible for the operation of the Anglo-Irish Agreement).

The outgoing government in 1992 was a Fianna Fáil caretaker administration, left in place after the Progressive Democrats had resigned from a coalition with Fianna Fáil following a bitter personal dispute between their respective leaders, Desmond O'Malley and Albert Reynolds. In both the caretaker government and the coalition that preceded it, Fianna Fáil controlled the key portfolios of finance and foreign affairs.

[12]The second-ranked portfolio in Ireland, according to the 1992 resurvey, was the Department of Industry, another important economic policy portfolio. After this came the Departments of the Environment (the main responsibilities of which concern local services) and of Foreign Affairs.

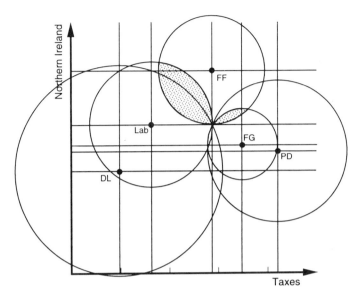

Figure 6.4. Two-dimensional Irish policy space: Indifference curves relating to FF-Labour coalition

The policy status quo of the outgoing government can thus be taken to be the ideal point of Fianna Fáil on these two important policy dimensions. This point is shown in Figure 6.3, together with the indifference curves showing how each of the other parties felt about the Fianna Fáil status quo.

The intersection of the Fine Gael (FG), Labour, and PD indifference curves shows that area of the policy space preferred by a legislative majority to the Fianna Fáil minority caretaker government. What is striking is that, despite the fact that Fianna Fáil had done very badly in the 1992 election, sinking to its lowest level for over 50 years, opposition parties controlling a legislative majority could agree on no alternative government that they all preferred to a Fianna Fáil minority government, and which excluded Fianna Fáil. Fianna Fáil was a participant in every cabinet in the winset of its ideal point, and hence was a strong party. According to our model, if Fianna Fáil could win standoffs with the other parties, then it could form an equilibrium minority administration on its own and take all portfolios. If Fianna Fáil was known not to be able to win standoffs with the other parties, then our model predicts that the equilibrium would be some cabinet in the winset of the FF ideal point. There are four such cabinets, including the dimension-by-dimension median cabinet, a coalition that gives finance to Fianna Fáil and foreign affairs to Labour. As Figure 6.4 shows, this dimension-by-dimension median cabinet has an empty winset.

Three of the cabinets in the winset of the Fianna Fáil ideal are ruled out, according to our model, by Proposition 4.3. This shows that, even if some cabinet is in the winset of the strong party ideal, and even if the strong party cannot win standoffs, a cabinet cannot be an equilibrium if the strong party prefers the dimension-by-dimension median to it. In this case the strong party, Fianna Fáil, prefers the dimension-by-dimension median cabinet – a Fianna Fáil–Labour coalition – to any other cabinet in the winset of its ideal point (i.e., to coalitions between Fianna Fáil and Fine Gael, the Progressive Democrats or Democratic Left). According to our model, this reduces the coalitional possibilities to two – a Fianna Fáil minority government and the dimension-by-dimension median cabinet, a Fianna Fáil-Labour coalition. If Fianna Fáil was forecast to win standoffs, the former should form; if not, the latter.

In the event, Fianna Fáil was in a much enfeebled position after its disastrous electoral performance in November 1992. Its leader, Albert Reynolds, faced a massive threat to his position on the grounds that he was alleged to have precipitated an unwanted election, which he then proceeded to lose. Immediately after the election, Fianna Fáil more or less withdrew from the government formation process, leaving this to a much vaunted "Rainbow Coalition" of Fine Gael, Labour, and the PD. This was an idea promoted by the Fine Gael leader during the election, and one that obsessed much of the news media after the results were declared.

Figure 6.3 in effect shows the area of the two-dimensional Irish policy space preferred by the Rainbow Coalition to the Fianna Fáil status quo. From this, we can very easily see something that took the news media, popular commentators, and indeed many politicians some time to realize – that every majority-preferred alternative to the status quo involved the participation of Fianna Fáil in some coalition or another. In our terms, since Fianna Fáil was a strong party, the opposition simply could not agree on a coalition that excluded it. However, the weakness of the Fianna Fáil leader meant that the party could not win standoffs and thus could not go it alone in a minority government.

In order to face down the opposition parties, credibly to refuse ever to enter any coalition, and to be allowed eventually to form a government on its own, Fianna Fáil needed the other parties to believe that, if it came to the crunch, FF would go back to the Dáil again and again, proposing its leader as prime minister of a minority cabinet and vetoing any other cabinet involving its participation. If the opposition parties had refused to relent and vote for the Fianna Fáil leader, then this would have precipitated a political crisis that would quickly have fed through into the financial system.[13] This would have been a severe test of political nerve for all concerned. Sooner or later, one side or the other would have had to give way. What the Irish opposition parties knew was that, if this scenario unfolded, it would have resulted in the removal of Albert Reynolds as FF leader, given his already weakened position within the party. Knowing this, and knowing that the opposition parties knew it, Reynolds was in no position to hang tough and face down the opposition in coalition negotiations, as he would have needed to do in order to establish a minority Fianna Fáil government. In order to stave off a leadership "heave" against him, he needed a Dáil majority sooner rather than later. Once installed as prime minister of a coalition cabinet, his position as party leader would be far more secure. The effect of all this was that it was common knowledge that the Fianna Fáil leader could not win standoffs. He thus had no alternative, according to our model, but to go into coalition with Labour and cede them the foreign affairs portfolio. As we have seen from Figure 6.4, this cabinet has an empty winset. In the event, it is the cabinet that formed in early 1993.[14]

All of this is a far cry from the traditional position of Fianna Fáil in the Irish party system. For over 50 years until 1989, the party had promoted single-party Fianna Fáil administrations, with or without a Dáil majority, as the alternative to "weak and unstable" coalition government, and refused to share power with anyone else. This is the classic stance of the strong party that can win standoffs. The credibility of this bargaining position had been enhanced when, on several occasions, Fianna Fáil had chosen to go into opposition rather than a coalition cabinet – an outcome that we can interpret as a periodic testing of the party's resolve by its opponents. Fianna Fáil's "no coalition" position, developed over this 50-year period and never deviated from, had assumed the status of what party stalwarts regarded as a core value.

The core value was shattered in 1989, when Reynolds' predecessor, Fianna Fáil leader Charles Haughey, led the party into coalition with the

---

[13]Ireland's membership of what at that time was the narrow-band European Exchange Rate Mechanism (ERM) meant that if political uncertainty led to uncertainty about the stability of the Irish currency in international markets, the only way for the government to maintain the exchange rate in the narrow band, given finite foreign currency reserves, was to raise domestic interest rates. As subsequent events in a number of open European economies showed in these circumstances, domestic interest rates can be forced so high (as high as 100 percent) that mass foreclosures and serious economic collapse are threatened. Such pressures led eventually to the effective abandonment of the ERM.

[14]If the recounts in Dublin South Central had ultimately awarded the disputed seat to the Democratic Left, changing the decisive structure, the equilibrium prediction of our model, a Fianna Fáil–Labour coalition with FF in finance and Labour in foreign affairs, would not have changed. However the stability of this equilibrium, conceived in a way that we elaborate in Chapter 10, would have been significantly lower.

Progressive Democrats. This was a traumatic event for the party faithful, and was once more in large measure a product of a major threat to the position of Haughey as party leader, reducing his ability to win standoffs (Laver and Arkins, 1990). It is also worth noting that both FF leaders were relatively old at the time when they "blinked" in the government formation negotiations, were approaching the end of their respective political careers, and almost certainly did not expect to lead their party beyond the full term of the coalition administration that they were forming. Having gone into coalition for whatever reason in 1989, however, Fianna Fáil's "no coalition" position, though halfheartedly reiterated in 1992, was impossible to retrieve once lost. Nobody with his head on straight in 1992 believed that Fianna Fáil would irrevocably refuse to share power with another party.

This is not of course to say that Fianna Fáil could not once more become a strong party able to win standoffs. It remains, after all, a strong party. This gives a tough leader whose threats are believed immense bargaining leverage. If a new Fianna Fáil leader stormed into power on a trenchant anticoalition platform, brought down the current coalition, called an election promising single-party government, and then refused implacably to talk turkey, it is quite possible, given Fianna Fáil's size and central location in the Irish legislative policy space, that the other parties would reassess their evaluation of FF's ability to win standoffs. This would reopen the credible possibility of a new series of Fianna Fáil minority governments. What the Irish example shows quite clearly is that, in order to consume the benefits of being a strong party, it is not enough merely to *be* strong. You also have to *act* strong.

CONCLUSION

We have not set out in this chapter to measure our model systematically against the real political world – we attempt this in Chapters 7, 8, and 9. Rather, after several chapters of rather closely argued theory, we have attempted to convey more informally the overall look and feel of our approach by going in some detail into a couple of particular cases. These were chosen not because they were representative in any precise sense, but because they allowed us to elaborate, in a real political context, several different features of our model.

Obviously, the representations of German and Irish politics that we have developed here have been selected from a range of plausible possibilities, each with a different set of key policy dimensions and a different way of measuring these. They are in no sense definitive analyses of the government formation situations concerned. What is quite clear, however, is that government formation in the two examples we discuss in this chapter can be analyzed quite plausibly using the technology provided by our model – this was our main objective. Alternative ways of describing the party system concerned could be discussed in the same way. It is worth noting, however, that we have often discovered when playing with examples ourselves that using different representations and operationalizations of a particular case may make little difference to our model's identification of the basic strategic realities of a particular government formation context.

In the German and Irish cases we have just discussed, these realities identify a particular centrally located coalition cabinet at the dimension-by-dimension median position. In each case, this cabinet is such that there is no alternative preferred by a legislative majority so that, if it forms, it will be in equilibrium. (In each case it did actually form and did remain in place.)

In both the German and Irish cases there is also one party that is in a stronger position than the others, by virtue of the fact that the only cabinets that are majority-preferred to one in which it gets all portfolios are those in which the "strong" party itself participates. In each case, there are indeed majority-preferred alternatives to a strong-party minority cabinet, so that the ultimate government equilibrium depends on forecasts about the willingness and ability of the strong party to win strategic standoffs with others. In the German case the CDs appear never to have attempted to impose a minority cabinet. In the Irish case, Fianna Fáil has quite often formed minority governments, and clearly would like to do so again, but leadership problems meant that it did not in 1992–1993 have the ability to face down its opponents.

Overall, and the reader will of course be a better judge of this than we are, it does seem that our model can be used in these cases to uncover interesting and nonobvious strategic features of the government formation process in a parliamentary democracy. This gives a feel for the way our model works and provides a qualitative context for the more intense quantitative evaluations that follow.

7

Theoretical implications, data,
and operationalization

The preceding chapter gave a glimpse of our model at work. The main purpose of that chapter, however, was to illustrate the model rather than to explore its empirical implications in a systematic way. Here we set off on a more comprehensive exploration with the ultimate objective of turning the model loose, so to speak, on the real world of government formation in particular countries. We do not do this because we have ambitions to take over the turf of the country specialists – we have no intention of trying to reproduce the qualitative analyses at which they excel. Rather we hope that an operational version of our model will provide a technology that allows us to be more systematic in how we go about specific aspects of particular country analyses. In this chapter, we begin the process of applying our model systematically to the formation of actual governments. After first presenting a series of theoretical implications of our model for government formation in the real world, we then turn to matters of operationalizing the model and using it to engage in comparative empirical analysis.

THEORETICAL IMPLICATIONS

The most fundamental principle of our entire approach states that, when the government formation process is triggered for some reason, either the status quo government remains in power or it is replaced by some alternative that is preferred to this by a parliamentary majority. We state this "ground zero" implication as:

> *Implication 0:* The status quo cabinet at the beginning of the government formation process either remains the cabinet in place at the end of the process or is replaced by some alternative in its winset. (Formally, if the status quo at time $t - 1$ is SQ_{t-1} and at time t is SQ_t, then: $SQ_t \in \{SQ_{t-1}\} \cup W(SQ_{t-1})$.)

Proposition 4.1 identifies the dimension-by-dimension median (DDM) cabinet as an equilibrium if it has an empty winset.[1] This allows us to make the following forecast:

> *Implication 1:* If the status quo cabinet at time t − 1 is at the dimension-by-dimension median, and this has an empty winset at time t, then this cabinet remains in place.
> (Formally if, at time t, $W(SQ_{t-1}) = \emptyset$, then $SQ_t = SQ_{t-1}$.)

That is to say, a sitting government with an empty winset cannot be displaced, since there is no alternative government on which any majority could agree. Such a government remains in place. However, because an empty-winset DDM cabinet need not be a *unique* equilibrium outcome of the government formation process, the cabinet need not become the government if it is not already the government at the start of the process.

When the DDM cabinet is some party's ideal point and has an empty winset, then the party in question is very strong. Implication 1, of course, holds in this instance. But we can say more:

> *Implication 2:* If a party is very strong, then it is assigned all portfolios in the government formation process.
> (Formally, if $W(s^*) = \emptyset$, then $SQ_t = s^*$.)

In this special instance of a party ideal point at the DDM position with an empty winset, Proposition 4.2 identifies this very strong party as the equilibrium outcome of the government formation process regardless of the government in place at the start of the process.[2]

Proposition 4.2 also has something to say about strong parties in general, whether they are merely strong or very strong:

> *Implication 3:* If a party is strong, then it participates in the cabinet that is the outcome of the government formation process.
> (Formally, if S participates in every element of $W(s^*)$, then S participates in SQ_t.)

In other words, our model of the making and breaking of governments implies that a strong party cannot be denied a place in the cabinet. It either controls the entire cabinet, obtaining all portfolios, or is awarded some subset of portfolios. Empirically, this has several more detailed corollaries that may be tested separately. Each of these implications elaborates the point that our model implies that we should see portfolios

---

[1] Recall that the *only* cabinet that may have an empty winset is the DDM, though it need not. Also recall that even if the DDM does have an empty winset, it need not be a *unique* equilibrium outcome of the government formation process as we model this.

[2] Proposition 4.2 identifies the equilibrium of the government formation as an element in $\{s^*\} \cup W(s^*)$, and the latter set is empty in this case.

assigned either to the strong party or to one of the parties participating in one of the governments in the winset of the strong-party ideal point.

Implication 3A: If there is a strong party and every government in the winset of its ideal point assigns a specific portfolio to that party, then the outcome of the government formation process will be a cabinet in which the strong party controls that portfolio.

(Formally: If party S is strong and every element of W(s*) assigns S a particular portfolio, then S receives that portfolio in SQ_t.)

Implication 3B: If there is a strong party, then the outcome of the government formation process will be a cabinet assigning each of the portfolios to the strong party or to one of its partners as identified in the winset of the strong party ideal.

(Formally: If party S is strong, then each portfolio in SQ_t is assigned to one of the parties identified in {s*} ∪ W(s*).)

We have now derived directly and explicitly from our model a series of statements about government formation in the real world. This allows us to apply our model systematically to actual instances of government formation and hence to evaluate whether it consistently provides us with some insight into the making and breaking of real governments. In order to do this, of course, we have to collect systematic information on government formation in a range of parliamentary democracies.

DATA AND OPERATIONALIZATIONS

In order to examine empirically the implications listed here, we collected information for every European parliamentary democracy since the end of World War II whose government formation process approximates our model. We exclude every legislature in which a single party controlled a majority of seats, since our theory would be trivially confirmed in every instance of this. We also excluded several countries that, for various reasons, did not seem appropriate to include.[3] This leaves us with a dataset covering the countries and elections listed in Table 7.1. The interval covered by the study period in each country is given in Table 7.2.

[3]France, Greece, and Switzerland were deleted because their respective government formation processes are not captured by our model, and their institutional arrangements depart in various ways from conventional parliamentary democracies. Portugal and Spain were deleted because of the difficulty of getting reliable estimates of party positions in their relatively new party systems. Finally, because virtually all elections manufactured a single-party majority government, Malta, Norway prior to 1961, and the United Kingdom were deleted. In some cases – for example, Ireland in 1954 and 1961 – the number of independent MPs for which data on issue positions were unavailable was a sufficient cause to exclude the case.

Table 7.1. Data set for empirical analysis

Country	Election
Austria	1949, 1953, 1956, 1959, 1970, 1983, 1986[a]
Belgium	1946, 1949, 1954, 1958, 1961, 1965, 1968, 1971, 1974, 1977, 1978, 1981, 1985, 1987[a]
Denmark	1945, 1947, 1950, 1953a, 1953b, 1957, 1960, 1964, 1966, 1968, 1971, 1973, 1975, 1977, 1979, 1981, 1984, 1987, 1988
Finland	1945, 1948, 1951, 1954, 1958, 1962, 1966, 1970, 1972, 1975, 1979, 1983, 1987[a]
Germany	1961, 1965, 1969, 1972, 1976, 1980, 1983, 1987[a]
Iceland	1946, 1949, 1953, 1956, 1959a,1959b, 1963, 1967, 1971, 1974, 1978, 1979, 1983, 1987[a]
Ireland	1965, 1973, 1981, 1982a, 1982b, 1987, 1989[a]
Italy	1953, 1958, 1963, 1968, 1972, 1976, 1979, 1983, 1987[a]
Luxembourg	1945, 1948, 1951, 1954, 1959, 1964, 1968, 1974, 1979, 1984, 1989
Netherlands	1977, 1981, 1982, 1986[a]
Norway	1961, 1965, 1969, 1973, 1977, 1981, 1985, 1989
Sweden	1948, 1952, 1956, 1958, 1960, 1964, 1970, 1973, 1976, 1979, 1982, 1985, 1988[a]

[a] Although there was another election before the end of the study period on January 1, 1993, the government that subsequently formed had not ended by the end of the study period.

For each of the government formation situations we investigate, we needed data on a number of items. First, we needed data on the legislative party system after each election in each country – the identity of parties with seats in parliament, the number of seats won by each party, and the number of seats required to pass an investiture or no-confidence motion.[4]

[4]Data on this are taken from Mackie and Rose (1991), supplemented by annual reports on election results by Mackie in the *European Journal of Political Research* and, after 1991, by the annual data issues of this journal.

Table 7.2. Length of study period

Country	Beginning	End
Austria (Not 1963-70)	7/11/49	17/12/90
Belgium (Not 1950-54)	11/3/46	7/3/92
Denmark	8/11/45	17/12/89
Finland	17/4/45	26/4/91
Germany	14/11/61	18/1/91
Iceland	4/2/47	30/4/91
Ireland (Not 1969-73, 1977-81)	1/4/65	5/2/92
Italy	17/7/53	4/7/92
Luxembourg	20/11/45	14/7/89
Netherlands	19/12/77	1/11/89
Norway	11/9/61	2/11/90
Sweden	28/10/48	3/10/91

Second, we needed data on which party held each government portfolio, both at the beginning and the end of each government formation process.[5]

Third, we needed data on party positions on salient issue dimensions. In order to describe how we have proceeded on this matter, it is necessary to identify a number of operational decisions that have had to be made. Most European cabinets comprise at least a dozen and sometimes as many as two dozen ministerial positions. This number does not exceed the capacity of our model, which can in principle handle any number of portfolios, but it does exceed our practical ability to collect and process data on party positions.[6]

More important than the practical problems associated with doing a complete analysis of the allocation of the full range of portfolios in any particular cabinet, however, is the fact that there are very sound theoretical reasons for not doing this. As we argue in Chapter 11, when party

[5]Data on this are taken from Woldendorp, Keman, and Budge (1993).

[6]The computing horsepower needed by WINSET to investigate completely a 10-party system with 15 cabinet portfolios involves comparing every cabinet on a lattice of 10^{15} points – that's 1,000,000,000,000,000 points – to every other. Even in these stirring times, this is something which exceeds the capacity of any supercomputer that might be put at our disposal. Printing the ensuing report would entail the destruction of an entire forest so that, even if the computer horsepower were available, only an environmental terrorist would conduct such an investigation.

positions on a number of policy dimensions are highly correlated to each other, one consequence of this is to reduce the effective dimensionality of the space in which the government formation process takes place. The effect of this is that a more straightforward and intuitive, yet just as valid, account of government formation can be conducted by concentrating on a relatively small number of the most important portfolios. Thus, for both practical and theoretical reasons, it is neither possible nor desirable to consider the allocation of every single cabinet portfolio when analyzing the formation of a particular government.

In the analyses that follow, therefore, we have confined ourselves to the allocation of *key* portfolios, those that clearly deal with highly salient policies. For each of these key portfolios (we will describe how we determine which portfolios are "key"), we assume that the jurisdiction for which a minister has responsibility can be described by a single policy dimension.[7] Thus we need to know three different things: Which portfolios are key in each country? What dimension of policy best describes the jurisdiction of each key portfolio? Where does each party stand on each of these policy dimensions? We use data from the expert survey administered in 1989 by Laver and Hunt (1992).[8]

Key portfolios?

In order to define key portfolios, we draw on the item in the Laver-Hunt questionnaire that asked respondents to rank-order cabinet positions in "their" country in terms of their importance in the government formation process. For each of the countries in Table 7.1 we have taken the mean ranking of the experts for that country as a measure of portfolio importance. Because there is some disagreement among experts on this matter, we also take the variance around this mean into account. For each country we are able to rank-order the top several ministries. Sometimes there is a clear-cut (statistically significant) difference between rankings of the first, second, and third most important portfolios. At other times, there is insufficient statistical difference to discriminate whether one is first and the other second, or the reverse. In any event, given the computational and data limitations alluded to, we operationalize key portfolios to mean the top two portfolios when there is a statistically significant difference between the mean expert rankings of the second- and third-ranked portfolios. If finance is one of these, as it always is in the countries of interest, then the next ranked ministry we consider is the next highest noneco-

[7]In Part II of this book, we referred to these as *simple jurisdictions.*

[8]For all of the world's parliamentary democracies, Laver and Hunt sent a postal questionnaire to a collection of country specialist experts. For countries listed in Table 7.1, there were from 5 to 36 respondents per country, with an average of 14.

Table 7.3. Policy jurisdictions of key cabinet portfolios

Country	1st portfolio	2nd portfolio	3rd portfolio
Austria	Finance	Interior	Foreign affairs
Belgium	Finance	Justice	–
Denmark	Finance	Foreign affairs	–
Finland	Finance	Foreign affairs	–
Germany	Finance	Foreign affairs	Interior
Iceland	Finance	Foreign affairs	–
Ireland	Finance	Foreign affairs	Agriculture
Italy	Finance	Foreign affairs	Interior
Luxembourg	Finance	Foreign affairs	–
Netherlands	Finance	Foreign affairs	Home affairs
Norway	Finance	Foreign affairs	–
Sweden	Finance	Foreign affairs	–

nomic portfolio. If, on the other hand, there is no statistical difference in the mean rankings of the second and third portfolios, then we operationalize key portfolios as the top three portfolios. Using this algorithm to identify key portfolios, the top portfolios were always finance, foreign affairs, and the most important internal affairs ministry, typically the Department of Justice or Interior.

The data to allow us to identify key portfolios are given in appendix B of Laver and Hunt (1992). Table 7.3 lists the key portfolios for each country in our study. As can be seen, finance is always top rated; foreign affairs is next in every country but Austria and Belgium, where domestic ministries are ranked higher.

We are acutely aware of the danger, when theorists test their own models empirically, that individual operational decisions may be made that favorably bias the tests. Accordingly, we have taken care to apply the algorithm given here mechanically and to avoid ad hoc adjustments. Readers with a detailed local knowledge of a particular country may feel an alternative operationalization is more appropriate. We felt, however, that comparative evaluation of our approach across a range of different countries was best served by adopting an arm's length approach to operationalization.

Another important feature of our operational definition of key portfolios is worthy of comment at this stage. While most readers will find the prominence given to financial matters very plausible, some may be surprised by the prominence that our definition gives to foreign affairs.

Empirical investigations

Taking party competition as a whole, and electoral competition in particular, foreign policy issues are often not the most salient. Remember, however, that we are dealing with the formation of real working governments. If we consider the practical policy decisions that must be taken, and cannot be avoided, by any government, then matters of foreign relations are clearly prominent. This, we believe, is what led country specialists in the Laver-Hunt expert survey to place the foreign affairs portfolio so high in their rankings. In effect, they are telling us, in country after country, that for *executive* politics, foreign affairs is a key policy dimension.

Policy jurisdictions?

The next empirical matter is to identify the policy dimensions falling under the jurisdictions of key portfolios in each country. Clearly any ministerial jurisdiction is in reality multidimensional. There is absolutely no problem for either our model or our computer program in analyzing multidimensional policy jurisdictions if reliable data are available on these and sensible interpretations can be made of them. Nonetheless, in order to keep our preliminary operationalization as straightforward as we can, we have restricted our description of cabinet policy jurisdictions to a single dimension in each case. For the finance portfolio we chose the question asked for the Laver-Hunt expert respondents on the trade-off between "raising taxes to increase public services" and "cutting public services to reduce taxes." For the foreign affairs portfolio, our operational definition consisted, except in the case of Ireland, of responses to the question of whether to "promote or oppose the development of friendly relations with the Soviet Union."[9] In the Irish case, the most salient foreign policy issue concerned attitudes toward the British presence in Northern Ireland, responsibility for which lies within the jurisdiction of the Department of Foreign Affairs. For the countries with a noneconomic domestic portfolio listed in Table 7.2, the question varied according to the ministry and country in question.[10]

[9]The survey was conducted in 1989, before the Berlin Wall came down and before the Soviet Union disintegrated. The question is certainly meaningful for the entire cold war period, essentially the period of our study.
[10]For Austria (interior), Italy (interior), and the Netherlands (home affairs), the issue defining this domestic noneconomic portfolio was support of or opposition to "permissive policies on matters such as abortion and homosexual law." For Belgium (justice) and Germany (interior), both federal countries, the question defining this ministry's jurisdiction involved promoting or opposing "decentralization of decision making." Finally, for Ireland (agriculture), the defining question was whether to "promote the interests of urban and industrial voters above all others or promote the interests of rural and agricultural voters above all others."

Implications, data, and operationalization

Party policy positions?

The next task is to locate the ideal points of the political parties on the dimensions in question. Although any other data source that gave party positions on a range of different policy dimensions characterizing the jurisdiction of key cabinet portfolios would have done equally well, no alternative to the Laver-Hunt survey is, to our knowledge, available for each policy dimension we use for every one of the range of countries in our analysis. Expert respondents were asked to place the political parties of their respective countries on each of the dimensions describing the jurisdictions of the key portfolios of Table 7.2. For each party we take the mean of these country-specific responses as the party's position on issues coming under the jurisdiction of the relevant portfolio.[11]

These data permit us to construct the lattice of governments that structures our theoretical model of government formation. It is important to bear the limitations of our data on party policy positions very firmly in mind, however, and, since one of us was responsible for collecting them, we are allowed to be quite brutal on this matter. Expert judgments are no more than surrogates for real data on party positions on key issues. At worst, they may be no better than aggregated professional folk wisdom, unsuitable for testing theories in political science because the political scientists who generated them are aware of the general thrust of the theories to which the data are to be applied. Far more valid measures would be based on elite surveys of party politicians and activists, or on the content analysis of policy documents, to name but two obvious possibilities.

At the current state of the discipline, however, theoretical models of party politics in multidimensional issue spaces have outstripped systematic comparative empirical accounts of real party positions on real issue dimensions other than the standard and very general "left–right" dimension. Thus, while a range of alternative data sources can be used as the basis for an empirical elaboration of unidimensional models of various aspects of party politics, very few sources are available for elaborating multidimensional models. To the best of our knowledge, as we have argued, none provides information on as many countries, as many parties, and as many policy dimensions as the Laver-Hunt study. The very real danger of limiting the analysis to a very few countries on which "harder" data on multidimensional policy positions are available is that results become highly susceptible to case selection bias, avoided by using

[11]In subsequent analysis we will also make use of the disagreement about party locations contained in these data – the variance in positions attributed by expert respondents.

a more comprehensive dataset.[12] For this reason, we make no apology for basing our initial empirical elaboration on expert data, although we must emphasize forcefully that our model can be elaborated with any systematic multidimensional data on party positions, and does not in any way depend upon the validity of the expert data methodology.[13]

In principle we might have extended the time series backward to the beginning of parliamentary democracy in each of the countries concerned. However, it is quite apparent that our expert opinion data on portfolio importance and party locations cannot be applied across any long expanse of time as if no change at all had taken place.[14] Indeed we believe we are pushing the estimates generated by these opinions, collected in 1989 about country-specific party politics in the late 1980s, to their very limits in taking them back to the mid-1940s.[15] In some cases such change has been so self-evident – with the emergence of new parties and the splitting and fusing of old ones – that our data clearly do not apply and we have excluded all preceding elections.[16]

In our theoretical development of Chapters 4 and 5 we implicitly treated all jurisdictions as being equally salient to each political party. This was done by employing Euclidean distance from a party ideal policy position as an inverse measure of preference – implying that a party's preference for a point is a decreasing function of its distance from that party's ideal. All of our theoretical results hold, however, if we relax this assumption in order to allow for the possibility that different policy dimensions (and hence jurisdictions) have different salience for different parties. A conservative party, for example, may care most about policy dimensions under the jurisdiction of the finance ministry, whereas a social

[12]The empirical elaboration of government formation theories may be particularly susceptible to case-selection bias, since theories do perform much better in some countries than in others. (See Laver and Schofield, 1990, for numerous examples of this phenomenon.) The original empirical elaboration of Axelrod's minimal winning theory, for example, used data from Italy, which he happened to have available (Axelrod, 1970). Subsequent more comparative evaluations (e.g., by Taylor and Laver, 1973), showed that Italy was far from a typical case, generating much better results for minimal-winning theory than most other countries.

[13]In fact, party positions estimated on the basis of the Laver-Hunt survey correlate very highly with positions on comparable scales derived from other sources, including the content analyses of party manifestos. See Laver and Hunt (1992: 41–42, 126–128).

[14]Even more problematical are the births and deaths of political parties no longer present in 1989 at the time the Laver-Hunt survey was conducted.

[15]In the multivariate analysis of Chapter 9, we will include decade dummies to help sort out statistical explanation in light of the "aging" of our opinion data as we push it back in time.

[16]As can be seen from Table 7.1, such changes in party systems led to the exclusion of legislatures in Germany before 1961, in Ireland before 1954, and in the Netherlands before 1977.

democratic party may care more about those under the jurisdiction of a Department of Social Welfare.[17]

In order to allow for the operationalization of models of party competition that take account of interparty variations in perceptions of dimension weights, the Laver-Hunt expert survey estimated the salience to political parties of the various policy dimensions that were considered. Thus, we were also able to conduct the analysis in Chapter 8 using sets of interparty policy distances that were weighted to take account of the particular policy dimensions for particular parties. We report only the results based on *unweighted* policy distances, however, for two reasons. First, sets of unweighted policy distances are so much more straightforward and intuitive (forming the basis for a single graphical representation of a party policy space that we can draw and easily envisage). Second, our empirical reanalysis of the entire set of cases based on weighted interparty policy distances made no substantial difference to any of the empirical conclusions we arrive at.

[17]Our results, as well as Kadane's Improvement Algorithm, continue to hold in such circumstances. Strictly, they hold even if indifference curves are ellipses instead of circles (or, in higher dimensions, ellipsoids instead of hyperspheres), so long as preferences are separable. Separable preferences imply that parties may differentially evaluate dimensions, but their evaluations on one dimension are effectively carried out independent of evaluations on other dimensions.

8

Exploring the model: A comparative perspective

INTRODUCTION

Thus far we have elaborated our model, set out some of its implications for coalition formation in the real world, explored these implications in a couple of particular settings, and discussed how these implications can be more generally evaluated using data that are actually available to us. We are now in a position to look in a more systematic manner at how well the model seems to capture important features of the making and breaking of real governments. We do this by determining whether each of the cabinets in our dataset conforms to each of the theoretical implications of our model set out in Chapter 7.

Using our data for each government formation situation that we consider, we use WINSET to calculate which of the possible cabinets that could have formed were consistent with the theoretical implications of our model. Since, out of very many cabinets that could possibly have formed, our model typically identified rather few as potential equilibriums, if the actual cabinet that formed was one of these equilibrium cabinets identified by our model, we regard this as an empirical "success."

Furthermore, since every day in politics is one in which the incumbent government must survive in the face of the possibility of being brought down, every day is in a sense a new government formation situation. If the parameters of the situation change in such a way that the incumbent government is no longer equilibrium, then our model implies that the government should change. We thus consider the duration over which the theoretical implications of our model are fulfilled in each case.

Note that looking at government formation in this way frees us from one of the traditional bugaboos of those who set out to "test" theories of government formation. The challenge is to find a definition of the unit of analysis – the government formation situation – that is independent of the theory being tested. In the literature on government durations, for example, many authors conclude that when the prime minister resigns for "nonpolitical" reasons a new government has not come into being so that a new case is not triggered (see Laver and Schofield, 1990: 145–147 for a review of this issue). Obviously, however, what is and is not "nonpolitical" is not exogenous to the model being tested; moreover, operational decisions on this can affect model evaluations in major ways. Our approach does not force us to make arbitrary choices on such matters.

Those who might object that we should have used hours, weeks, or months, rather than days, as the fundamental clock tick in our evaluations should note that – unless we are talking about years or decades – the duration of a clock tick makes not a blind bit of difference to our results, except at the level of rounding error. The figures we report can easily be rescaled to reflect different durations of clock tick. What is crucial is the notion that the government formation process is continuous, rather than one that is divided into a set of episodes, the beginning and end of which must be determined in some arbitrary manner by the analyst.

It is quite straightforward, if a little tedious, to evaluate the success of our theoretical implications on a case-by-case basis. We ourselves have had to do this in order to generate the results that follow, but a case-by-case report of every one of these evaluations would drive even the most dedicated and abstemious reader to strong drink and leave us all unable to see the forest for the trees. We are thus left with the problem of how to present information on a large number of case-based evaluations in a manner that allows us to get some overall feel for what is going on. This is not as straightfoward as it might seem at first glance. The essential problem is one of finding a yardstick that can be used in assessing the success rate of each implication, since these success rates are not very meaningful in themselves. We have learned very little, for example, when we hear that portfolio allocations in Austria were consistent with the forecast of Implication 0 for 5,738 days during our study period. Is that good or bad?

In the next chapter, we crunch all of our data through one of the more conventional statistical machines. In this chapter, however, in an effort to keep our empirical evaluation intuitively meaningful, we report a more direct investigation of the extent to which governments that formed in each country during the postwar era are consistent with the implications of our model. But this leaves us with the problem of finding a yardstick for success.

The ideal yardstick, of course, would be to compare the performance of our theory against serious competitor theories. Our problem is that the main current alternatives to our approach are the respective game-theoretic models of Baron and of Schofield. These are indeed well enough specified to be programmed, *but they each make spatial forecasts of government policy, rather than forecasting government membership and portfolio allocation,* so that the outcome they forecast cannot be directly compared with that of our approach.

At this stage in our work, therefore, we confine ourselves initially to comparing the success of our theoretical propositions with how well we would be able to predict portfolio allocations if we had no model at all of the government formation process, which would amount to saying that each portfolio allocation is as likely as any other. Anyone who objects that each portfolio allocation is obviously not as likely as any other in effect has an implicit model of portfolio allocation in mind. But only if such a model were well enough specified to generate unambiguous empirical implications could it be included in a comparative evaluation. It is the absence of such well-specified models that forces us initially to compare our predictions with the null hypothesis that there is no systematic pattern in portfolio allocation. In the next chapter we operationalize intuitive alternatives to our theory that constitute more challenging null hypotheses.

The big advantage of comparing our model forecast with a null hypothesis such as this is that it allows us to take into account the fact that different government formation situations present our model with different challenges. In almost the simplest possible case, when we are forecasting the allocation of two portfolios in a three-party system, there are nine possible portfolio allocations. (The first portfolio can be given to one of three parties; for every one of these allocations, the second portfolio can also be given to one of three parties.) In the most complex case that we tend to confront in practice, forecasting three key portfolios in a ten-party system, there are by the same logic $10 \times 10 \times 10 = 1,000$ possible portfolio allocations. Obviously, the more complex case presents our model with a far sterner test. In the simpler case, even a person with no model who simply made a random guess at the exact portfolio allocation would be right 1 time in 9. In the more complex case, a random guess would be right only 1 time in 1,000.[1]

[1]It might of course be objected that, by comparing our model with a random null – in effect with no model at all – we have given ourselves too easy a task. There are three responses to this objection. The first is that we do not present the quite strong results in this chapter as if they were a test of our model in any conclusive sense. A more comprehensive analysis of the data, much more closely approaching such a test, can be found in the next chapter. Rather, we see this chapter as a first pass through the data, giving us a general idea of whether our model is at the races at all. Second, contrasting the implications of our model with those of a random null provides an essential baseline that allows us to compare the performance of a given model-based implication in different countries, and of different implications in the same country. In this way the random null allows us to calibrate our analysis. Finally, we would be happy to compare our approach to other equivalent models but, as we have argued, there appears to be no other candidate.

Exploring the model

In the remainder of this chapter, therefore, we compare two numbers for each theoretical implication of our model, drawn from the experience of each country over the full period of our study. The first is a measure of the predictive success of our theoretical implications; it is the *observed* number of days that the incumbent conformed to each of the various implications of our model. The second provides a baseline against which to measure this success; this is the *expected* number of days that a government would have conformed to the theoretical implications if the null hypothesis held.

To make this concrete, consider the specific case of Austria in 1953. The finance, foreign affairs, and interior portfolios – the key portfolios described in the previous chapter – were held by the People's Party (ÖVP), the ÖVP, and the Socialist Party (SPÖ) respectively, just prior to the election of 1953. Implication 0 of the previous chapter states that either this government remains in power after the election, or it is replaced with one of the portfolio allocations in its winset (where the winset is now based on the new set of legislative weights produced by the election). As it happened, the ÖVP-ÖVP-SPÖ continued in power. How impressive is this? That is, how much more confident in our theory should you, the reader, be after learning of this successful forecast?

There were four parties in the Austrian legislature after the 1953 election. This means that there were $4 \times 4 \times 4 = 64$ possible ways to allocate the three key portfolios. Of these, a quick consultation with our trusty computer program, WINSET, tells us that 16 allocations were in the winset of ÖVP-ÖVP-SPÖ. Thus, including the incumbent coalition itself, 17 of the 64 possible portfolio allocations were compatible with Implication 0. Thus, the probability that the null hypothesis would select an outcome compatible with Implication 0 in this case is 17/64. Using this type of information we can calculate the expected number of days during the study period that the null hypothesis would forecast the cabinet in a manner compatible with the implication. We then use this as a baseline against which to assess the number of actual days that the cabinet was compatible with our model-based implications.[2]

---

[2]The theoretical implications we examine predict points, and sets of points. The empirical question we pose is whether these point or set predictions are fulfilled or not – whether we have a hit or a miss. A generalization of this deterministic type of forecast would be to generate a probability distribution over feasible portfolio allocations. There are many ways to do this – we could consider possible errors of perception of party positions, for example, generating a forecast for every probable misperception, weighted by the probability that this misperception holds. This would permit more discrimination among "misses," for example, allowing some weight to be given to "near hits." This more sophisticated testing lies beyond the scope of the current book, but deserves future attention. We are grateful to Gary King for some stimulating discussions on this point.

Empirical investigations

Implication 0: The status quo cabinet at the beginning of the government formation process either remains the cabinet in place at the end of the process or is replaced by some alternative in its winset.[3]

This implication is probably the most fundamental for our entire approach. There is a sitting government which either continues in power or is replaced. If it is indeed replaced, then its replacement must, according to our approach, be a cabinet that is preferred by a legislative majority to the sitting government. Table 8.1 presents the country-by-country evidence on this.

For each country we first give the total number of days during the study period in which the implication, according to our theory, should have been observed to hold. Then we provide the actual number of days in which Implication 0 correctly specified the allocation of key portfolios in the incumbent government. Finally, we give the expected number of days a random guess would have identified a portfolio allocation consistent with the implication, calculated in the way we elaborated in the previous section. In parenthesis below each country name, we give the actual number of governments for which Implication 0 correctly, and incorrectly, specified the portfolio allocation. For example, consider Germany. Table 8.1 shows that of the 17 occasions of government formation that we consider, 12 are correctly predicted by our theory. In terms of duration, the study period covers 10,552 days. Implication 0 would have held by chance on 3,736 days; it actually held on 8,889 days. Thus our theoretical proposition provides a massive improvement over chance alone in the case of Germany.

Overall, Implication 0 clearly outperforms the null hypothesis by a wide margin in every one of the countries studied. Taking into account the number of governments considered and the length of the time period involved, we can be quite confident that Implication 0 is systematically providing us with useful information about government formation. This is despite the fact that the implication is rather general and thus can generate quite large prediction sets. This can be seen from the rather high figures for expected success from random guessing, in comparison to those in subsequent tables. Even taking this into account, we were rarely less than about twice as likely to be right about portfolio allocation in the incumbent government as compared with the null hypothesis, and sometimes (e.g., in Sweden) as much as ten times more likely to be right. In raw numerical terms, a total of 162 of the 221 actual governments that

---

[3]$SQ_t \in \{SQ_{t-1}\} \cup W(SQ_{t-1})$.

Table 8.1. *Assessment of Implication 0:* $SQ_t \in \{SQ_{t-1}\} \cup W(SQ_{t-1})$

Country (hits, misses)	Days implication		
	Could have held	Actually held	Held by chance
Austria (7, 2)	6,761	5,738	3,099
Belgium (17, 9)	14,279	9,846	4,349
Denmark (18, 4)	13,392	10,685	3,624
Finland (19, 9)	10,023	5,930	3,823
Germany (12, 5)	10,552	8,889	3,736
Iceland (11, 7)	15,339	9,377	6,010
Ireland (4, 3)	5,977	4,592	1,795
Italy (30, 11)	13,741	9,835	4,985
Luxembourg (10, 4)	17,326	10,780	2,297
Netherlands (6, 1)	4,635	4,581	832
Norway (13, 4)	11,808	9,392	4,392
Sweden (15, 0)	11,471	11,471	1,079
Total (162, 59)	135,304	100,116	40,021

formed were consistent with Implication 0.[4] Denominated in terms of the total number of days in which the implication should, in principle, have held, we see that it performed as our theory expects about three-fourths of the time; by chance alone it would have performed correctly less than one-third of the time.

> *Implication 1:* If the status quo cabinet at time t − 1 is at the dimension-by-dimension median, and this has an empty winset at time t, then this cabinet remains in place.[5]

There is always an incumbent government and the legislature always has views about this, so every government in our study provides evidence on Implication 0. This is not true for the other implications, which deal with particular government formation situations that may or may not arise at any given time in any given country. For example, as Table 8.2 shows, the government formation situation specified in Implication 1 – in which the previous status quo government happened to have an empty winset at the next time period – did not arise at all in some countries (such as Austria, Germany, and the Netherlands), and rarely in others (such as Belgium, Denmark, Finland, Iceland, and Ireland).

Table 8.2 also shows, however, that in those countries in which the premises were satisfied, there is strong evidence in support of the implication, which outperforms the null hypothesis by a very wide margin indeed. In Finland and Iceland, the premises of Implication 1 were satisfied a few times, but the conclusion failed to hold.[6] The reverse occurred in Belgium, Denmark, and Ireland: few occurrences of the premises, but the evidence strongly supports the implication. Finally, providing the large majority of cases in which the premises of Implication 1 come into play are Italy, Luxembourg, Norway, and Sweden. In these cases, we see that Implication 1 provides a truly massive improvement over the null hypothesis in our ability to forecast portfolio allocations.

Implication 1 makes a very precise forecast in a very precise circumstance and this forecast turns out to be really rather accurate. The very precision of the forecast, moreover, means that the expected success of a random guess is typically quite low. Overall, the evidence in Table 8.2 is

---

[4]A formal test of statistical significance for each country is complicated by the fact that, throughout a country's time series, there are variations in the number of parties and in the cardinality of winsets, both of which affect chance guessing. So we do not report them here, though we are convinced that differences are easily significant at conventional confidence levels.

[5]If, at time t, $W(SQ_{t-1}) = \emptyset$, then $SQ_t = SQ_{t-1}$.

[6]The entries in the last column for these two countries reveal that some combination prevailed of (1) an unpredicted government that lasted a short time and (2) the actual unpredicted government constituted an unlikely event according to chance probabilities.

Exploring the model

Table 8.2. *Assessment of Implication 1: If , at time t,*
$W(SQ_{t-1}) = ø$, *then* $SQ_t = SQ_{t-1}$

Country (hits, misses)	Days implication		
	Could have held	Actually held	Held by chance
Austria (0, 0)	NA	NA	NA
Belgium (1, 1)	458	164	6
Denmark (1, 1)	1,083	429	42
Finland (0, 2)	1,773	0	32
Germany (0, 0)	NA	NA	NA
Iceland (0, 3)	1,911	0	86
Ireland (1, 1)	841	589	26
Italy (8, 3)	3,000	2,022	8
Luxembourg (8, 0)	7,107	7,107	444
Netherlands (0, 0)	NA	NA	NA
Norway (4, 1)	2,844	2,816	72
Sweden (11, 0)	9,440	9,440	351
Total (34, 12)	28,457	22,557	1,067

crystal clear in its compatibility with Implication 1. The implication is true for a very high proportion of the time for which it applies, and thus gives us very good information about what is likely to happen in government formation. When a previous status quo government has an empty winset, *on the basis of the current configuration of the legislature,* the data show, in line with the predictions of our model, that this government is clearly very likely indeed to continue in office with the same portfolio allocation.

> *Implication 2:* If a party is very strong, then it is assigned all portfolios in the government formation process.[7]

As with Implication 1, this implication did not always come into play since it forecasts that a very strong party receives all key portfolios, regardless of which government preceded it in office. The implication applies to all situations in which there is a very strong party, since the power of a very strong party, according to our model, does not depend upon the preceding status quo. But it obviously does not apply when there is no very strong party, as there never was in Austria, Germany, and the Netherlands.

Table 8.3 shows that this implication also performs vastly better than the null hypothesis, improving by many times our ability to forecast portfolio allocations in those circumstances where the implication applies. It should also be noted, however, that in crude numerical terms the forecast was wrong as often as it was right (with 46 hits as against 43 misses). This fact, however, allows us to emphasize two points about the nature of the empirical evaluations we are conducting.

First, in predicting a unique portfolio allocation, Implication 2 is making a highly precise forecast, on the one hand, and may only barely miss, on the other. For example, even if the very strong party dominates the government and controls all but one of the key portfolios, this will, in our terms, count as a predictive failure, since it did not control every single key portfolio, as forecast under Implication 2. In this light, it is actually quite amazing that the forecast is dead-on half the time. In Italy, for instance, with as many as 10 parties, there are as many as 1,000 possible portfolio allocations. The forecast of Implication 2, consequently, is that 1 specific government out of as many as 1,000 possible will form; forecasting 11 out of 16 correct under these circumstances is thus a very strong performance.

The second point is illustrated by the Swedish case – rather typical of our data in terms of overall forecasting success. On a number of occasions, the Center Party was very strong. Although a major party in Swedish

[7] If $W(s^*) = \emptyset$, then $SQ_t = s^*$.

Table 8.3. *Assessment of Implication 2: If $W(s^*) = ø$, then $SQ_t = s^*$*

| Country (hits, misses) | Days implication | | |
	Could have held	Actually held	Held by chance
Austria (0, 0)	NA	NA	NA
Belgium (2, 10)	3,603	667	92
Denmark (2, 1)	1,835	1,181	68
Finland (0, 4)	2,062	0	47
Germany (0, 0)	NA	NA	NA
Iceland (1, 4)	4,658	1,172	233
Ireland (3, 1)	1,974	1,722	34
Italy (11, 5)	5139	3,011	13
Luxembourg (9, 6)	15,942	6,503	1,259
Netherlands (0, 0)	NA	NA	NA
Norway (6, 5)	7,316	4,384	205
Sweden (12, 7)	14,105	10,471	844
Total (46, 43)	55,634	39,111	2,795

politics, it is rarely a very large party. In 1973, 1976, and 1979 this party was very strong, yet controlled between 18 and 25 percent of the *Riksdag* seats. In 1952, 1956, and 1958, when it was also very strong, the Agrarian Party (as the Center Party was then known) controlled only between 8 and 14 percent of the seats. Small, centrally located parties play an important role in our model, and may even be very strong. In such circumstances, however, it may well be that factors quite outside our model (an obvious example is that a small party may have insufficient competent legislators to staff the entire cabinet) may mean that the forecast that the very strong party will take all cabinet portfolios is unrealistic. In such circumstances, our model may be "right" in identifying the central strategic role of the very strong party – as in the Swedish case we have just discussed – but "wrong" in the precise portfolio allocation it forecasts.

> *Implication 3:* If a party is strong, then it participates in the cabinet that is the outcome of the government formation process.[8]

The third implication of our model concerns strong parties. In essence, as we have seen, it forecasts that a strong party will be a member of every equilibrium government. The evidence on this is in Table 8.4. Once more, the model considerably outperforms random guessing, but by a less impressive margin than some of the previous implications. In two countries – Denmark and Germany – it does not even outperform random guessing. For example, by our reckoning the Christian Democrats were a strong party in Germany from 1969 until the early 1980s, but they nonetheless failed to get into government for the whole of that period. The ÖVP was often the strong party in Austria, but there were long-lived governments of which it was not a member. In neither case would the identity of the strong party seem in anyway bizarre to country specialists. What fails in these cases is the prediction that a strong party will always get into government. However, in a number of other countries – Belgium, Luxembourg, and Sweden, for example – our generalization provides a very considerable boost to our ability to forecast the allocation of cabinet portfolios. Overall, it does appear that strong parties are considerably more likely than others to go into government, though there are some important exceptions to this pattern.

> *Implication 3A:* If there is a strong party and every government in the winset of its ideal point assigns a specific portfolio to that party, then the outcome of the government formation process will be a cabinet in which the strong party controls that portfolio.[9]

[8]If S participates in every element of $W(s^*)$, then S is in SQ_t.
[9]If S is strong and if every element in $W(s^*)$ assigns a particular portfolio to S, then S receives that portfolio in SQ_t.

Table 8.4. *Assessment of Implication 3: If S participates in every element of W(s*), then S participates in SQ$_t$*

Country (hits, misses)	Days implication		
	Could have held	Actually held	Held by chance
Austria (7, 3)	8,004	6,152	4,982
Belgium (15, 15)	15,319	8,638	4,916
Denmark (3, 11)	8,589	1,875	2,670
Finland (11, 7)	5,720	2,901	1,885
Germany (10, 7)	9,552	5,823	7,123
Iceland (9, 10)	16,324	8,315	6,444
Ireland (3, 1)	1,894	1,642	1,019
Italy (14, 10)	7,918	5,257	3,333
Luxembourg (14, 1)	17,822	15,966	7,225
Netherlands (0, 0)	NA	NA	NA
Norway (9, 8)	10,708	6,703	3,527
Sweden (13, 6)	14,070	11,176	4,939
Total (108, 79)	115,920	74,448	48,63

This implication makes a very precise forecast in the circumstance in which every element in the winset of the strong party ideal point gives the strong party the same portfolio. As it happens, as can be inferred by comparing the individual country totals in Tables 8.4 and 8.5, if there is a strong party, then this circumstance is quite common. This implication thus has quite wide applicability. As can be seen from Table 8.5, there were over 300 portfolios that satisfied this condition in our dataset. For example, consider Italy. During the study period, in those cases in which there was a strong party, there were 77 portfolios covered by Implication 3A. Of these, our theory correctly forecasts 53. In terms of duration, given the large number of Italian parties, the proposition would have held by chance in only 594 of 9,854 possible days. In fact, the theoretical proposition holds nearly eight times as often. Overall the table shows that, in every country except Denmark, our generalization gives us a massive improvement over the null hypothesis of random guessing if we wish to forecast precise portfolio assignments, holding nearly four times as often as chance alone. Our theoretical implication is clearly tapping a systematic pattern – when the strong party is assigned the same portfolio in every element in its winset, then it is much more likely to receive the portfolio in question.

> *Implication 3B:* If there is a strong party, then the outcome of the government formation process will be a cabinet assigning each of the portfolios to the strong party or to one of its partners as identi-fied in the winset of the strong-party ideal.[10]

This implication applies to all circumstances in which there is a strong party, and deals with all key portfolios in these circumstances. Uncertain-ties over how effective the strong party is at winning standoffs mean that we may not be able to forecast precisely which cabinet in $W(s^*)$ will form. Nonetheless our model clearly implies that, since every equilibrium portfolio allocation must be in $\{s^*\} \cup W(s^*)$, every individual portfolio must be allocated to a party associated with $\{s^*\} \cup W(s^*)$.[11] The evidence in Table 8.6 is incontrovertible. The forecast of our model outperforms the null hypothesis in every country by a very wide margin. Overall it held nearly six times more frequently than chance guessing yields. The model once more gives us a very considerable boost in forecasting the allocation of key cabinet portfolios.

[10]If S is strong, then every portfolio in SQ_t is assigned to one of the parties identified in $\{s^*\} \cup W(s^*)$.

[11] In a five-party system, $\{A,B,C,D,E\}$, if Party A is strong and $W(AA) = \{BA, AC\}$, then Implication 3B says that the first portfolio should be assigned to A or B and the second to A or C. That is, neither C, D, nor E should get the first portfolio, and neither B, D, nor E should get the second.

Table 8.5. *Assessment of Implication 3A: If S is strong and if every element of*
$W(s^*)$ *assigns a particular portfolio to S, then S receives that portfolio in* SQ_t

Country (hits, misses)	Days implication		
	Could have held	Actually held	Held by chance
Austria (2, 0)	1,117	1,117	70
Belgium (7, 17)	14,066	7,450	2,838
Denmark (5, 16)	11,351	1,508	1,741
Finland (10, 25)	9,031	2,135	800
Germany (6, 11)	11,552	4,145	2,038
Iceland (8, 16)	15,989	5,089	3,585
Ireland (9, 3)	1,974	1,722	34
Italy (53, 24)	9,854	4,460	594
Luxembourg (23, 7)	17,735	11,235	2,568
Netherlands (0, 0)	NA	NA	NA
Norway (15, 13)	10,708	5,644	1,296
Sweden (25, 13)	14,105	10,841	651
Total (163, 145)	117,482	55,146	16,195

Table 8.6. *Assessment of Implication 3B: If S is strong, then each portfolio in SQ_t is assigned to one of the parties identified in {s*} ∪W(s*)*

Country (hits, misses)	Days implication		
	Could have held	Actually held	Held by chance
Austria (10, 20)	8,468	3,706	873
Belgium (26, 34)	14,823	7,883	1,809
Denmark (12, 24)	8,689	3,607	1,158
Finland (16, 38)	7,561	2,175	707
Germany (40, 11)	10,552	8,150	834
Iceland (20, 18)	16,332	9,306	2,837
Ireland (9, 3)	1,974	1,722	34
Italy (67, 20)	9,503	7,213	132
Luxembourg (23, 7)	17,817	11,235	2,568
Netherlands (0, 0)	NA	NA	NA
Norway (16, 19)	11,907	5,644	1,008
Sweden (25, 13)	14,105	10,841	651
Total (264, 207)	121,731	71,382	12,623

Exploring the model

Taken together, Implications 3A and 3B have a very good track record at predicting precise portfolio assignments. These particular empirical findings, therefore, give us confidence not only that we are getting the right answers but that we are getting them for the right reasons. They seem to us to be the clearest possible evidence that portfolio allocation matters quite a lot in government formation. *Implication 3A, in particular, is a very precise and nonobvious statement, derived explicitly and directly from our model and going to the heart of our approach.* Given what is often a wide range of possibilities, it is very easy, furthermore, for predictions from these implications to be wrong. We therefore feel that the results in Tables 8.5 and 8.6 provide a convincing demonstration that we are on to something.

CONCLUSIONS

Formal theories of government formation are not unusual, although those dealing with the allocation of cabinet portfolios remain a rare breed. A range of empirical studies of government formation can also be found in the literature. What is quite unusual, however, is a fully specified formal model used to derive explicit empirical statements that are then assessed against data from real-world cabinet formations. It was therefore with considerable trepidation (to be honest with the reader!) that we sought to tease out explicit and nonobvious empirical forecasts from our formal model and compare these forecasts with what actually happened in postwar western Europe. We worried, and continue to worry, about the operational compromises that were required. We worried, and continue to worry, about the crudeness of our data on party policy positions. These concerns, moreover, were magnified by our decision to analyze government formation over a period of nearly half a century.

Given these concerns, we are actually very gratified at how well the theory has performed. All of the implications we derived from our model have received considerable empirical support. Of course the generalizations were not right every single time – any reader would have been justifiably suspicious if we had reported that they were. But they were right very much more often than they would have been if they had nothing at all to do with the government formation process and were no better than random guesses. Furthermore, the empirical performance of Implications 3A and 3B, which, as we have argued, deal with precise details of portfolio allocation that go to the heart of our model, gives us particular confidence that portfolio allocation is indeed central to the government formation process.

173

9

A multivariate investigation of
portfolio allocation

In the preceding chapter we made a determined attempt to derive testable empirical implications from our model of government formation and to evaluate these using data on actual government formations in 12 postwar European democracies. We found considerable empirical support for our approach. Many of the implications we derived – in particular those dealing with the cabinet membership of very strong and merely strong parties – give the analyst a massive improvement over chance in making forecasts about the allocation of cabinet portfolios. In this chapter we extend our empirical analysis in three substantive directions, using more powerful statistical techniques.

The substantive extensions of our empirical analysis are concerned with two important features of the strategic position of any legislative party in the government formation process – its size and its position in the policy space. In Chapter 5 we investigated the relationship between size, policy, and strong-party status in large numbers of simulated legislatures. In the present chapter, we investigate this relationship in real legislatures. We have three key objectives in this phase of the analysis. First, we know from Chapter 5 that, in simulated legislatures, strength is strongly related both to the weight of parties and to their position in the policy space. Larger parties, and parties at a median position on at least one policy dimension, are far more likely to be strong or very strong in our simulations. We noted when reporting these simulations that party positions in real party systems are not randomly located; in this chapter we assess the extent to which a party's strength is related to its weight and policy position in the real world.

This is a necessary precursor to a second and more fundamental part of our empirical analysis. We know that whether a party is strong, in both simulated and real party systems, is intimately related to both its weight and its position in the policy space. We also know that whether or not a party is strong is a function of the configuration of weights and policy

174

positions of all parties in the system, not just those of the party under consideration. It is possible, therefore, that parties get into government because they are large or because they are central, rather than because they are strong per se. In the second empirical section of this chapter, therefore, we assess the ability of the concepts in our model to account for government participation, controlling for the weight and policy centrality of the parties concerned.

Given the absence of alternative models of government formation that make detailed forecasts about cabinet membership, models that would have provided benchmarks against which we could have evaluated our approach, our analysis of the government participation of strong parties, controlling for weight and policy position, provides a more rigorous evaluation of our model than measuring our success against a null hypothesis based on the random selection of government participants. In effect it assesses whether the proposition that strong parties get into government adds anything to the implicit proposition that large parties and central parties are more likely to get into government than others. While these implicit theories have not, to our knowledge, been articulated by any particular author in the context of a rigorously specified model of government formation, they do nonetheless seem to us to be sensible benchmarks against which to assess our approach.

The third phase of the analysis in this chapter deals with something that we have not yet considered in empirical terms, namely the performance of our model when no strong party exists. If no strong party exists and if some portfolio allocation has an empty winset, then this portfolio allocation is an equilibrium in our model. We are silent on the matter of whether, in such circumstances, alternative equilibriums may exist. In such circumstances, participants in the empty winset allocation will receive key cabinet portfolios, a proposition we evaluate later in this chapter.

Before going on to report on our empirical findings, however, we must outline the data and statistical techniques that we used.

DATA AND METHODS

Our portfolio allocation model makes a rather precise prediction. Proposition 4.2, our main theorem, states that if a strong party exists – whether it is very strong or merely strong – then either the strong party secures all the key portfolios or the portfolios are distributed to one of the coalitions of parties whose policy point is in the winset of the strong party's ideal. Empirically, then, we want to estimate the likelihood of a party getting into government as a function of our key theoretical variables:

175

- Is a party merely strong? (MSP)
- Is a party very strong? (VSP)
- Is a party a partner of a strong party in a coalition in its winset? (PSP)

We are interested whether these theoretical variables enhance our ability to forecast party participation in government. Each of these variables is coded one if the logical condition is fulfilled and zero otherwise. We are also interested in the ability of the theoretical variables to do this *over and above knowledge about the weight and centrality of the party in question.*

In all of the statistical models that follow, we employ a dichotomous dependent variable – either whether or not a party is in government, or whether or not it is strong. Thus the multivariate technique most suitable for our purposes is probit analysis, which we use to estimate the likelihood that a party is in government (or is merely strong or very strong, depending on the statistical model under consideration), conditional on a range of independent variables. We formally specify several statistical models and sketch the specific hypotheses to be tested momentarily. First, however, we describe the data from which these models will be estimated.

Our dataset covers the postwar government formation experiences of the 12 European democracies described in Chapter 7. We have excluded all situations in which a single party controls a majority of the parliamentary seats.[1] We have also excluded government formation situations, typically early in a country's postwar history, in which a nonpartisan is assigned a major portfolio. From the remaining postwar history we take, as our unit of analysis, a specific party in a specific country at a specific time.

Several classes of party have been deleted from the analysis. We have excluded some minor parties, also typically early in a country's postwar history, that "died" without leaving a political trace. By this we mean parties that did not fuse with or transform themselves into other ongoing parties. We did this because it was impossible to obtain any information, either from party histories (as reported in Mackie and Rose, 1991) or from experts (in the Laver-Hunt survey data), about their policy preferences – information that figures prominently in our analysis. Likewise we excluded some contemporary minor parties for which there was no information on policy preferences. Each of these classes of exclusion occurred very infrequently, on the one hand, and often involved "extremist" or non-*ministrable* parties, on the other; so we do not believe their omission has affected our analysis.

---

[1]In principle, there is no reason to exclude these, since our theory applies to this case as well. However, our theory will be confirmed trivially here, thus favorably biasing its aggregate performance. For this reason we have deleted single-party majority governments.

A multivariate investigation

Table 9.1. Variables

Variable name	Variable label	Operationalization	Source
Government	G	1 = party obtains key portfolio 0 = otherwise	EJPR
"Merely" strong party	MSP	1 = "merely" strong 0 = otherwise	WINSET
"Very" strong party	VSP	1 = "very" strong 0 = otherwise	WINSET
Partner of strong party	PSP	1 = partner 0 = otherwise	WINSET
Weight	W	Percentage of seats	MR
Centrality	MD_i	$\lvert D_i - \text{mean}(D_i) \rvert$ [a]	LH

[a]Where D_i is the position of the party on Dimesion 1 and mean D_i is the mean position of all parties on Dimension 1.

Sources:
EJPR: European Journal of Political Research 24 (July 1993) – a special issue, edited by Jaap Woldendorp, Hans Keman, and Ian Budge, giving party government data in 20 democracies for 1945-1990.
WINSET: A computer program that analyzes spatial party distributions.
MR: Mackie and Rose, 1991.
LH: Laver and Hunt, 1992.

There were 250 government formation situations during this time period meeting our criteria, ranging from 6 in the Netherlands to 43 in Finland and Italy. In all, 1,516 parties had opportunities to secure a key governmental portfolio.[2] For each of these observations (a party in a government formation situation in a country), we collected the data displayed in Table 9.1. The dependent variable in which we are interested is G – whether or not a party is in government. Our theoretical variables concern whether a party is merely strong, very strong, or a partner of a strong party in a coalition in the winset of the strong-party ideal point – MSP, VSP, or PSP. Our measure of party size is W, and a

[2]The time periods for each country are given in Table 7.2.

177

party's centrality on each of the two policy dimensions we use is captured by MD_1 and MD_2.[3]

In the dataset used to estimate the equations to be set out here, although we have as many as 1,516 observations (depending upon the particular equation), these are not entirely independent since groups of observations are of parties that come from the same country at the same time period. This has no effect on the estimates of coefficients, but does exaggerate the t-statistics used to evaluate their significance. Consequently, we have also coded dummy variables for country and decade for each observation. When included in the regression equations, the dummy variables mitigate this effect. We will not report coefficients for these dummies in the equations, but the reader should be aware that, in fact, a dummy for each country (with one deleted) and for each decade (with one deleted) is included in each estimation, something of which we remind the reader at appropriate points.[4]

DO STRONG PARTIES GET INTO GOVERNMENT MORE OFTEN THAN OTHERS?

In order to provide a link with the empirical analyses in the previous chapter, we first focus on whether strong parties and their partners are more likely to secure key portfolios than other parties. We therefore restrict ourselves to those government formation settings in which there is a strong party. This yields 1,125 party observations.[5]

We first estimate the model that gives the clearest indication of the empirical power of our theory. Our principal theoretical finding is that strong parties secure key portfolios, either on their own or in coalition with specific partners (namely those associated with points in the winset of the strong-party ideal). This is the gist of Proposition 4.2. Implications 2 and 3, derived from it, received considerable empirical support in Chapter 8. We now put this proposition to a more comprehensive statistical

[3]From Table 7.3 it is seen that the appropriate number of portfolios is two for seven countries and three for five countries. To keep things as parallel as possible, we have only employed MD_1 and MD_2 – centrality on the first two portfolio dimensions – in each case.

[4]Since sets of variables cannot be perfect linear combinations of one another, one country and one decade dummy must be omitted from each model specification. The coefficients reported in Equations 0–6 were estimated omitting the dummies for Austria and the 1940s. In addition, when a country or decade contributed no cases to a particular analysis, its dummy was also omitted. Note that the constant reported for Equations 0–6 is very much a product of omitted dummies, and is thus not of much theoretical interest in this context.

[5]That is to say, 391 of the party observations in our dataset occurred in circumstances in which there is no strong party. We shall examine these cases shortly.

test in Equation 0, where S = 1 if a party is merely strong, very strong, or a partner of a strong party; S = 0 otherwise.[6]

$$G = -0.72 + 1.01S$$
$$(-2.72) \quad (10.93) \tag{0}$$

As is clearly apparent from the t-statistic, reported underneath the coefficient for S in Equation 0, this variable is highly significant. The unequivocal empirical lesson to be drawn from Equation 0 is that, if a party is strong, it is very much more likely to get into government than if it is not.

Equation 1 distinguishes between the government participation of merely strong parties (MSP), very strong parties (VSP), and strong-party partners (PSP). All three coefficients relating to the theoretical variables are highly significant.

$$G = -0.51 + 0.68 \text{ MSP} + 1.66 \text{ VSP} + 0.73 \text{ PSP}$$
$$(-1.90) \quad (4.62) \quad\quad (11.01) \quad\quad (5.86) \tag{1}$$

Since a party is either merely strong, very strong, a partner of a strong party, or "none of the above," the independent variables in Equation 1 classify every party in a government formation situation. While parties in each of the first three categories are clearly more likely to get into government than other parties, the relative magnitude of the coefficients indicates that very strong parties (1.66) are much more likely to get into government than merely strong parties (0.68), or the partners of strong parties (0.73).[7]

We can more clearly see the effect on securing a key portfolio of being very strong, merely strong, or the partner of a strong party, as well as the relative performance of our model in different countries and decades, by computing the probabilities of getting into government that are implied by Equation 1. These probabilities are presented in Tables 9.2 through 9.5. Table 9.2 gives the probability of government participation for parties that are neither strong themselves nor partners of strong parties.[8]

[6]In terms of the variables defined in Table 9.1, S = MSP + VSP + PSP.

[7]There is no statistically significant difference between the coefficient for MSP and PSP. The reader should also recall that, for any particular strong party, there may be more than one potential partner.

[8]The cell entries (in this and the three succeeding tables) are computed as follows. Consider the case of Italy during the 1960s, where the likelihood that one of these "none of the above" parties participates in government is 0.12. In equation (1), since MSP = VSP = PSP = 0 in this instance, the only effects come from the constant term (- 0.51), the Italy dummy coefficient (- 0.88), and the 1960s dummy coefficient (0.22). (The latter two coefficients are not reported in Equation 1.) Summing these yields - 1.17. From the probit model this number is a z-score of the standard normal distribution. A statistical table of the cumulative normal distribution associates this z-score with a probability of 0.12. Other cell entries are computed in a similar manner, each with its own combination of country and decade dummy coefficients.

Table 9.2 *Probability of a party securing a key portfolio if it is neither strong nor the partner of a strong party[a](by country and decade)*

| Country | Decade[b] | | | | |
	1940s	1950s	1960s	1970s	1980s
Austria	0.30	0.35	0.38	0.29	0.29
Belgium	0.12	0.15	0.17	0.11	0.11
Denmark	0.10	0.13	0.15	0.10	0.09
Finland	0.12	0.15	0.17	0.11	0.11
Germany	0.28	0.33	0.37	0.27	0.26
Iceland	0.20	0.24	0.26	0.19	0.18
Ireland	0.09	0.12	0.14	0.13	0.12
Italy	0.08	0.11	0.12	0.08	0.08
Luxembourg	0.19	0.23	0.25	0.18	0.18
Norway	0.11	0.14	0.16	0.10	0.10
Sweden	0.09	0.12	0.13	0.09	0.09

[a] The Netherlands is absent because at no time during the period of our data was a strong party present; hence we have no country dummy for the Netherlands estimated.
[b] The number of cases of governments forming after January 1, 1990, but concluding before January 1, 1993, is small, so we have merged these cases with those from the 1980s.

Several features are worth noting. First, the overall probability of getting into government for a party not identified by our approach is very low. It ranges from 0.08 (in Italy in various decades) to 0.38 in the worst set of cases for our model (in Austria in the 1960s). Overall, therefore, these figures, by identifying those parties unlikely to be in government, provide further confirmation that our model is identifying the parties that *are* likely to participate in government. Second, reading across the rows for each country, there is little variation by decade; we might have expected more variation if our data were less valid in earlier decades, as we move further back from the date of the expert survey in 1989. Third,

Table 9.3. *Probability of a merely strong party securing a key portfolio[a]*
(by country and decade)

Country	Decade[b]				
	1940s	1950s	1960s	1970s	1980s
Austria	0.57	0.62	0.65	0.55	0.55
Belgium	0.31	0.36	0.39	0.30	0.29
Denmark	0.28	0.33	0.36	0.35	0.34
Finland	0.31	0.36	0.39	0.38	0.37
Germany	0.54	0.60	0.63	0.53	0.53
Iceland	0.44	0.49	0.52	0.43	0.42
Ireland	0.27	0.32	0.35	0.34	0.33
Italy	0.24	0.29	0.32	0.23	0.22
Luxembourg	0.43	0.48	0.51	0.42	0.41
Norway	0.30	0.35	0.38	0.37	0.36
Sweden	0.25	0.30	0.33	0.24	0.23

[a] The Netherlands is absent because at no time during the period of our data was a strong party present; hence we have no country dummy for the Netherlands estimated.
[b] The number of cases of governments forming after January 1, 1990, but concluding before January 1, 1993, is small, so we have merged these cases with those from the 1980s.

there is some variation within each decade across countries. In some systems with few parties, such as Germany and Austria throughout the entire time period, the odds of a party not identified by our model getting into government were better than one in four. In other small party systems, such as Belgium, Iceland, and Luxembourg in the 1940s and 1950s, these odds are much lower. In nearly all large party systems, the odds on government participation are quite low for a party that is neither strong nor a partner of a strong party – such a party is in general unlikely to secure a key government portfolio. This is especially evident when we

Table 9.4. *Probability of a partner of a merely strong party securing a key portfolio[a]*
(by country and decade)

| Country | Decade[b] | | | | |
	1940s	1950s	1960s	1970s	1980s
Austria	0.58	0.64	0.67	0.57	0.57
Belgium	0.33	0.38	0.40	0.32	0.31
Denmark	0.30	0.35	0.37	0.36	0.35
Finland	0.33	0.38	0.41	0.32	0.31
Germany	0.56	0.62	0.65	0.55	0.55
Iceland	0.46	0.51	0.53	0.45	0.44
Ireland	0.29	0.34	0.36	0.35	0.34
Italy	0.26	0.31	0.34	0.25	0.24
Luxembourg	0.45	0.50	0.53	0.44	0.43
Norway	0.32	0.37	0.39	0.38	0.37
Sweden	0.27	0.32	0.35	0.26	0.25

[a] The Netherlands is absent because at no time during the period of our data was a strong party present; hence we have no country dummy for the Netherlands estimated.
[b] The number of cases of governments forming after January 1, 1990, but concluding before January 1, 1993, is small, so we have merged these cases with those from the 1980s.

compare corresponding cell entries in this table with those of the next three tables, relating to the government participation of parties identified by our model.

Tables 9.3 and 9.4 give the probability of a merely strong party or one of its partners securing a key portfolio. There is not much difference between corresponding cell entries in these two tables, since the coefficients for MSP and PSP in Equation 1 are not very different. However, entries in corresponding cells in either of these tables are much larger than in Table 9.2. The probability of one of these two categories of party securing a key

Table 9.5. *Probability of a very strong party securing a key portfolio[a]*
(by country and decade)

Country	Decade[b]				
	1940s	1950s	1960s	1970s	1980s
Austria	0.85	0.90	0.91	0.87	0.87
Belgium	0.68	0.73	0.76	0.67	0.66
Denmark	0.65	0.71	0.73	0.72	0.71
Finland	0.68	0.73	0.76	0.67	0.66
Germany	0.84	0.89	0.90	0.86	0.86
Iceland	0.79	0.83	0.85	0.79	0.78
Ireland	0.64	0.70	0.73	0.72	0.71
Italy	0.60	0.66	0.69	0.60	0.59
Luxembourg	0.78	0.82	0.84	0.78	0.77
Norway	0.67	0.72	0.75	0.66	0.65
Sweden	0.61	0.67	0.70	0.61	0.60

[a] The Netherlands is absent because at no time during the period of our data was a strong party present; hence we have no country dummy for the Netherlands estimated.
[b] The number of cases of governments forming after January 1, 1990, but concluding before January 1, 1993, is small, so we have merged these cases with those from the 1980s.

portfolio ranges, on average, from about one-quarter to about two-thirds. The "bite" of our theoretical variables can clearly be detected.

The odds on getting into government are especially high for very strong parties, reflecting the large and highly significant coefficient for VSP in Equation 1. In Table 9.5 the odds of a very strong party being in government range from 2 chances in 3 to better than 9 in 10. Even in very large party systems, such as Denmark, Finland, and Italy in the 1970s and 1980s, a very strong party is highly likely to be in government. The most dramatic comparisons of all, of course, involve corresponding cells of Tables 9.2 and 9.5.

Empirical investigations

These tables reiterate, on the basis of estimates of empirical probabilities of government participation, the fundamental point highlighted by our model, that strong parties and their partners are very much more likely than others to get into government.

WHAT MAKES A PARTY STRONG?

We know from our simulations in Chapter 5 that, other things being equal, parties are more likely to be strong if they are large and if they are central. We now estimate the extent to which this is true in real party systems.

Equation 2 shows the empirical relationship between a party's weight and centrality and whether or not it is a merely strong party (MSP).[9] It clearly shows that if a party is large, central, or both, it is significantly more likely to be merely strong.[10] Centrality on the first dimension is more crucial than centrality on the second – in other words merely strong parties are more likely to be central on the most important policy dimension than on the next most important one.[11] All coefficients have the expected sign. (Note that, if a party is at the mean party position on dimension i, then $MD_i = 0$. The greater MD_i, the less central a party is on that dimension. Thus we expect strength to be negatively related to MD_i.)

$$MSP = -0.77 + 0.03 \ W - 0.49 \ MD_1 - 0.03 \ MD_2$$
$$(-5.23) \quad (6.24) \quad (-8.79) \quad (-0.55) \tag{2}$$

Equation 3 shows the empirical relationship between a party's weight and centrality and whether it is a very strong party (VSP). These results are even stronger. We know both analytically and from our simulations that very strong parties are highly likely to be central on both policy dimensions. Equation 3 shows that, empirically, very strong parties do indeed tend to be large and central on both dimensions.

$$VSP = -1.77 + 0.05 \ W - 0.29 \ MD_1 - 0.10 \ MD_2$$
$$(-9.67) \quad (10.19) \quad (-6.43) \quad (-1.61) \tag{3}$$

Finally, Equation 4 shows the empirical relationship between a party's weight and centrality and whether or not it is a partner of a strong party, participating in a cabinet in the winset of the strong party's ideal point. The sign for the coefficient estimating the impact of centrality on the

[9]Recall that W is the percentage of seats, empirically ranging no higher that 50 percent. MD_i is measured relative to a 20-point scale; empirically MD_i does not exceed 10.

[10]The statistical significance of these coefficients is indicated by the t-statistic in parenthesis.

[11]This is a product of the empirical pattern in which there is less variation in party positions on the second dimension than on the first (economic policy) dimension.

most important policy dimension, MD_1, is positive yet highly significant.[12] The sign estimating the impact of centrality on the second policy
dimension, MD_2, is negative and highly significant. This reflects the fact
that merely strong parties tend to be central on the most important policy
dimension (as we see from Equation 2), and hence the partners of these
parties cannot also be central on this dimension. The partners of merely
strong parties do, however, tend to be central on the second most important policy dimension. (Very strong parties have no partners and tend, as
we have seen, to be central on both policy dimensions.) The important
finding in this context, however, is that the partners of strong parties –
identified by our model as potential government participants – also tend
to be centrally located in the party system, having a central position on
the second most important policy dimension.

$$PSP = -0.86 + 0.01 \ W + 0.18 \ MD_1 - 0.45 \ MD_2$$
$$(-6.96) \quad (2.89) \quad\quad (6.75) \quad\quad (-10.51) \quad\quad (4)$$

What is quite clear from all of this is that real political parties are
much more likely to be strong, or to be the partners of strong parties, if
they are large and if they are central.

STRENGTH, SIZE, CENTRALITY, AND GOVERNMENT PARTICIPATION

While, both analytically and empirically, size and centrality enhance a
party's prospects of being strong, whether a party is strong depends on
the entire configuration of the legislative party system. Two parties in two
different party systems could have the same share of the total legislative
weight, and the same policy position, but one could be strong and the
other not, depending on the configuration of weights and policy positions
of the other parties. In effect, *the calculation of whether a party is strong
uses more information than just the size and centrality of the party in
question, even though both of these factors are also closely related to
strength.* This suggests an altogether tougher empirical test for our approach. We can investigate whether a party's strong-party status, *controlling for its size and centrality,* contributes to its chances of getting into
government. In other words we can investigate whether there is any bite
in the aspects of party strength that go beyond size and centrality. We
shortly turn to this matter but, before we go any further, we consider how
party weight and centrality have traditionally been considered to be related to government participation.

[12]Meaning: A party that is *not* centrally located on the most important dimension is
more likely to be a partner of a strong party.

Party weight

Models of government formation that assume politicians to be motivated only by the desire to get into office tend to imply a role for a minimal winning criterion. Minimal winning coalitions comprise only parties that are essential to the coalition's winning status. As we have seen, given a majority decision rule, if a coalition is less than minimal winning, then a majority opposition that also wants to get into office, and indeed can get into office, does not actually do so – clearly a contradiction. If in contrast a coalition is more than minimal winning, then members of the winning coalition are sharing the rewards of office with parties that they do not need in order to control those rewards – there is no incentive for office-seeking parties to do this.

The minimal winning criterion implies that large parties tend to have more bargaining power, other things being equal, than small ones. The principal reason for this is that large parties figure more conspicuously in the decisive structure of the government formation game. They participate more frequently in winning coalitions (an "opportunities" advantage), on the one hand, and if, on the other hand, other parties try to assemble a winning coalition that excludes a large party, negotiations are more prolonged and difficult (a "transaction cost" advantage). For example, in a standard four-party configuration, in which the distribution of seats is (40, 20, 20, 20), the big party can form a majority coalition by two-way negotiation with any of the smaller parties (an opportunities advantage for the large party). In order to exclude the big party, all of the smaller parties must coalesce with each other on the basis of three-way negotiations (a transaction cost advantage for the large party). These weight-related advantages do not always manifest themselves; in some strategic settings, differences in weight are strategically irrelevant. In a three-party legislature where the party weights are (48, 26, 26), for example, no weight advantage accrues to the largest party. All three parties are strategically equivalent, despite differences in weight, since any pair of them can form a winning coalition. Nevertheless, more often than not, gaining weight increases bargaining power.

Party centrality

Once we go beyond office-seeking assumptions to assume that politicians are also motivated by policy when they bargain over government formation, the centrality of a party's policy positions has a bearing on its bargaining power. According to this line of argument, parties seek spatially closer coalition partners because they forecast eventual government policy to be closer to their own preferred policy as a result. It is also easier to arrive at a joint policy position with those whose preferences are substantively similar than with those whose preferences are different – each side needs to concede less to reach an agreement. Centrally located parties find themselves in the desirable situation of being spatially closer to a wider set of parties. They are thus at an advantage in coalition bargaining, so the story goes, since there are more potential coalition partners for them to negotiate realistic policy compromises with. Theories that emphasize this spatial advantage, especially multidimensional theories, are often somewhat vague about exactly how the advantage materializes. (That is to say, they rarely make explicit the process of government formation in which such an advantage does indeed materialize.) Nevertheless, more often than not, central policy positions are held to increase bargaining power.

Weight and centrality

Two caveats need to be entered at this point. First, as we have noted, the arguments for weight and centrality derive from *different* motivational sources. Weight is important when parties are exclusively office-oriented. Weight combines with policy position when policy concerns predominate. And, of course, when party motivations are mixtures of policy seeking and office seeking, then both weight and location make a difference.

Second, weight and location may be related to one another. Indeed this is precisely the point of spatial models of the larger electoral game – namely, that weight is a function of the distribution of party locations relative to the distribution of voter preferences.

Let us be clear, furthermore, that our own portfolio allocation model is also based fundamentally on party weight and centrality. As we have demonstrated, a strong party must typically be at the median position on at least one policy dimension. Moreover, larger parties are more likely to be at the median position both for logical and empirical reasons. As a logical matter, if one examines the set of feasible ways to order parties along a dimension, the larger a party, the more frequently it will be median on that dimension, and therefore the more likely it will be strong. From an empirical perspective, parties are large in the spatial electoral game, in part because they are central. In our own data, as we have just seen in Equations 2 and 3, strength is related to both weight and centrality.

Overall therefore, the model that we discuss does not in any sense pit our concepts of strength against weight or centrality as explanations of government participation. They do, however, investigate the effects of strength on government participation, controlling for weight and centrality. As we indicated in the introduction to this section, the main reason to do this is to investigate the extent to which government participation is affected by aspects of strength that are a function of the party system as a whole, rather than by strength as a product of the size and centrality of the particular party in question. This will in effect tell us whether, for given levels of size and centrality, being a strong party still enhances the chances of getting into government. Thus, while much of a party's strength will be a product of its size and centrality, if party strength enhances participation even controlling for these matters, the notion of a strong or very strong party clearly has even more powerful analytical bite.

An alternative interpretation of the same equations is that they show statistically whether our equilibrium concepts add to our ability to predict government participation, taking the implicit assumptions that large and central parties are more likely to participate in government as the basis in informal surrogate benchmark models. At the very least, these informal models are likely to provide a tougher "test" for our model than the "random allocation" null hypothesis used in the previous chapter.

Equation 1 has of course already shown that our concepts do indeed very significantly increase our ability to predict government participation. Subsequent results put this finding in context, rather than undermine it. It might be, for example, that a party's strength was entirely a product of its own weight and policy position. This would make it no less a strong party, and no less likely to get into government. What this would tell us is that party strength is a simple function of weight and centrality. If party strength increases our predictive ability over and above size and centrality, considered additively, then this tells us that party strength is an altogether more complex phenomenon. It is to these matters that we now turn.

Equation 5 shows the empirical relationship between our various concepts of party strength, controlling for party size and centrality, along with a t-statistic (in parenthesis) for each coefficient. We reiterate that dummy variables for country and decade were also included in these estimations, though we do not report their coefficients. Two of the three theoretical coefficients are statistically significant; the third is of the wrong sign, but insignificant statistically. The independent weight and centrality variables are of the right sign and have important effects. The joint null hypothesis that the three theoretical coefficients (of MSP, VSP, and PSP) are zero may be rejected at the 99.9 percent confidence level.[13]

[13]This joint hypothesis is tested as follows. Calculate the log likelihood of Equation 5. Run the probit identical to Equation 5 with the three theoretical variables deleted and calculate its log likelihood. The number $-$ 2(log likelihood(Equation 5 with restrictions) - log likelihood(Equation 5)) has a χ^2 distribution with degrees of freedom equal to the number of restricted coefficients (in this case, three). A table of the χ^2 distribution gives the significance level reported in the text. Specifically, the log likelihood test yields a χ^2_3 statistic of 19.46, allowing us to reject the joint null hypothesis at the .001 level of significance that the coefficients of MSP, VSP, and PSP are 0.

Since every day in politics presents the incumbent government with new challenges,

$$G = -0.970 \quad - \quad 0.151 \text{ MSP} \; + 0.630 \text{ VSP} + 0.248 \text{ PSP}$$
$$(-2.85) \qquad (-0.82) \qquad (3.46) \qquad (1.72)$$
$$+ 0.041 \text{ W} - \quad 0.047 \text{ MD}_1 \; - 0.157 \text{ MD}_2$$
$$(10.53) \qquad (-1.54) \qquad (-3.84) \qquad\qquad\qquad (5)$$

The coefficients in Equation 5 thus give a very clear picture of the systematic operation of our model in the real world. First, as already noted, the rejection of the joint null hypothesis that the coefficients of our three model-generated variables are all zero, even controlling for size and centrality, means our concepts of party strength are adding significantly to our ability to predict whether particular parties participate in government. This implies that the overall configuration of the party system, over and above the size and centrality of specific parties, is an important consideration in determining government participation. Second, note that, holding size and centrality constant, very strong parties are much more likely to get into government than others. This is a

it is arguable that each probit regression reported in this chapter, and Equation 5 in particular, should be estimated using a dataset in which each case is weighted by the number of days that the cabinet it refers to was in existence. If cabinets predicted by our model last a long time while out-of-equilibrium cabinets form and fall much more rapidly, there will be more cases out of equilibrium than are in equilibrium *in any fixed time period,* reducing the apparent potency of our model. Not weighting cases for duration results in a situation in which, if our model was successful in predicting a government that lasted many years, then this would count for a single case, and be weighted equally with an out-of-equilibrium government that lasted a few days. For most people, we suspect, these relative durations would be seen as evidence in favor of our model, not just as one success and one failure.

If we rerun Equation 5 with cases weighted by duration, then the following coefficients emerge, with coefficients generated from the unweighted dataset being given for comparison. (Note that, since it is largely a product of omitted dummies, the constant is omitted.)

	Coefficient	
Variable	Weighted	Unweighted
MSP	− 0.101	− 0.151
VSP	+ 1.025	+ 0.630
PSP	+ 0.336	+ 0.248
W	+ 0.046	+ 0.041
MD$_1$	+ 0.023	− 0.047
MD$_2$	− 0.146	− 0.157

The most striking difference between weighted and unweighted regressions is of course the increase in the coefficient for VSP when cases are weighted. In other words, once the duration of cabinets is taken into consideration, the presence of very strong parties in government, *controlling for weight and ideological position,* is even more pervasive. (Note from the t-statistics reported in the text that the only coefficient that changes sign, that for MD$_1$, is not statistically significant.)

Although we can increase the size of our model coefficients by running weighted regressions, we report the results of the unweighted analyses, since these results have the same basic structure as those of the weighted regressions, but provide the sterner test for our model.

189

particularly striking result. Very strong parties are quite likely to be large and central. However, not all large and central parties are very strong. Equation 5 thus shows, among other things, that *large and central parties that are very strong are more likely to get into government than large and central parties that are not very strong*. Third, note that, although we know from Equation 1 that merely strong parties are indeed more likely to get into government than others, Equation 5 shows that merely strong parties are not more likely to go into government than other parties of equivalent size and strength. In other words, empirically, mere strength arises as a straightforward product of the size and centrality of the party in question. This finding echoes the relative size of the coefficients in Equation 1, and the relative performance of Implications 2 and 3 in Chapter 8.

Overall, knowing whether a party is very strong adds greatly to our ability to predict government participation, even controlling for the size and centrality of the party in question. Knowing whether a party is merely strong (and such parties must threaten credible vetoes in order to assert their bargaining position) also helps us to predict government participation, but in a way that is more readily derived from its size and centrality, without regard to the overall configuration of the party system.

WHAT HAPPENS WHEN THERE IS NO STRONG PARTY?

We have so far confined our attention to cases in which there is a strong party. We also have something important to say in those cases in which there is no strong party. Proposition 4.1 states that the dimension-by-dimension median (DDM) cabinet, in which the median party on each dimension is assigned the portfolio with jurisdiction over this, is an equilibrium of the government formation process if this cabinet is majority-preferred to all others – if the winset of the DDM cabinet is empty. This proposition can be directly tested using our dataset, which has 391 party observations from government formation situations in which no strong party exists.[14] Nearly 20 percent of these (76 cases) are drawn from circumstances in which the DDM cabinet has an empty winset. We may thus test Proposition 4.1 by estimating one last probit equation.

Define M as unity if a party is median on at least one dimension and the party system is one in which the DDM cabinet has an empty winset. Define M as zero otherwise. Our model suggests that median parties that participate in empty-winset DDMs (for which M = 1) are more likely to

[14]These occurred in Denmark (76), Finland (120), Ireland (13), Italy (119), the Netherlands (58), and Norway (5).

participate in government than others (for which M = 0). Equation 6 estimates the strength of this relationship in practice.

$$G = \begin{matrix} -0.97 \\ (-11.99) \end{matrix} \begin{matrix} + & 0.68 \text{ M} \\ & (3.50) \end{matrix} \qquad (6)$$

The t-statistic on the coefficient for M is highly significant. Thus, even in those cases with no strong party, our theory receives strong empirical support. Parties that participate in empty-winset DDMs are in practice much more likely to get into government than others.

SOME CONCLUDING THOUGHTS

Needless to say we have done little more than scratch the surface of the empirical inquiries suggested by our theory. We believe, however, that the evidence presented justifies considerable confidence in the broad outlines of our approach. The factors we identified as affecting government participation – whether a party is very strong, merely strong, or a partner of a merely strong party, and whether a party was a participant in an empty-winset DDM cabinet – have proved to be quite important. Our comparative empirical investigation has shown that every one of these properties does significantly increase the odds of government participation in the real world.

In addition to investigating our theoretical concepts, we have also shown weight and policy centrality interact with strong-party status to contribute to the prospect of a party securing a key portfolio in a parliamentary government. We have seen that being a very strong party significantly increases the odds of government participation over and above the impact of size and centrality. This implies that important features of very-strong-party status have to do with the overall configuration of the party system. We have also seen that merely strong parties do get into government more than others, but at a rate that appears to be a direct function of the fact that strong parties tend to be both larger and more central than others.

This empirical evidence thus suggests that *centripetal forces* are extraordinarily important in the making and breaking of governments. What comes through powerfully from our results is the role of empty-winset points as attractors. If there is a strong party, then this is reflected in the consistently very significant coefficient for the *very* strong party variable. A very strong party is a party whose ideal point has an empty winset. From the Kadane Theorem (extended to the lattice), this point must be the DDM. If there is no strong party, then it is the participants in an empty-winset DDM that are more likely to secure key governmental portfolios. Thus we have both a coherent theoretical rationale and strong empirical support for the proposition that a central policy position, always known to have drawing power in one-dimensional spatial formulations, also is highly attractive (in several senses of that word) in a multidimensional framework. Parties with central policy positions are more likely to be strong, are more likely to participate in empty winset DDMs, and hence are more likely to get into government.

PART IV

Applications, extensions, and conclusions

10

Party systems and cabinet stability

Thus far in this book we may appear to have talked more about the making than the breaking of governments. In fact, we model a continuous process characterizing the birth, life, and death of governments. Our model of government formation, therefore, is also a model of government duration and government termination. Each government that is born inevitably rises from the ashes of its predecessor. Thus, one of the most significant reasons to understand the government formation process has to do with the stability of governments. In most countries, government formation takes a relatively short time – a matter of days, at most a few weeks rather than months. Uncertainty about the partisan composition of the new government is thus typically resolved quite quickly. Something that is never fully revealed as events unfold, however, at least until the government actually falls, is how long the incumbent cabinet will last. An effective model of cabinet government should clearly provide an account of what breaks governments as well as what makes them, an account that can be used to estimate the durability of an incumbent government – or, indeed, of any prospective government. In this chapter, therefore, we set out to develop our model in a way that allows us to analyze the potential stability of governments.

Previous approaches to the analysis of government stability have for the most part been inductive, approaching the problem from one of two basic directions. The first has been to attempt to identify various attributes of particular cabinets (e.g., their majority status) and of the general bargaining environment in which they find themselves (such as the number of parties in the legislature), attributes that seem on the face of things to be related to cabinet durability. The main thrust of the argument has then rested upon the empirical relationship between these attributes and cabinet stability. Essentially, this approach is deterministic – assuming implicitly that the eventual duration of any government is theoretically knowable, even if in practice unknown, at the moment of its formation.

195

The second approach is probabilistic, on the assumption that the eventual duration of any government cannot be known when it is formed, even if some governments can be plausibly forecast to last longer than others. This approach sees a cabinet as existing in a stream of random events, some of which are capable of bringing it down. The more likely a cabinet is to be destroyed by a particular random event, the less stable it is.[1]

Neither of these approaches is based upon an explicit model of what it takes to make and break a government, however. For this reason, our approach has rather more to say in a systematic way about the stability of different types of cabinet. One of our main concerns has been to characterize equilibrium features of the process of making and breaking governments in parliamentary democracies. We are therefore able to make a number of rather precise statements about the ways in which an equilibrium cabinet can be destroyed. Indeed, as we shall shortly see, our approach allows us to characterize each equilibrium cabinet, a priori, in terms of how stable it is likely to be.

RATIONAL FORESIGHT, SHOCKS, AND GOVERNMENT STABILITY

In very general terms, every cabinet that forms does so as a result of equilibrium processes, modeled or unmodeled. If the key parameters do not change, then the equilibrium cabinet should not change. Thus a general model of cabinet stability must identify the key parameters and specify the types of change in these that are likely to destabilize the government.

This argument applies with particular force to our own approach. This is because one consequence of the rational foresight approach with which we have been working is that we assume that everything that *can* be anticipated to affect the life cycle of a government *will* in fact be anticipated by all key actors before they form the cabinet. The effects of all such anticipated events will thus be impounded in the strategic calculations that underpin the process of forming the cabinet in the first place. This implies that an equilibrium cabinet ought not to be destabilized by an event that was anticipated at the time of its formation. Put another way, only unanticipated events – shocks – can destabilize an equilibrium cabinet.

Shocks may destabilize a cabinet that was previously in equilibrium by shifting key parameters of the government formation environment in

---

[1]For a review and evaluation of these approaches, see Laver and Schofield (1990: chap. 6). The literature has since been supplemented by Paul Warwick (Warwick, 1992a, 1992b, 1994; Warwick and Easton, 1992).

ways that were not taken into account when the government was put together. A most obvious and dramatic example of this would arise if a party forming a majority single-party cabinet split as a result of some unexpected dispute, creating a new decisive structure in which there was no majority party. It is now possible for the dissident faction of the former majority party to combine with the opposition and defeat the government. On similar if less dramatic lines, any government, whether a single-party administration or a coalition, may lose its legislative majority as a result of defections, by-election defeats, or other mischances that could not have been foreseen at the time the government was formed.

Another type of shock that might destabilize an equilibrium government is the emergence of a new issue. In its most dramatic form, this may result in the creation of a completely new policy dimension, just as the collapse of the former Soviet Union posed completely new and unanticipated policy dilemmas in many parliamentary democracies in the early 1990s. In a less dramatic form, it may result in the perturbation of party positions on existing policy dimensions, changing interparty distances and therefore the locations of indifference curves defining winsets that underpin the strategic basis for a particular equilibrium government.

A third type of shock that may affect government stability concerns the parties' perceptions of each other. Even in a world of perfect and complete information about bargaining weights and policy positions, we have seen that the making and breaking of governments can depend on at least one other parameter, the ability of a strong party to win standoffs against other parties. If a strong party is forecast to win standoffs, then a minority government in which the strong party controls all portfolios will be in equilibrium, according to our model. On the other hand, if the strong party is not forecast to win standoffs, then such a minority government is not in equilibrium, and the equilibrium government will be in the winset of the strong party ideal. This has the important effect that a shock that leads to a change in expectations about whether a strong party can win standoffs, such as an unforeseen change in party leader, may destabilize an incumbent government. If a new leader takes control of the strong party in sole control of a minority cabinet, for example, then other parties may upgrade their estimates of whether they can win standoffs and as a result of this decide to take on the strong party.

Many other shocks may also have an impact on the government formation process, but our model is essentially concerned with the bargaining weights of the parties, their policy positions, and actors' evaluations of who can win standoffs. It is unanticipated shocks that change these parameters which our model suggests may destabilize an equilibrium cabinet. Other shocks appear as white noise in our model, and have no systematic or predictable effect.

197

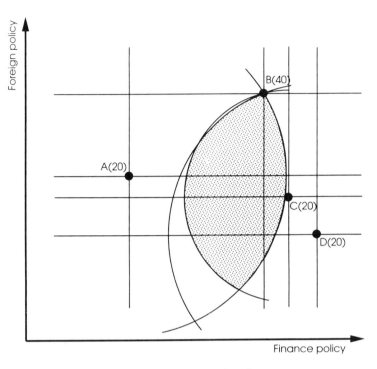

Figure 10.1. A minority government in a four-party system

In the remaining sections of this chapter we concentrate on two of the main types of shock that we are able to analyze in a systematic manner – shocks to interparty distances and shocks to the decisive structure of the government formation process.

PARTY POLICY AND GOVERNMENT STABILITY

According to our model, one of the most important factors affecting whether a particular cabinet is in equilibrium is the identity of the cabinets in its winset. Shocks that change party policy positions can obviously change the shape and content of winsets.

This can easily be seen from Figure 10.1. The example shows a four-party legislature with a strong party, Party B. The winset of Party B's ideal point is shown as the shaded area. It can be seen that B participates in every cabinet in this winset, and can therefore veto each of them. If Party B were forecast to win standoffs, and if the status quo cabinet were one in which B took all portfolios, then this cabinet would, according to our model, be in equilibrium. Notice, however, that the position of Party C is such that a very slight leftward move by it on the (horizontal) economic policy dimension would put two points involving Party C (including Party C's ideal point) into the winset of the Party B minority government.[2]

A similar effect would result from a small rightward movement by Party A – this would also, by shifting A's indifference curve to the right, place Party C's ideal point in the winset of the Party B government. Obviously, Party B would no longer be a strong party – there are now majority-preferred cabinets that Party B cannot veto. For this reason, the Party B minority government is no longer in equilibrium. In this sense, because it is vulnerable to very slight perturbations in the positions of either or both of Party C and Party A, the Party B minority government might be seen as being not particularly stable. Another way of looking at this is to see the Party B minority government as being close to a strategic threshold, the crossing of which in some unexpected way would destabilize it.

In contrast to the situation in Figure 10.1, Figure 10.2 shows a party system in which Party C has fused with Party D, at D's ideal point. The result is that the Party B minority cabinet is considerably more stable. Far greater movements in the positions of Party A or Party D are needed before the winset of Party B's ideal contains any cabinet in which Party B does not participate. If Party B is forecast to win standoffs, and if the status quo is a cabinet in which Party B controls all portfolios, then far greater shocks to the system will be needed to destabilize the status quo.

The difference between the Party B minority cabinets shown in Figures 10.1 and 10.2, then, has to do with the scale of shocks to party positions needed to change the contents of the winset of Party B's ideal point. Since only very slight shocks are needed in the situation shown in Figure 10.1, we think of it as unstable. Since much greater shocks are needed in the situation shown in Figure 10.2, we think of it as more stable.

SIMULATING INSTABILITY

For the purposes of illustration, we analyzed the stability of the minority cabinet in Figures 10.1 and 10.2 in an ad hoc manner, looking only at the effect of moving the position of one party in one direction on one dimension. Of course this is only a very small part of the picture. Many different types of policy shock may disturb the relative party positions shown in Figure 10.1. Party B might move to the left more than Party C, for

[2]The indifference curve centered on C would also shift, of course, but this would not effect the content of the winset in question. What is important in this case is the movement of cabinets involving Party C from one side to the other of the indifference curve centered on Party A.

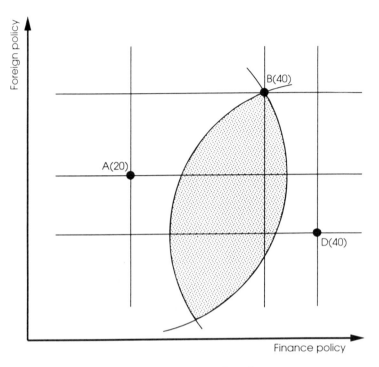

Figure 10.2. A minority government in a three-party system

example, maintaining its strong party position. Party A might move to the right, destroying it, and so on. It is effectively impossible, even in a simple example such as this, to explore all of the possible strategic discontinuities that might arise from particular movements of the four parties on the two dimensions in question. So how can we proceed to a systematic analysis of the stability of some particular cabinet?

The solution we adopt is to simulate the process that might bring about instability. Since a cabinet is stable until the strategic environment in which it is located is disturbed by some random shock, we can simulate the random shocks that might disturb a particular party system, and observe the effects that our model predicts these shocks to have on the strategic environment of the government. We concentrate in the first instance on shocks to party positions, assuming party weights to be fixed. This amounts to an assumption, for the time being, that party splits will not happen, and a concentration on events that might destabilize cabinets between scheduled elections. (We will consider the effects of shocks to party weights.)

200

Party systems and cabinet stability

We assume that every cabinet exists in a stream of random events and that each event causes unforeseen perturbations of relative party policy positions and, therefore, of interparty distances. We might think of each random event as being like a meteorite, of greater or lesser size, that hits the political world and shakes it around a little. After each random event, we recalculate the key strategic parameters of the government formation process and assess whether the status quo cabinet remains in equilibrium.

We simulate the effect of random events on the party system by taking each party position on each dimension at the time of government formation, and perturbing this by adding a random "shock" term. The shock term is a number randomly drawn from a normal distribution with a mean of zero and a standard deviation, relative to the range of party positions, that reflects the roughness of the ride to which we wish to subject the cabinet. If the standard deviation of the shock terms is set to zero, for example, then the shock terms will always be zero and random events do not perturb party positions at all – providing the government with a perfectly smooth ride, and nothing that might destabilize it, even if it is right up against some strategic threshold. If the standard deviation of the shock terms is on the other order of magnitude of the entire range of party positions on each dimension, then random shocks will as a matter of routine create an entirely new constellation of party positions, a completely different party system. This is of course a very rough ride indeed and in practice we will need to set the level of variation in the shock terms considerably below this if we wish our simulation to be realistic.

The question of how to calibrate the level of the random shocks that we apply to the party systems under investigation highlights the very important point that the purpose of these simulations is to compare the relative stability of equilibrium cabinets forming under two different party configurations. We apply the same distribution of shocks to the two party configurations, and calculate the proportion of cases in each configuration for which the cabinet under investigation remains in equilibrium. By doing this, we can estimate the *relative* stability of the two cabinets; we need make no assumption about the real-time frequency of the type of shock with which we are dealing. Although we cannot forecast the actual life expectancy (in days, months, years) of any cabinet, we can use our model to compare two cabinets and form an opinion about which is likely to last longer than the other.

We conduct our comparisons of cabinet durability by generating a large random dataset for each party configuration under investigation. Each case in the dataset represents a version of the party configuration, after it has been on the receiving end of a shock. Each party position on each dimension is given by the "base" position of the party on the dimensions at the time of government formation, plus a random shock term drawn from a normal distribution with mean zero and particular standard deviation.[3] The standard deviations we shall use in the examples that follow have been arbitrarily fixed at either 5 or 10 percent of the maximum range of party positions on some dimension in the system. Such shocks shake the base party configurations around quite considerably, but do not destroy them altogether.

We can use this technique to compare the relative stability of the strong party minority cabinets described in Figures 10.1 and 10.2. First, we generate 1,000 versions of System I, the party configuration in Figure 10.1. Each version has identical party weights, and bases the positions of each party on those shown in Figure 10.1, with a shock term added to each position that is independently drawn from a normal distribution with mean zero and a standard deviation on each dimension of 5 percent of the distance between the extreme parties on the dimension in question (i.e., between Parties A and D for the taxation dimension, and between Parties B and D for the foreign policy dimension). We call this a *5 percent SD shock stream*. We then use our WINSET computer program to calculate the proportion of these 1,000 different "shocked" versions of the base configuration in which Party B is no longer a strong party. A similar analysis is performed on System II, the party configuration in Figure 10.2 using another 1,000 random shock terms drawn from the same distribution. (To keep things simple, the ranges of party positions on each dimension are identical to those in

[3]A very important question concerns whether the political impact of shocks can accumulate. We could model such cumulation by starting each simulation from a base configuration, adding a set of shock terms, then applying a second set of shock terms to the already shocked base configuration, rather than to the (unshocked) base configuration as we do at present. This could be done just as easily from a programming point of view but we must make a choice and have chosen not to do it. From the perspective of our comparative estimations of the relative stability of different cabinets, we argue here that this choice makes no difference, provided there is no systematic pattern of shocks in the sense that one type of shock at Time 1 affects the probability of different types of shock at Time 2. If each shock is independent, then party positions at Time t will be base positions plus a random shock term, whether this is calculated as a single random number or the sum of an independent series of t − 1 random numbers. While, instinctively, it might be felt that a system could move away from its base configuration "more quickly" if shocks cumulate in this way, note that we make no argument about real time in this context, only about *comparative* durations. Note in particular that we do not model the impact of shocks as being analogous to body blows to a boxer, in the sense that a new cabinet has a certain initial stock of resilience that is eroded by each shock it is subjected to – nothing in our formal model speaks to this sort of process, which is implicit in certain atheoretical and inductive "events models" of government stability that have been formulated (e.g., Browne et al., 1984, 1986, 1988). Rather, we see an equilibrium cabinet as being just as much in equilibrium however this equilibrium has been arrived at, whether this is immediately after a cabinet has formed, or after it has been battered by shocks to the far ends of the political universe and back again.

Table 10.1. *Relative vulnerability to shocks of two strong-party cabinets*

	Shocks, per 1,000, that leave Party B no longer strong	
Standard deviation of shock term	*System I*	*System II*
5% max party range	423	19
10% max party range	509	36

Figure 10.1.) We repeat both analyses, giving the two governments a rougher ride by drawing the shock terms from a normal distribution with mean zero and a standard deviation of 10 percent of the range of party positions on the dimension in question (a *10 percent SD shock stream*). The results are in Table 10.1.

The results in Table 10.1 systematically and dramatically confirm the intuitions we developed from looking at Figures 10.1 and 10.2. The party system in Figure 10.1 is very much more vulnerable to shocks than the party system in Figure 10.2. Considering first the 5 percent shock stream, 42 percent of such shocks (423 out of 1,000) destabilize the Party B minority government in System I, destroying B's strong party status. Only 2 percent of equivalent shocks (19 out of 1,000) in this way destabilize the Party B minority government in System II. Repeating the analysis for a 10 percent shock stream (thus with more substantial shocks), we see a similar massive difference in vulnerability to shocks between the two systems.[4]

SHOCKS TO GENERIC PARTY SYSTEMS

The preceding analysis focused on a couple of particular examples. In order to extend the discussion to a more comprehensive characterization of the stability of cabinets that form in different types of party systems,

[4]Note also that the incidence of lethal shocks is increasing at a more rapid rate for the more stable System II. This also makes intuitive sense – the relative stability of different systems should converge as the size of the shocks increases. We can turn up the shock meter (increase the standard deviation of the distribution of the random shock terms relative to the distribution of party positions) to generate a stream of whopper shocks that will destabilize anything, even the most stable of cabinets.

we now consider a number of "generic" two-dimensional party systems that can be used as a baseline for future analysis. We describe and analyze generic three-, four-, and five-party systems – when there are more parties than this, the range of possible party configurations becomes so large as to make nonsense of the concept of a generic party system.

There are, of course, many different three-party systems in which no party wins a majority, but these reduce, in effective strategic terms, to the same basic system, since any nondictatorial set of weights yields the same decisive structure. Austen-Smith and Banks (1990) have already shown analytically that the DDM always has an empty lattice winset in a three-party system, so the existence or absence of an empty-winset point is not a potential source of variation. As we showed in our general discussion of strong parties, although most two-dimensional three-party configurations also have a strong party, not all do. Thus we explore two different three-party systems, each with the type of triangular configurations of parties that we tend to find in real data (see Laver and Hunt, 1992, for examples) – one has a strong party and one does not.[5] These configurations can be seen in the appendix to this chapter, in Figures 10A.1 and 10A.2, respectively. Substantively, taking the horizontal dimension to reflect economic policy and the vertical dimension to represent the second policy dimension, whether this is social policy or foreign affairs, the generic configurations can be interpreted as party systems anchored on the left by a social democratic party (Party A), with the right divided between a more centrist populist conservative or Christian democratic party (Party B) and a classical liberal party (Party C).

In a similar vein, for all of the potential variety in two-dimensional four-party systems, we can identify a limited number of types of these. In the first place, we eliminate distributions of weights with blocking coalitions whose weights sum to precisely 50 percent of the total, which we consider to be pathological rather than generic. Interestingly, this leaves only two nondictatorial types of decisive structure. One has a dummy party and three others, any two of which can form a majority coalition. We concentrate here on the decisive structure with no dummy, however, which puts one party in a dominant position, able to form a majority coalition with any one of the other parties, while all three of the others are needed to form a majority that excludes the dominant party.

As far as policy configurations of the four parties go, we can start with the generic triangular three-party system we have already considered and add a fourth party. This can be either inside (Figures 10A.3, 10A.5, and 10A.7) or outside (Figures 10A.4, 10A.6, and 10A.8) the Pareto region of

---

[5]Note that the triangular location of three parties in two dimensions is generic. The only two-dimensional configuration of three parties that is not triangular is when all parties are precisely arranged along a straight line, which we take to be pathological.

the other three parties. We combine the spatial configuration of parties with the decisive structure by making the dominant party the one that is median on one dimension only (Figures 10A.3 and 10A.4), on both dimensions (Figures 10A.5 and 10A.6), or on neither dimension (Figures 10A.7 and 10A.8). Obviously, six generic party systems do not cover every possible strategic permutation of a two-dimensional four-party system, but they seem to us to cover a fair range of them. Substantively, Party D might be seen as a third bourgeois party – adding Christian Democrats to the conservatives or vice versa, or perhaps adding an agrarian or center party.

As the range of possible party configurations increases dramatically with the number of parties, it is not sensible to attempt to cover the entire gamut of strategic possibilities. Our generic five-party systems, therefore, are derived from the types of two-dimensional five-party system that we tend to encounter in practice. We do this by adding a second left-wing party (Party E) – to the left of the social democrats on both dimensions. Substantively, this can be taken to be a Communist or New Left party. In terms of structure we use the "dominated" decisive structure we tend to observe quite often in practice in five-party systems, whereby one party can form a majority with any of the others, but a coalition of all of the other "dominated" parties is needed to form a majority that excludes the dominant party. We vary this according to whether the dominant party is social democratic as in Scandinavia (Figure 10A.9), centrist as in Ireland (Figure 10A.10), or conservative (Figure 10A.11).

We now take the 11 generic party systems we have described here and expose each of them to a stream of random shocks in order to gain some insight into the stability of their respective equilibrium features, concentrating on the existence and identity of a strong-party and an empty-winset DDM. Remember from Proposition 4.1 that if the status quo is an empty-winset DDM, then it remains an equilibrium cabinet. Similarly, from Statement A of the appendix to Chapter 4, if the strong-party ideal point is the status quo, then this too remains in equilibrium unless there is a change in the others parties' assessments of the strong party's ability to win standoffs. More generally, the identity of the strong party determines the winset of the strong-party ideal point and, from Proposition 4.2, we know that every equilibrium government is either the strong-party ideal point or an element in the winset of this. A change in the identity of the strong party, therefore, is almost certain to be disequilibrating.

The results of this analysis are reported in two rather daunting tables, Tables 10.2 and 10.3. Table 10.2 shows the results of exposing our generic governments to a 5 percent SD shock stream, Table 10.3 of exposing them to a 10 percent SD shock stream. Perhaps the most striking pattern to emerge from these displays is that *equilibriums based on*

Table 10.2

Table 10.2. The impact of 5% shock streams on generic party systems

Party system	Cases with same strong party	Cases with same empty-winset DDM
Three party		
Fig 10A.1: strong party	766	1,000
Fig 10A.2: no strong party	no s*	912
Four party (Party D central)		
Fig 10A.3: big party median on 1 dimension	889	1,000
Fig 10A.5: big party median on 2 dimensions	1,000	997
Fig 10A.7: big party median on no dimension	no s*	no m**
Four party (Party D noncentral)		
Fig 10A.4: big party median on 1 dimension	915	999
Fig 10A.6: big party median on 2 dimensions	1,000	1,000
Fig 10A.8: big party median on no dimension	no s*	no m**
Five party		
Fig 10A.9: SD median on 2 dimensions	1,000	998
Fig 10A.10: Center median on 1 dimension	661	1,000
Fig 10A.11: SD median on 2 dimensions	1,000	993

empty-winset DDMs are more robust to shock than those based upon strong parties. In almost every case, the identity of an empty-winset DDM changes much less frequently than the identity of a strong party when the system is subjected to shocks. Other things being equal, an equilibrium cabinet at the DDM seems likely to be more stable, in the same party system, than one controlled by a strong party, since shocks are more likely to change the existence and/or identity of the strong party than that of an empty-winset DDM.

Predictably, though comforting nonetheless, the stability of equilibriums based on both strong parties and empty-winset DDMs declines as the amplitude of the shock stream is turned up from a standard deviation of 5 percent to one of 10 percent of the maximum range of party positions (in which the system is thereby subjected to a rougher ride).

In the four- and five-party systems in which the large party is at the median on both dimensions (Figures 10A.5, 10A.6, 10A.9, and 10A.11), increasing the amplitude of the shocks does not make much of a differ-

Table 10.3. *The impact of 10% shock streams on generic party systems*

Party system	Cases with same strong party	Cases with same empty-winset DDM
Three party		
Fig 10A.1: strong party	615	969
Fig 10A.2: no strong party	no s*	747
Four party (Party D central)		
Fig 10A.3: big party median on 1 dimension	730	956
Fig 10A.5: big party median on 2 dimensions	978	885
Fig 10A.7: big party median on no dimension	no s*	no m**
Four party (Party D noncentral)		
Fig 10A.4: big party median on 1 dimension	734	952
Fig 10A.6: big party median on 2 dimensions	1,000	995
Fig 10A.8: big party median on no dimension	no s*	no m**
Five party		
Fig 10A.9: SD median on 2 dimensions	1,000	896
Fig 10A.10: Center median on 1 dimension	530	938
Fig 10A.11: SD median on 2 dimensions	986	856

ence to the identity of either the strong party or the empty-winset DDM. In these cases the dominant party is typically very strong, and the only shocks that disrupt this are those that have the effect of putting the dominant party at one end or the other of some policy dimension. There are no delicate thresholds to be crossed here; what is needed to change the equilibrium is major surgery on party positions.

In contrast, the least stable systems – those most susceptible to disequilibrating shocks – are those in which the dominant party is at no median position. Given the decisive structure, it must thus be at one end or the other of both policy dimensions (Figures 10A.7 and 10A.8). There is no strong party in this case, and the three-party configuration with no strong party (Figure 10A.2) is also more unstable in this sense. In such party systems, even the kinder, gentler (5 percent SD) shock stream is likely to generate a new strong party – and the rough (10 percent SD) rise is very likely to do so. It is also the case that the stability of the empty-winset DDM is also lower in such party systems, especially when subjected to more robust shock streams.

Applications, extensions, and conclusions

Party systems in which the dominant party is median on only one of the two dimensions (Figures 10A.3, 10A.4, and 10A.10) are also noticeably less stable than those in which it is median on both dimensions. Especially in the more vigorous shock streams, the identity of the strong party is quite likely to change, although the existence and identity of the empty-winset DDM remains stable.

In general, then, what can we learn from all of this? It would of course be unwise to generalize in too cavalier a manner from our limited analyses of a few generic party systems, but some interesting patterns do seem to emerge quite clearly. The most striking is the relative stability of equilibrium cabinets at the empty-winset DDM. Shocks seem much less likely to disrupt these than they do to disrupt cabinets that are dependent on the identity of the strong party. Related to this we note that, if the empty-winset DDM is also an ideal point, and particularly if it is the ideal point of the dominant party, then the equilibrium is much less susceptible to shocks.

The least stable systems seem to be those with a dominant party at a nonmedian position. Not being strong, the dominant party may well be excluded from government, but relatively small shocks can change this and put it back in the catbird seat.

INVESTIGATING INSTABILITY IN REAL CABINETS

The techniques elaborated in the previous section can of course be applied to the investigation of real-world cases. As an example, consider the government that formed in Ireland in January 1993, the formation of which we discussed in Chapter 6. The status quo during the period of government formation was a Fianna Fáil minority caretaker administration, holding all portfolios. The key cabinet jurisdictions identified in Chapter 6 were the Department of Finance, with jurisdiction over economic policy, and the Department of Foreign Affairs, with responsibility for Northern Ireland policy. Party seat totals and policy positions are given in Tables 6.7 and 6.8, respectively.

As Figure 6.3 shows, Fianna Fáil was a strong party after the election, raising the possibility, since the status quo was a Fianna Fáil caretaker administration, of a Fianna Fáil minority government. Given a forecast by the other parties that Fianna Fáil could not win standoffs, however, as we saw in Chapter 6, our model predicts the formation of the dimension-by-dimension median cabinet. This is a coalition giving the finance portfolio to Fianna Fáil and foreign affairs to Labour. This has an empty winset and is in fact the cabinet that formed.

In order to assess the potential stability of this cabinet, we can use our model to investigate the effect of bombarding it with a stream of random shocks, calculating the frequency of occasions, for a given level of variation in the shock, for which the party system has the same DDM cabinet and this cabinet has an empty winset. This analysis can give us some intuition about how stable the incumbent DDM cabinet in Ireland is likely to be, relative to other cabinets.

First, we can give the coalition a relatively easy ride by using a 5 percent shock stream. If we simulate 1,000 party systems, each shocked in this way, what we are interested in is the percentage of shocked systems for which the Fianna Fáil–Labour DDM cabinet has an empty winset, and hence remains in equilibrium. For the 5 percent SD shocks, this figure was 99.9 percent. In only 1 case out of 1,000 was the DDM cabinet not the Fianna Fáil–Labour coalition. If we crank up the shock meter to expose the coalition to a rougher simulated ride, using a 10 percent shock stream, then the relevant figure is 93.1 percent.[6]

In order to give a sense of perspective to these figures, a similar analysis was run for the very stable DDM cabinet involving CDU and FDP that formed after the 1987 election in Germany, also discussed in detail in Chapter 6. A total of 99.8 percent of empty winset DDMs remained in equilibrium in the face of a 5 percent SD shock stream, while 92.8 percent survived the 10 percent SD shock stream. On this interpretation, therefore, the FF-Labour coalition that formed in Ireland in 1993 should have a resilience to policy shocks analogous to that of the CDU-FDP government in Germany.[7]

SHOCKS TO SEAT DISTRIBUTIONS

Thus far we have been holding the decisive structure constant and modeling instability in the system in terms of the implicit effect that policy shocks might have on interparty policy distances. Changes in the equilibrium properties of the system thus result from changes in the configuration of interparty distances, not from changes in the decisive structure. The rationale for this approach is that for the most part the decisive structure of a legislature does not change between elections. To be sure, there may be deaths and illnesses among legislators, but many European PR systems provide for the appointment of a replacement legislator from the same party in such circumstances, rather than for a by-election that might change the allocation of seats. The main potential sources of actual

[6]This percentage was calculated after 66 cases with blocking coalitions were eliminated from the analysis, in which there was no unique median party on one dimension or another.

[7]Of course we do not know whether the shock streams in the two countries are drawn from the same underlying distribution, and, as it happens, the FF-Labour coalition fell in very acrimonious circumstances, the result of a breakdown of trust between the parties, in November 1994.

change in the decisive structure between elections arise from party splits and fusions. Obviously if an existing party splits, or two existing parties fuse, this can make a big difference to the decisive structure. Such events, however, are rare and we do not consider them in this context.

However, a far more pervasive source of change in the *effective* decisive structure may arise from a particular feature of most European parliamentary democracies, coupled with our rational foresight assumption about how legislators calculate the best course of action. In most European countries the prime minister may recommend, to a titular head of state who is unlikely to refuse, the dissolution of the legislature and the holding of new elections. (Laver and Schofield, 1990: 64, indicate that this provision applies in 16 of the 20 European parliamentary democracies they consider.) This introduces an interesting strategic asymmetry in the cabinet government game, since the prime minister's party can in effect choose between two legislatures, the current legislature and the legislature forecast to result if the current one were to be dissolved and new elections held. If the forecast legislature generates a strategic environment more favorable to the prime minister's party than the current one, an election can be called and the new legislature substituted.

There are two ways of interpreting this. One is that it creates an incentive for the prime minister to call an early election, thereby destabilizing the current government. The second is that, in a world in which actors calculate on the basis of rational foresight, it should not be necessary for the new election actually to be held. Rather, recognizing that it *could* be held, the actors will impound this effect into beliefs about bargaining weights in the current legislature. The current legislature will then behave *as if* an election had been held. But either way there will be a reallocation of power in the legislature, and a potential destabilization of the status quo.

So how do prime ministers and other actors estimate the prospective result of an election that might be held at a particular point in time? The answer is that they may read tea leaves, go to fortune-tellers, and use many other pieces of information to do this. One obvious and systematic source of information, however, comes from opinion polls. (This is not of course to say that experienced politicians automatically assume that opinion polls are right. Rather it is to assume that, whatever they may say in public when a poll result is published, politicians learn to decode opinion polls to derive their best forecast of how, given a particular poll result, the election might actually turn out.)

All forecasts of election results are obviously subject to shocks, in the same way as other expectations, as a result of all sorts of unforeseen events. Thus a prominent politician may be caught with a hand in the wrong till or shoes under the wrong bed. Disasters such as floods, storms, or air crashes may put the government under pressure in unexpected ways. Almost anything can happen to change peoples' views of either government or opposition parties. Such shocks can feed through quickly into opinion poll ratings, and thence into expectations about the result of calling a snap election. Thus, effective seat distributions can in this way be shocked during the lifetime of a legislature, but only in a way that benefits, or at least cannot harm, the prime minister's party. The asymmetry arises because, if the shocks benefit the PM, they can be capitalized on by the PM calling an early election. If they harm the PM, there is no need to call an early election, and the PM can continue with the existing legislature.

Such shocks might nonetheless be destabilizing if they provide incentives for the prime minister to terminate the current coalition and form another more favorable one. In particular, if the prime minister's party is a member of an equilibrium DDM coalition, there will be a big incentive to dissolve the legislature if the forecast result would make the PM's party strong when it was not, or very strong when it was merely strong, for example. Indeed within our approach, the only reason for a PM to call, or to threaten, an early election is if the PM's party is favored by the equilibrium cabinet that is the ultimate outcome of the new decisive structure forecast to result from the early election.

This argument can best be illustrated by expanding the two real-world examples we developed in detail in Chapter 6 and briefly examined the stability of earlier in the present chapter – Germany in 1987 and Ireland in 1992–1993. In each case the prime minister's party was merely strong and a member of an equilibrium DDM coalition with an empty winset. (The PM's party was Fianna Fáil in the Irish case and the Christian Democrats in the case of Germany.) A change in the legislature which made the PM's party very strong would have created destabilizing incentives for the PM's party – either to call an actual election or to force the other parties to behave as if an election had been called. We can investigate this possibility systematically by applying a stream of random shocks, not to policy positions as before, but to the seat distribution. We can then investigate the proportion of these that generate a situation in which the PM's party becomes very strong. These shocks model the impact of unanticipated changes in the forecast results of holding a snap election, reflected in shocks to opinion poll findings, for example, or in how these are interpreted. They reflect changes in the incentives for the PM's party to terminate the government and call an immediate election.

Once more, an operational decision that must be made concerns the amplitude of the shock stream to apply to the seat distribution. This in turn depends on forecasts of electoral volatility. For want of a better estimate, we rely here on historical variations in the seat distribution, assuming that future seat distributions will fall within these broad parameters. Thus we calculate the change in seats at each election in the recent past, calculate the standard deviation of these changes, and apply a random shock term to each party's seat total drawn from a normal distribution with a mean of zero and the observed historical standard deviation for the party in question. In the case of Germany we calculated the standard deviation, for each party, of changes in its seat total since 1972.[8] In the case of Ireland, we began a little later, in 1981, since this was the first election held to a new set of Dáil constituencies, with subsequent constituency revisions handled by an independent boundary commissioner, considerably reducing the variation in election results.[9]

We can now run a 1,000-case simulation on the situation in Germany in 1987, fixing party positions as those estimated by Laver and Hunt, but adding a random shock term to the seat total for each party in each case. The shock term is a seat change randomly drawn from a normal distribution with a mean of zero and a standard deviation equal to the observed standard deviation in seat changes for the party for the period in question. We can then investigate the equilibrium properties of every case, each of which represents a version of the German party system in 1987, shocked to change expectations of the results of calling an immediate legislative election.

In this particular simulation, based on Germany in 1987, the same empty-winset DDM, a CDU-FDP coalition, arises in 891 of 1,000 cases. Of the 109 cases in which a new empty-winset DDM arises, 72 of these arise at the SPD ideal point, making the SPD a very strong party. If the opposition SPD had the power to force an election on a majority government whenever it wanted, these shocks to expected election results would be destabilizing. But, given the rules of parliamentary democracy in Germany, it did not have this power. Thus the incumbent government can, as a result of institutional design, ride out shocks generating expected election results favoring the SPD – a useful bonus arising from being in power. However, the remaining 37 cases generating a new empty-winset

[8]The relevant standard deviations in seat changes for German parties over this period were: CDU, 19.97; SPD, 13.16; FDP, 13.92; Greens, 8.49.

[9]The relevant standard deviations used for seat changes for Irish parties over this period were: Fianna Fáil, 5.85; Fine Gael, 14.24; Labour, 7.89; PDs 3.50; Democratic Left, 1.50. The PD figure was reduced from its actual figure to prevent the generation of (clearly unrealistic and uninterpretable) negative PD seat totals in the simulation runs – and as a new party its actual standard deviation was probably too high as an estimate of future variations in its seat total. The DL figure was reduced slightly (to prevent the generation of negative DL seat totals) from the standard deviation of Workers Party seat totals, since the party was formed out of the Workers Party and comprised all but one of former WP legislators.

DDM in Germany place this at the CDU ideal point. In other words, 3.7 percent of shocks to electoral expectations in Germany in 1987 generate a prediction that, if an election were to be called immediately, the CDU would be returned as a very strong party, able to control all cabinet portfolios. With the CDU controlling the premiership, these shocks may well be destabilizing, creating a situation with strong incentives for the chancellor to call an early election, in the expectation of this returning the CDU as a very strong party. Alternatively, as a result of changes in the expectations of all of the legislative actors, deriving from this electoral forecast, the same effect may result without actually calling the election.

To gain some insight into the scale of the destabilizing effect of the incentives that may arise for the PM to call an early election, we can repeat a similar analysis for Ireland in 1992. In this situation, the incumbent empty-winset DDM, a Fianna Fáil–Labour coalition, arises in 845 of 1,000 cases. In 23 of 1,000 cases, this cabinet loses its empty winset – potentially destabilizing if the opposition could force an election on a government with a secure legislative majority, but not according to the rules of the game in Ireland. In 14 of 1,000 cases a new DDM, less favored by Fianna Fáil, is generated. In 118 cases, however, there is a new empty-winset DDM at the Fianna Fáil ideal point, making Fianna Fáil a very strong party and clearly creating an incentive for the Fianna Fáil prime minister to call an early election with the expectation of forming a single-party government controlling all portfolios. If one assumes rational foresight this may, of course, not actually result in an early election, but rather in a reallocation of power within the existing party configuration – either way, the equilibrium cabinet will change, however.

Thus, although we saw that the Irish and German cases were very similar in terms of the destabilizing effects of *policy* shocks on interparty distances, the Irish status quo in 1992–1993 was potentially quite a bit less stable than that in Germany in 1987, when we consider the effect of shocks to the *electoral expectations* of the PM's party.[10] Over 10 percent of these shocks created an incentive for the Irish PM to cut and run for an early election, with the expectation of being in a significantly stronger bargaining position after the results have been declared. These incentives were much less likely to arise in the case of Germany in 1987, which we may therefore characterize as the more stable status quo.

For this important reason, therefore, we may feel that the Irish government is less stable than the government that formed in Germany in 1987. This is not because of some policy shock that might break the government, but because the decisive structure is closer to a strategic threshold

---

[10]This is particularly true once we consider the cumulative survival probabilities based on a stream of such shocks.

in Ireland. It takes smaller shifts in opinion polls to generate incentives for the Irish prime minister to hold an early election. Note that this analysis also says something about the most likely manner in which the Irish government will fall. It implies that the government in question will not be broken apart by an unexpected policy dilemma, but rather will be brought down from within, by a prime minister eager to capitalize on the possibility of leading a very strong party.

We conclude this section with a speculation that the application of our model to the impact on cabinet stability of shocks to seat distributions gives us the possibility of understanding a process that represents one of the more interesting unstudied mysteries of politics. Why do governments with secure majorities change policy in response to midterm opinion poll shocks, when they do not have to face an election until so far into the future that opinion polls will undoubtedly be saying something different? Impressionistically, at least, governments do respond to midterm poll shocks when on the face of things, they have no need to.

One possible answer to this puzzle can be found in the preceding account of shocks to anticipated seat distributions. If the PM's party expects to improve its position vis-à-vis the current legislature by holding an early election, then it can use the rational foresight of this improvement to extract concessions from its partners in government. If the PM's party expects to stay in the same position or do worse in any early election, then one need not be held. However, if partners in government of the PM's party expect to do better as a result of early elections, then they can leave the government, or threaten to leave, and do what they can to force one – combining with the opposition to vote no confidence in the government, for example. The PM's partners can also use rational foresight to extract concessions from the PM's party in such circumstances. In short, opinion poll shocks may combine with rational foresight to change the balance of power within a government coalition, and may thereby result in changes in government policy, even when no election is required for some considerable time. Our model provides a tool that could be used to explore specific examples of this process in the real world.

CONCLUSION

There may have been points in this chapter when readers came to the conclusion that we have gone completely mad. Certainly, making arguments about important political processes on the basis of simulations using thousands of randomly generated party systems is still rather unconventional in political science. One of the reasons for this is precisely the main virtue of our approach, however. It is still rather rare to make arguments about important political processes using a fully specified and

214

programmable model of that process. The great benefit of such models, however, is that they allow the analyst to deal systematically and rigorously in counterfactuals, answering the "what if" questions that provide the main reasons to do political science in the first place. Of its very essence, the problem of understanding government stability requires that we deal in counterfactuals. "What if this were to happen?" "What if that were to happen?" "Would the government be destabilized?" Thus, rather than engaging in cross-national aggregate data analysis in an attempt to identify empirical factors associated with government stability – the approach used by all of our predecessors in this field – we have used our model to explore counterfactuals.

Obviously, we might in particular cases be interested in particular counterfactuals. "What if the Social Democrats moved to the left?" "What if the Liberals split down the middle?" Our model can of course be used to explore these possibilities, and to provide an analysis of the likely impact of such changes on the government equilibrium. If we are interested in the general stability of some cabinet, however, we are in a sense interested in the impact of a wide range of different counterfactuals. We cannot sensibly investigate all of these analytically, and it is for this reason that we turn to simulations. Each of our simulated deviations from some "base" legislature under investigation represents a counterfactual for that legislature. Since we have an explicit model, we can systematically investigate the impact of each simulated counterfactual in turn on the government equilibrium. Aggregating these analyses over a wide range of different counterfactuals, we get a systematic sense of how robust the equilibrium government is to things that might happen to it. We can thereby investigate the stability of any equilibrium government in a systematic manner.

Without repeating the detailed findings in previous sections two basic conclusions stand out very clearly. The first is that equilibrium governments at the dimension-by-dimension median seem to be substantially more stable than those based on the bargaining power of strong parties. In every base case we analyze, far fewer shocks destabilize empty-winset DDMs than destabilize the existence and/or identity of strong parties. This applies whether the shocks in question are policy shocks or shocks to anticipated seat distributions.

The second conclusion is that our model can be used to understand why governments might change tack between elections. Because we have an operational model, furthermore, we do not have to confine ourselves to the general observation that governments may change tack because shocks to policy distances or anticipated seat distributions undermine the strategic calculations that formed the original basis of the government. We can build substantively on that observation in particular cases to make more precise statements about how particular types of shock might have particular types of effect for particular governments. We did this, for example, when we investigated the incentive that a Fianna Fáil prime minister in Ireland might have to bring down a government he was leading by calling an early election, when it was doing well in the opinion polls. Our model allows us to make quite specific statements about such circumstances.

Overall, therefore, this chapter shows quite clearly that, once we have a comprehensive model of cabinet government, this gives us the theoretical purchase to develop a systematic account of government stability. This in itself is one of the most important reasons to want to model the making and breaking of governments.

Appendix

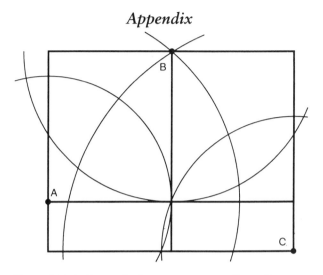

Figure 10A.1. A generic three-party system; Party B strong

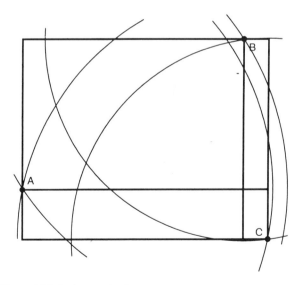

Figure 10A.2. A generic three-party system; no party strong

217

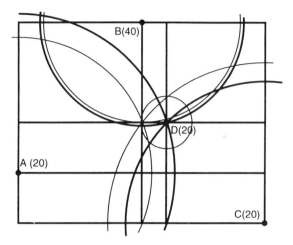

Figure 10A.3. A generic four-party system; Party B median on horizontal dimension, Party D central

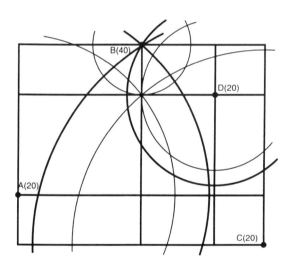

Figure 10A.4. A generic four-party system; Party B median on horizontal dimension, Party D noncentral

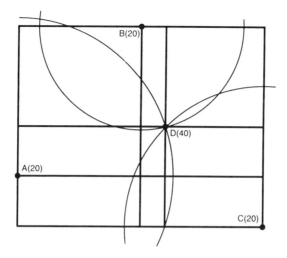

Figure 10A.5. A generic four-party system; Party D median on both dimensions and central

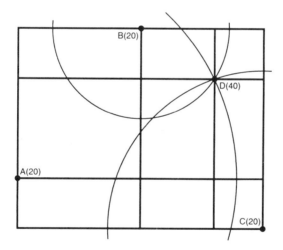

Figure 10A.6. A generic four-party system; Party D median on both dimension but noncentral

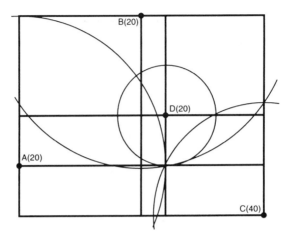

Figure 10A.7. A generic four-party system; Party C median on no dimension, Party D central

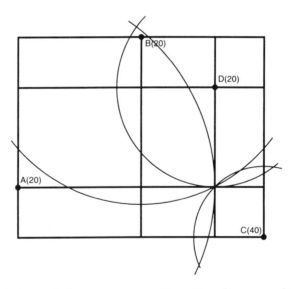

Figure 10A.8. A generic four-party system; Party C median on no dimension, Party D noncentral

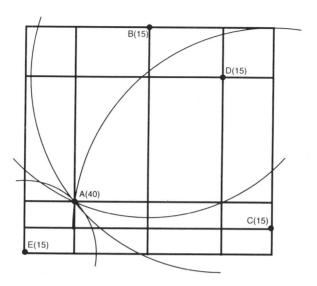

Figure 10A.9. A generic five-party system; "Scandinavia"

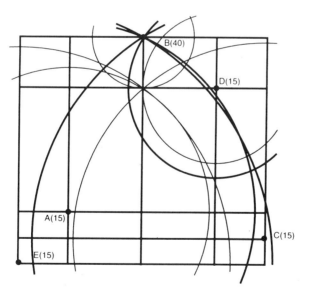

Figure 10A.10. A generic five-party system; "Ireland"

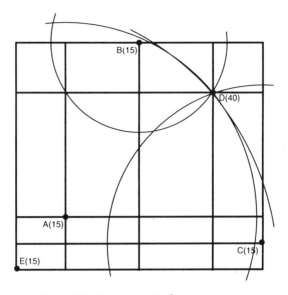

Figure 10A.11. A generic five-party system

11

Making the model more realistic

INTRODUCTION

We did a number of things in the first three parts of this book. In Part I we described the context surrounding the making and breaking of governments in parliamentary democracies. In Part II we developed an explicit model of government formation, derived theoretical propositions from this model, and used simulations to explore parts of our model that these propositions could not reach. In Part III we confronted our model with the real world. We looked at two case studies of government formation, teased out empirical implications from our propositions, and brought real-world data to bear on these implications in an attempt to evaluate them. In Part IV, we apply and extend our model. We began in Chapter 10 by interrogating our model on the question of cabinet stability. In the present chapter we reexamine some of our assumptions and explore the extent to which our approach is affected by relaxing them. In the next chapter we look at some specific applications of our approach. In the final chapter of the book, we draw some lessons from our approach for the study of party competition in general and government formation in particular.

As the reader well appreciates, any theory is based on assumptions and conceptualizations. Once stated, these must be taken as fixed for the purposes both of theorizing and of exploring the empirical consequences of theory. Otherwise, we do not know where we stand. It is at this early stage that compromises must be made and restrictions imposed in order to get on with the business at hand. Of course, this is as true of informal arguments as it is of formal theories (the primary difference being that the latter are typically more explicit and self-conscious about doing it). We have not departed from this practice. We do, however, feel obliged both to relax restrictive assumptions as much as we can and to provide persuasive justifications for assumptions that we are unable or unwilling to relax. We do this in the present chapter.

We reconsider our assumptions on three different aspects of the issue space within which the making and breaking of governments takes place. First, we consider the dimensionality of this space. Our theory is not restricted in its dimensionality; it applies to politics represented by two-dimensional, or two hundred–dimensional, issue spaces. Both our paper-and-pencil exercises and our empirical analyses, however, have for practical reasons typically used two- or three-dimensional issue spaces. In the next section we discuss why correlations among party positions might well provide very sound theoretical reasons for doing this.

Our second reconsideration of the issue space focuses on the independence of preferences across issue dimensions. In assuming that actors possess Euclidean, or distance-based, preferences, we have ignored the possibility that a party's preferences in one policy jurisdiction may depend on what policies are being pursued in other jurisdictions. We discuss the ways in which assuming such interdependent preferences affects the analysis presented earlier in this volume.

Our third reconsideration of the issue space relaxes the assumption of simple jurisdictions. Throughout we have assumed that ministerial jurisdictions are unidimensional, clearly a restrictive assumption. The tax structure, for example, a major responsibility of the Finance Ministry or Treasury is, itself, multifaceted. And finance ministries typically have expenditure as well as revenue responsibilities. The foreign policy portfolio covers not only cold war–related policy issues (on which basis we empirically characterized the policy domain of the Ministry on Foreign Affairs), but a wide range of other issues as well – North–South relations, European affairs, specific bilateral relationships, and so on. We move at the end of this chapter to explore the theoretical consequences of multidimensional portfolios and thus of complex jurisdictions.

THE IMPACT OF CORRELATED ISSUE PREFERENCES

Our model of cabinet government in parliamentary democracies assumes that the allocation of cabinet portfolios among parties is determined by the interaction of three key sets of variables. Once we have data on each of these sets of variables, we have all of the information used by our model to analyze government formation in a given setting. The first set of variables concerns the decisive structure of the legislature – determined by the distribution of seats between parties and the decision rule employed in the key legislative votes that make and break governments. A second factor concerns the ability of strong parties to win standoffs when they find themselves in head-to-head confrontation with others. The third set of variables concerns the policies of political parties – in particular the positions of parties on key policy dimensions and the relative importance they attach to each policy dimension. This third set of concerns touches upon a deep and interesting problem in political science, which has to do with the difference between a "key" policy dimension that should form part of our analysis and a policy dimension that we should ignore as a "mere" detail, a distraction from the big picture of politics in the party system we are dealing with. Such choices are vital for empirical elaborations of all spatial models of politics, including our own.

In the general spatial model of voting, as we have seen, the chaos results imply that the set of dimensions chosen has a vital bearing upon the possibility for political equilibrium. Whenever more than one dimension is important and the outcome cannot be determined by a single actor, equilibrium is more or less impossible to achieve. Our model, as we have seen, allows for the possibility of equilibrium in policy spaces of any dimensionality and, as we have argued, this is one of its major assets, since informal observation suggests there is not as much chaos in the real political world as the chaos results imply. Nonetheless, we also saw from simulations estimating the frequency of features such as strong parties and empty-winset DDMs in random party systems that the potential for equilibrium in our model declines steeply, though never disappearing completely, as the number of salient policy dimensions increases. Thus, even for our model, the dimensionality of the relevant policy space remains firmly on the agenda.

As we have already seen, there are two approaches to assessing the dimensionality of the policy space within which the making and breaking of governments goes on. The first is determined by the set of cabinet portfolios in place at the start of the government formation process, which we may take to be immutable in the short term. (We return later in the next chapter to consider the possibility that the set of cabinet portfolios is endogenously determined as part of government formation.) For the moment, we can think of the set of cabinet portfolios in place at the beginning of this process as being the result of a sort of giant historical dimensional analysis of the wider policy space, in which the key policy dimensions on which the government may have to take action have been identified and allocated to a set of policy jurisdictions. However this situation might have arisen, the result is that, if there are 15 portfolios in a given cabinet, giving control over 15 key departments of state, then there are 15 real-world policy jurisdictions for parties to allocate as part of government formation. Decisions on each of these cannot be avoided. If we wish to be comprehensive in our analysis of government formation, on this view, we are dealing with a 15-dimensional space at the very least (since every portfolio has jurisdiction over at least one policy dimension).

The second approach to describing the dimensionality of the policy space is determined by the empirical structure of the policy positions of key actors, who can be taken to have some position or other on any policy dimension on which decisions potentially have to be made. Since there is a huge but indeterminate number of potential decisions, this means that the policy space within which government formation takes place has a huge but indeterminate number of policy dimensions.

Both approaches to specifying the dimensionality of policy spaces generate the problem that estimates of dimensionality are "too high" for both tractability and intuitive plausibility. If we use the number of cabinet portfolios to determine the dimensionality of the space, then this generates a lattice of high dimensionality, which, in anything other than the smallest of party systems, will have a huge number of points. A 10-party system with a 15-seat cabinet, for example, would generate a lattice of 1,000,000,000,000,000 – one million billion – points, and each of these must be compared with every other in order to complete a comprehensive strategic evaluation. Even our trusty nontalking pal, WINSET, running on the fastest kit in the business, gives up and lies down when faced with tasks of this enormity. And commonsense extrapolation of the simulation results we have already generated suggests that the potential for equilibrium in such systems is as close to zero as makes no difference.

The use of giant lattices such as this is clearly not sensible, for a number of reasons. First, the theoretical potential for equilibrium is reduced effectively to zero, despite the fact that we do in practice observe what are clearly equilibrium governments, even in large party systems.[1] Second, the computing power required to determine the strategic possibilities in a given scenario is so gigantic we might well assume that it lies beyond the scope of ordinary politicians. Third, even if ordinary politicians can do it, mere political scientists cannot, so we cannot estimate such high-dimensional models. Each of these problems is essentially the same, though even more acute, if we estimate dimensionality on the basis of the number of potentially salient issues. All of this implies that, while we must of course admit the theoretical possibility that the policy space in which politicians make and break governments has a very large number of dimensions, it seems intuitively plausible that real-world policy spaces can more usefully be described in terms of a relatively small number of "key" policy dimensions.

In addition to the argument that politics in the real world appears to be more stable than would be implied if things happened in policy spaces of high dimensionality, another important phenomenon also has the implication that the space for government formation may effectively be of much lower dimensionality than is implied by the number of cabinet

[1]It should be said, however, that research into government stability suggests that stability declines as the number of parties in the system increases, so that increasing the number of lattice points does in practice increase instability. See King et al., 1990.

Table 11.1. *Pearson correlations between individual party positions on eight policy dimensions in the Netherlands*

	A Taxes vs. spending	B Foreign policy	C Public owner-ship	D Social policy	E Relig-ious policy	F Urban vs. rural	G Cent-raliz-ation	H Envir-onment
A	1.000							
B	0.927	1.000						
C	0.986	0.950	1.000					
D	0.791	0.908	0.821	1.000				
E	0.778	0.904	0.830	0.988	1.000			
F	0.855	0.936	0.897	0.974	0.988	1.000		
G	0.375	0.596	0.386	0.711	0.652	0.581	1.000	
H	0.895	0.850	0.865	0.814	0.770	0.812	0.637	1.000

Source: Calculated from data in Laver and Hunt, 1992: 262-265.

portfolios or the number of potentially salient issues. This is that a party's position on one key policy dimension is often in practice quite closely related to its position on another key dimension. Thus its position on public ownership, for example, may in practice be closely related to its position on welfare policy, or even on aspects of foreign policy, despite the fact that these policy dimensions are conceptually quite distinct and typically fall into entirely different governmental jurisdictions. This can be seen from Table 11.1, which shows the correlations, for the party system in the Netherlands, between party positions on eight different policy dimensions for the 10 parties for which Laver and Hunt (1992) collected data. These high correlations show that it is typically very easy to predict a party's position on one policy dimension from its position on another. Equivalent correlation matrices, with coefficients of very similar orders of magnitude, can be calculated for any other country for which Laver and Hunt collected data.

Table 11.1 shows that correlations between party positions on differ-ent issue dimensions in the Netherlands are in practice very high, half at .85 or more. Thus, reading down column A of the table, we see that the correlation between the positions of Dutch parties on the main economic policy dimension and their positions on the foreign policy dimension – substantively a quite distinct dimension – is 0.927. Squaring this figure to get an estimate of explained variance, we thus find that about 86 percent of the variation in the foreign policy positions of Dutch parties can be accounted for by their positions on economic policy. Parties on the left on economic policy tended to promote foreign policies more favorable to the

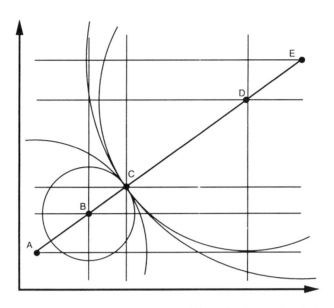

Fig 11.1. A very strong party in a system with perfectly correlated dimensions

Soviet Union, and vice versa. When the substantive relationship between distinct policy dimensions was more direct, correlations were higher still. Party positions on public spending were correlated at the level of 0.986 to positions on public ownership, for example – 97 percent of the variation in positions on one dimension was explained by positions on the other.

These correlations between policy positions on different dimensions are highly significant for the possibility of equilibrium in the government formation process. Increasing the correlation between party positions on different dimensions in a policy space of given dimensionality dramatically increases the likelihood, all other things being held equal, of equilibrium-inducing strong parties and empty-winset DDMs. This can clearly be seen for two perfectly correlated policy dimensions in the hypothetical party system displayed in Figure 11.1. The figure shows a five-party system with a decisive structure in which any three parties can form a winning coalition (each of the parties has roughly the same weight). Party positions on one dimension are *perfectly* correlated with positions on the other, with the result that these positions are arrayed along a straight line running diagonally between the two dimensions. Obviously in such circumstances, the same party will be median on both dimensions, so that the dimension-by-dimension median must be an ideal point – in this case the ideal point of Party C. Since three parties are needed to form

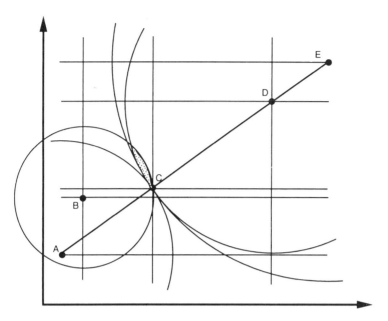

Fig 11.2. A very strong party in a system with imperfectly correlated dimensions

a majority, the only lattice points that are majority-preferred to CC are those within the intersection of the indifference curves through CC of three of the four other parties. This intersection is empty, making the median party very strong.

This phenomenon is general. When party positions on different dimensions are perfectly correlated, and hence arranged in a straight line in a space of any dimensionality, the ideal point of a single party will be at the median position on all dimensions and on the single line representing them. The winset of this median party ideal will be empty (Black, 1958).

As the correlation between party policy positions on different dimensions is reduced from unity, the possibility emerges of a nonempty intersection between the indifference curves of parties on "opposite sides" of the party at the median position on both dimensions, and hence of a nonempty winset for this party ideal point. In Figure 11.2 we have modified the hypothetical party system in Figure 11.1 by pulling Party B off the line joining all party ideals. The correlation between party positions on the two dimensions, although still very high, is now not perfect, though Party C remains at the median on both dimensions. Now that the party ideals are not all on a straight line, the ideal of the median party has a nonempty policy winset. Parties B, D, and E, who between them control a legislative majority, all prefer policies in the shaded area in Figure 11.2. As a result of this, there would now be no majority-rule equilibrium point in the general spatial model, but we note that the lattice winset of the median party ideal remains empty, so that Party C remains very strong and its ideal point remains an equilibrium.

As the correlation between party positions on the two dimensions declines, so too does the probability that the same party will be median on both dimensions and that, even if a party does have an ideal at the median on both dimensions, it will have an empty-lattice winset. As the correlation between party positions approaches zero, so that a party's position on one dimension is totally unrelated to its position on the other dimension, the relevant probabilities will approach those we estimated in Table 5.1, where we assumed that positions on each dimension were completely independent of one another.

We can use simulations to get a sense of the way in which correlations between party positions on different dimensions affect the probabilities of various equilibrium features of the government formation process. The results of some simulations are given in Table 11.2 and displayed in Figure 11.3. These show, for a two-dimensional party space with a range of different decisive structures, the effect of progressively increasing the proportion of the variation in party positions on Dimension 2 that is accounted for by their positions on Dimension 1.[2]

The result of these simulations is striking and, as we shall see from Table 11.3, is not merely the consequence of collapsing a two-dimensional space into a space with an effective dimensionality approaching one. As the correlation between party positions on the two dimensions increases, so too does likelihood of the various equilibrium features identified by our model. The empirical findings in Table 11.1 suggest that, in the case of the

---

[2]This is achieved, for each case, by setting the position of party i on Dimension 1, d_{i1}, to a number randomly drawn from a uniform distribution on the [0,1] interval. Party i's position on Dimension 2, d_{i2}, is a function of both its position on Dimension 1 and a random-error term. Specifically, for each party:

$$d_{i1} = \epsilon_1$$
$$d_{i2} = x \cdot d_{i1} + (1 - x) \cdot \epsilon_2$$

where ϵ_1 and ϵ_2 are numbers randomly drawn from a uniform distribution on the [0,1] interval and x is a parameter with a value between 0 and 1 that can be varied to increase or decrease the contribution of the party's position on Dimension 1 to its position on Dimension 2. If x is set to 1, then $(1 - x)$ is zero and the party's position on Dimension 2 is equal to its position on Dimension 1. If x is set to 0, then $(1 - x)$ is 1 and its position on Dimension 2 is completely uncorrelated with its position on Dimension 1 and is simply another number randomly drawn from a uniform distribution on the [0,1] interval. Indeed, x represents the proportion of the variation in party positions on Dimension 2 that is accounted for by their positions on Dimension 1, and is thus closely analogous to the squared coefficient of correlation between party positions on the two dimensions.

Making the model more realistic

Table 11.2. *The effects of correlations between party positions on two dimensions*

Proportion of variation in positions on Dim 2 accounted for by variation in positions on Dim 1	Frequency of		
	Strong party	Very strong party	Empty-winset DDM
Three party systems (.33, .33, 33)			
1.00	1,000	1,000	1,000
0.99	1,000	990	1,000
0.95	1,000	940	1,000
0.90	999	885	1,000
0.75	989	725	1,000
0.50	962	479	1,000
0.25	910	358	1,000
0.00	899	326	1,000
Four party systems (.40, .20, .20. .20)			
1.00	1,000	1,000	1,000
0.99	1,000	990	1,000
0.95	999	939	1,000
0.90	997	887	994
0.75	971	725	987
0.50	878	474	926
0.25	827	345	890
0.00	786	312	876
Five party systems (.20, .20, .20. .20. .20)			
1.00	1,000	1,000	1,000
0.99	1,000	980	1,000
0.95	998	908	1,000
0.90	993	845	996
0.75	950	595	970
0.50	752	270	867
0.25	668	222	810
0.00	623	186	782
Seven party systems (.14, .14, .14, .14, .14, .14, .14)			
1.00	1,000	1,000	1,000
0.99	1,000	981	1,000
0.95	998	891	999
0.90	989	800	997
0.75	895	508	940
0.50	615	165	752
0.25	481	129	664
0.00	436	113	630

Note: Simulation equations: $d_{i1} = \varepsilon_1$; $d_{i2} = x \cdot d_{i1} + (1-x) \cdot \varepsilon_2$

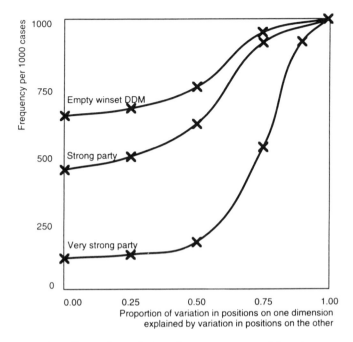

Figure 11.3. The effects of correlations between party positions in a two-dimensional seven-party "egalitarian" system

dimensions studied in the Netherlands at least, around 0.90 of the variation in the position of a party on one dimension can be explained by its position on another. This implies that a value of 0.90 in column 1 is the one we should pay particular attention to in Table 11.2. Column 3 shows that the frequency of very strong parties in random three-party systems increases from 326/1,000, about one-third of all cases, when there is no correlation between policy positions on the two dimensions to 885/1,000, almost 90 percent of all cases, when the correlation between positions on the two dimensions is on the order of 0.90. Even more dramatic effects can be observed in larger party systems. The incidence of very strong parties in the seven-party decisive structure we investigate increases from around 11 percent with no correlation between positions on different dimensions to around 80 percent of all cases in which 90 percent of the variation in one dimension is explained by party positions on the other. Looking at columns 2 and 4 of Table 11.2, we see that the frequencies of both empty-winset DDMs and of strong parties increase as the correlation between policy positions on different dimensions increases, though at a less dramatic rate than for very strong parties.

232

Table 11.3. *The effects of correlations between party positions on four dimensions*

Proportion of variation in positions on Dim 2 accounted for by variation in positions on Dim 1	Frequency of		
	Strong party	Very strong party	Empty-winset DDM
Five party (.20, .20, .20. .20. .20)			
1.00	1,000	1,000	1,000
0.90	959	649	952
0.75	754	251	742
0.50	319	19	281
0.00	150	1	198

Note: Simulation equations:

$$d_{i1} = \varepsilon_1; \quad d_{i2} = x \cdot d_{i1} + (1\text{-}x) \cdot \varepsilon_2; \quad d_{i3} = x \cdot d_{i1} + (1\text{-}x) \cdot \varepsilon_3; \quad d_{i4} = x \cdot d_{i1} + (1\text{-}x) \cdot \varepsilon_4$$

When we look at party systems with more policy dimensions, all of which are correlated to each other, the effects are even more striking. To illustrate this, a set of simulation results based upon a hypothetical five-party, four-dimensional system is given in Table 11.3. Our simulations, which are also displayed in Figure 11.4, suggest that there is a 1 in 1,000 chance of a very strong party in a random four-dimensional, five-party system. When positions on three dimensions are 90 percent explained by their positions on a fourth, the incidence of very strong parties increases to 649/1,000.

The thrust of this analysis is clear. It is simply not the case in the real world that a party's position on one policy dimension is totally unrelated to its positions on at least some other policy dimensions of importance in government formation. Correlations between party positions on different policy dimensions imply that in practice the effective dimensionality of policy spaces may not be as high as it appears to be from the number of substantively different issues that parties may be called to take positions on. When positions on two dimensions are perfectly correlated, taking into account party positions on the second dimension in addition to positions on the first adds no new information to our analysis.

This has the further implication that in practice it is possible to capture almost all of the information contained in party positions on a wide range of different policy dimensions using positions on a small number of "key" policy dimensions. Thus, when we concentrate on a small number

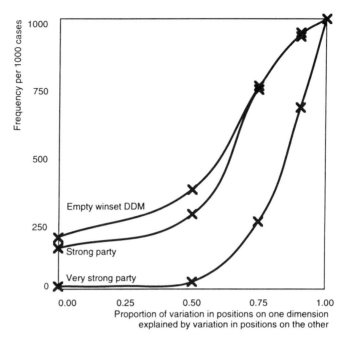

Figure 11.4. The effects of correlations between party positions in a four-dimensional five-party "egalitarian" system

of key dimensions, we are not necessarily assuming that only these dimensions are important in government formation. We are in effect assuming that positions on these dimensions contain all of the information we need to describe the policy space in which government formation takes place, and that the consideration of further dimensions will provide us with no new information on this.

The argument in this section has two important consequences for our overall analysis of making and breaking governments. One of these is substantive and one technical. The technical implication is that, provided we can identify the "right" policy dimensions, we are justified in basing our analyses of particular cases on relatively low-dimensional representations of the policy space in question. Nothing of substance is added to the analysis by using more complicated higher-dimensional representations. In this very important sense, we should not regard low-dimensional representations of the government formation process as in some sense second-best analyses, used only because we did not have the data or the computer firepower to do better. The implication is that, even when the data and the computer firepower are available, low-dimensional operationalizations of the government formation process may capture most of its important features, while having the considerable benefit of being much easier to interpret than those with more dimensions.[3]

The substantive point is that the structure of policy positions in the system has a significant impact on the frequency of our equilibrium concepts, all other things being equal. Our simulations show very clearly that, in a party system of a given size with a policy space of a given dimensional structure, *the likelihood of there being a strong party, or an empty-winset DDM, varies dramatically with the extent to which policy positions are correlated. Other things being equal, if policy positions on one dimension are related to policy positions on another dimension, then the possibilities for equilibrium are much greater.* Conversely, when positions on different dimensions are totally unrelated to one another, the possibilities for equilibrium are much less. Even in the same party system, therefore, changes in the extent to which two issues are perceived to be related to each other alter the possibilities for equilibrium governments.

INTERDEPENDENT PREFERENCES

The matter of correlated issues, which we have just discussed, involves *inter*party relationships among preferences on issues. When preferences on issues are correlated, parties that are extreme on one issue, relative to other parties, will tend to be extreme on other issues as well; parties centrist on one issue will tend to be centrist on others. The matter of interdependent preferences, on the other hand, involves *intra*party relationships among preferences on issues.

Throughout this volume so far, we have operationalized policy preferences in terms of Euclidean distance. A party possesses an ideal point – the policies it would implement if given all the levers of power – and prefers one package of policies to another if and only if the spatial location of the first is closer in distance from its ideal point than the spatial location of the second. Thus, party indifference curves are circles in two dimensions.[4]

An assumed preference structure with these characteristics has a very important property: A party's preferences on one policy dimension are not affected by the policies that are implemented on any other dimension.

---

[3]Reinforcing this point, we should consider the possibility that measurement error in the estimation of positions on two dimensions that are "really" perfectly correlated will create an illusion of two partially independent dimensions where in fact only one exists. The mirror-image probability of measurement error creating the illusion of a single dimension where in fact two exist is obviously much smaller.

[4]They are spheroids in higher dimensions.

Put differently, a party's preferences on a dimension are *independent* of outcomes on other dimensions. To see this, consult any of our diagrams of policy spaces and lattices, say Figure 11.2. In this figure Party B has an ideal point indicated by the black dot. The vertical line passing through this point is Party B's horizontal *reaction function*. This gives the policy that Party B would implement, if it controlled the horizontal dimension, for all possible policies implemented on the vertical dimension. Notice that this reaction function is *constant* – Party B will implement the same policy on the horizontal dimension, regardless of the policy implemented on the vertical dimension. Likewise, the horizontal line passing through B's ideal point in Figure 11.2 is its vertical reaction function, giving the policy it would implement on the vertical dimension as a function of various policies implemented on the horizontal dimension. Again, the reader will note that this is constant. Party B's behavior if it controlled the vertical portfolio is unaffected by what is happening in the horizontal portfolio.

The assumption of Euclidean distance-based preferences such as these is a strong requirement. It embodies two restrictive components. First, it asserts that the party weighs each dimension equally (the *equal salience condition*). This would seem to fly in the face of empirical experience in which conservative parties tend to weigh finance-related policies heavily, social democratic parties care a great deal about domestic welfare policies, classical liberal parties reckon justice-portfolio issues most important, religious parties are often most interested in education matters, rural parties place considerable weight on farm issues, and so on (see Budge and Keman, 1990, for a review of this empirical evidence).

Second, the assumption of distance-based preferences embodies the restriction that what a party does if it controls a specific portfolio is independent of, and unvarying with, who its coalition partners are and what they do in the jurisdiction they control (the *separability condition*). Thus, Party B in our running example will implement the same horizontal policy when it controls that portfolio, whether it also controls the vertical portfolio, whether Party A controls the vertical portfolio, or whether Party C, D, or E controls it. Its actions are separable by dimension because its preferences on each dimension are independent of the policy implemented on the other.

As we noted theoretically in Chapter 2 and empirically in Chapter 7, while the equal-salience condition sounds incredibly restrictive, it turns out to be nonproblematical. If we allow variations in salience – so that Party B in Figure 11.2, say, weighs changes of policy in the horizontal direction much more heavily than changes in the vertical direction – then all of our theoretical results continue to hold. Neither the definition of lattice points nor that of party reaction functions is affected. The reason for this is that a party that differentially weighs dimensions continues to have preferences that satisfy the separability condition.[5] Consequently, all our theoretical propositions continue to hold.

This does not mean that the equal salience condition has no theoretical bite, for it does. In Figure 11.2 the set of cabinets that Party B prefers to some cabinet under investigation, and hence quite possibly the winset of the cabinet under investigation, will depend on whether B's indifference contours are circular or elliptical. Consequently, while the theoretical propositions of Chapter 4 continue to hold, the expected frequency with which various of our analytical concepts (strong party, very strong party, empty-winset DDM, holdout point) occur, both in random and in real data, is almost certain to be affected.[6] In practice, however, as we noted in Chapter 7, we actually ran our empirical analyses in two different ways – with and without differential salience weights – with no substantial effect on our results. So, at least for the range of variation in party-specific salience weights observed in our data, the assumption of equal salience does not do too much injustice to our picture of empirical reality.

Our theoretical model is considerably more dependent on the separability condition, however. Most of our propositions, as well as Kadane's Theorem, will require reworking if this condition is relaxed. To see what is involved, let us think again about a party's jurisdictional reaction functions. In the Euclidean case, such as that shown in Figure 11.2, the reaction functions for each party define our lattice of credible governments. For example, the intersection of Party B's reaction function for the horizontal portfolio (the vertical line through B's ideal point) and Party A's reaction function for the vertical portfolio (the horizontal line through A's ideal point) defines the lattice point BA. Because this point is an intersection of reaction functions, it gives each party's "best response" in the jurisdiction it controls to the action of the other party in the latter's jurisdiction. Thus, in the language of game theory, it is the unique *Nash equilibrium* policy of that cabinet and distribution of portfolios – neither party has an incentive to react differently to the actions of its partner. If, as just discussed, we abandon the equal salience condition, this does not

[5]Differential salience weights imply that the party's preferences may be characterized in terms of *weighted* Euclidean distance (where the weights are the salience weights). Indifference curves are now ellipses in two dimensions (ellipsoids in higher dimensions), with major and minor axes parallel to the dimensions on which the policy space is based. That is, the "egg-shaped" indifference curves are oriented parallel to the dimensions of the issue space, with (somewhat counterintuitively until you think about it) the "long" (or major) axis oriented parallel to the lower-weighted issue and the "short" (or minor) axis parallel to the more salient issue.

[6]We have not explored precisely *how* departures from equal salience would affect these theoretical frequencies. Such an exploration would constitute a sufficiently major undertaking as to take us fairly far afield, though it is certainly not beyond the realm of analytical or computational capacities.

change the lattice because it leaves reaction functions intact – namely, linear curves parallel and perpendicular to the portfolio dimensions.

If, however, we abandon the separability condition, then the lattice is very much affected. In Figure 11.5 we display the preferences of three parties in two dimensions. Party C's preferences are Euclidean – its indifference curves are circles and its reaction functions are lines parallel and perpendicular to the issue dimensions. Parties A and B, however, have nonseparable preferences, reflected in "skewed" elliptical indifference curves and reaction functions that are still linear and still pass through each party's ideal point, but are no longer parallel and perpendicular to the issue dimensions.[7] As before, the intersections of various reaction functions produce the lattice, but it is no longer "orthogonal," as it was in the Euclidean case.

In principle we can conduct an analysis based on skewed lattices in a manner similar to that done for the rectangular lattices analyzed in the first three parts of this book. However, our propositions are no longer established for this case because, in the theoretical proofs of the appendix to Chapter 4, we relied heavily on Kadane's Theorem (which, in turn, assumes separability) and on elementary geometry that no longer is appropriate. Government formation when preferences are nonseparable, therefore, remains an area ripe for further theoretical development.

If this were merely a subject for mathematical generalization, then further theoretical development along the lines suggested would thrill modeling jocks but few others. We believe, however, that substantive gains are involved. Impressionistically, it is our belief that the behavior of individual government parties in their respective portfolio jurisdictions depends on the entire composition of that government.[8] Partly this may reflect varying bargaining situations and strengths – wherein a specific party is in a more powerful position to work its will in the portfolios it controls with one set of partners as compared with another set (about which matter our theory says nothing). But, even if differential bargaining factors do not arise, it still may be the case that parties behave differently, depending on government composition, because policy choice in one jurisdiction spills over into others, affecting optimizing behavior in

[7] To compute these reaction curves, consider Party B's best response on the finance dimension. The reaction function is the locus of points in which different horizontal lines are just tangent to B's elliptical indifference curves. This traces out the tilted vertical line passing through BB. Because it is not perfectly vertical, it follows that what B does on the horizontal issue dimension, if it controlled the finance portfolio, varies with what is done on the foreign affairs issue dimension. B's best response, that is, is no longer constant.

[8] Obviously, this impression entails a counterfactual claim that a party of government would behave differently in a government of different composition. Thus, we cannot provide an empirical basis for our impression. It is just a hunch.

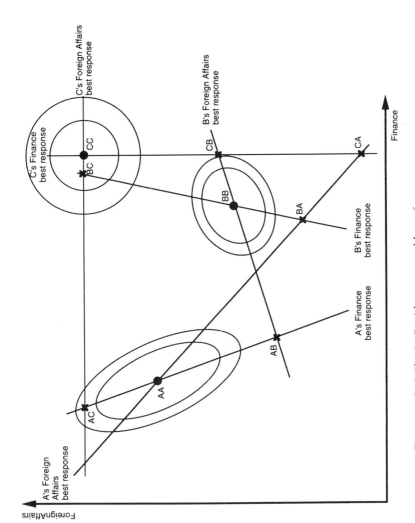

Figure 11.5. A "lattice" with nonseparable preferences

the latter. Thus, we regard theoretical progress on the circumstance of nonseparable preferences to constitute more than a marginal mathematical generalization.

COMPLEX JURISDICTIONS

Throughout the analysis in this volume, we have distinguished between *dimensions* and *jurisdictions*. A dimension has served as a spatial method for characterizing policy outcomes in terms of a single continuously varying parameter. Politicians, parties, voters, and interest groups have preferences defined in terms of this parameter. When conceived of in spatial terms, these preferences may be represented in a geometric fashion as single-peaked curves. In some instances, the parameter is well defined – for example, revenue policy may be measured by the preferred tax rate on incomes or social welfare policy measured by the preferred rate of unemployment benefit. In other instances, the parameter is metaphorical, as when "policy toward the (former) Soviet Union" varies from friendly to hostile. These spatial dimensions, of which there are as many as there are policy issues that require official resolution, constitute the domain of state ministries. That is, a ministerial portfolio consists of authority over a bundle of issue dimensions. We have referred to such bundles as *ministerial jurisdictions*.

In both our modeling and our empirical analyses, we have made two powerful assumptions, each of which bears further scrutiny. First, we have assumed that each policy jurisdiction is unidimensional. In light of the discussion in the first part of this chapter, we may now rephrase this to mean that party preferences across what may be many nominal dimensions of a portfolio are so highly correlated that the effective dimensionality of a portfolio is one. We now relax this assumption, allowing party preferences across the many dimensions of a portfolio to be imperfectly correlated enough that the effective dimensionality of at least some of the jurisdictions is greater than one. In relaxing this assumption, we are moving from a policy space partitioned into simple jurisdictions to one with complex jurisdictions.

Second, we have assumed that the assignment of policy dimensions to cabinet portfolios – a matter of governmental organization – is fixed and exogenous. This is a perfectly serviceable assumption for the purposes of analyzing government formation phenomena, since any theory must take some things as fixed in the short term and/or determined outside the bounds of the model. However, several reasons occur to us for relaxing this stricture. For one thing, organizational matters are inextricably bound up in the authority, and hence the value, of ministerial positions, suggesting that the politics of allocating issues to portfolios is no less important than, and hardly separable from, that of allocating portfolios to parties. For another thing, administrative reorganizations do, in fact, take place. Sometimes these reorganizations are part and parcel of government formation, constituting an element of a coalitional agreement; sometimes they are stimulated by bolts out of the blue, like the energy shocks of the 1970s; sometimes they are the results of long-standing interministerial policy initiatives that are hived off into separate jurisdictions (environmental issues, as well as those of urban regeneration, come to mind). For these reasons and undoubtedly others, it would be useful to incorporate the (re)assignment of policy dimensions to portfolio jurisdictions into our model of government formation. We will take this topic up in Chapter 12; in the present chapter we concentrate our attention on the equilibrium effects of moving from simple (unidimensional) jurisdictions to complex (multidimensional) ones.[9]

We retain the assumption that the party holding a portfolio implements its ideal policies on those dimensions of policy over which it has jurisdiction. Thus imagine a case in which there are two portfolios. The foreign affairs portfolio comprises two policy dimensions (e.g., policy toward the European Union and policy toward the United States); the finance portfolio comprises one dimension (e.g., the preferred share of national income devoted to public spending). If Parties A and B form a government, with Party A taking the foreign affairs portfolio and Party B taking finance, then Party A will be forecast to implement its ideal policies on both foreign policy dimensions under its jurisdiction (i.e., on both EU and U.S.A. policy), while Party B will be forecast to implement its ideal policy on public spending.[10] The principal impact of having complex jurisdictions, for a given policy space, is a *reduction* in the number of lattice points relative to that associated with a simple jurisdictional arrangement. We state this as our first preliminary fact:

The set of lattice points associated with a complex jurisdictional arrangement is a subset of those associated with the simple jurisdictional arrangement consisting of the same policy dimensions.

[9]Formally, we assume that the n spatial dimensions, however they have originated from the politics of a given country, are partitioned into J jurisdictions, where the ith jurisdiction has j_1 dimensions. Obviously, $\Sigma_i \; j_i \; = n$. If $j_i = 1$ for every i, then the jurisdictional structure is *simple* (the theoretical arrangement for most of this book), whereas if $j_i > 1$ for some i, then the structure is *complex*. This distinction concerning jurisdictions first appeared in the context of the committee system of the U.S. Congress. See Shepsle (1979).

[10]That is, this government implements (a_1, a_2, b_3) – the first two components the respective projections from A's ideal and the last component the respective projection from B's ideal.

Some lattice points that arise in the simple jurisdictional arrangement are no longer available when jurisdictions are complex. In the previous example, if each policy dimension was allocated to a separate jurisdiction, then it would be possible to assign the portfolios so that Party A could control policy on the European Union, and Party B control policy on the United States. If both foreign policy dimensions are under the jurisdiction of the same portfolio, then this is not possible. There are now fewer ways of allocating party control over the set of policy dimensions.

Consider a government formation environment with three parties and five policy dimensions. If portfolio jurisdictions are simple, then there will be five jurisdictions and each jurisdiction can be allocated to one of three parties, yielding $3^5 = 243$ lattice points. Imagine now that portfolio jurisdictions are complex in that the first two policy dimensions are in the jurisdiction of one portfolio, the third and fourth dimension are under the jurisdiction of a second portfolio, and the fifth dimension is under the jurisdiction of a third portfolio. There are thus three ways to assign the first two dimensions to a party *as a bundle*, three ways to assign the third and fourth dimensions *again as a bundle*, and three ways to assign the last dimension, yielding only $3^3 = 27$ lattice points, a dramatic reduction in the number of possible portfolio allocations. A number of interesting consequences flow from this.

A second important preliminary fact on which several subsequent results are predicated is the following:

Party ideals are lattice points in all jurisdictional arrangements.

Since the difference between the simple jurisdictional arrangement and any complex arrangement is that some lattice points in the former involve the possibility of dividing authority among parties on dimensions that are bundled together in the latter, such points are no longer feasible in a complex structure. But ideal-point allocations of portfolios – giving every portfolio to the party with the stipulated ideal point – do *not* involve such divided authority, so the ideal points will survive on the lattice under any jurisdictional arrangement involving bundled dimensions. This is no more apparent than in the most extreme of the complex jurisdictional arrangements in which *all* dimensions are part of a single "grand" jurisdiction.[11] In this case, *no* division of authority is feasible; hence, *the only possible cabinets are the party ideals.* Any jurisdictional arrangement other than the grand jurisdiction will have additional lattice points –

---

[11]One may view extreme prime ministerial government as consisting of a single grand jurisdiction. Policy, in this instance, is under control of the prime minister and her party, and ministers are no more than perfectly disciplined agents with no autonomy of their own.

never more than in the simple jurisdictional structure but always including the party ideal points.

These facts about complexity lead to our first two results:

Proposition 11.1: If a party is strong under the simple jurisdictional arrangement, then it is strong under any complex arrangement of jurisdictions covering the same set of policy dimensions.

Proposition 11.2: If a party is very strong under simple jurisdictions, then it remains very strong under any complex jurisdictional arrangement covering the same set of policy dimensions.

From our facts, we know that party ideal points are in the lattice associated with every jurisdictional arrangement, and that the lattice associated with a complex jurisdiction is a version of the simple-jurisdictional lattice, but with fewer points. Consequently, the issue of whether a party is (very) strong is most demanding in the simple jurisdictional scheme of things, since it must satisfy a theoretical criterion against the broadest domain of alternatives. A party that participates in every point in the winset of its ideal will still do so if we remove points from the lattice – the thrust of Proposition 11.1. Likewise, if there are no points in the winset of a party ideal, this will remain true if we remove points from the lattice – the thrust of Proposition 11.2.

From these two propositions, it follows that Proposition 4.2 holds in all complex jurisdictional arrangements:

Proposition 11.3: If a strong party exists in the simple jurisdictional arrangement, then, for every complex jurisdictional arrangement covering the same set of policy dimensions, the equilibrium of the government formation game is either the strong party ideal or an element in its winset.

By precisely the same kind of reasoning, we may state a parallel result for empty-winset DDMs, though with a twist:

Proposition 11.4: If the DDM cabinet has an empty winset in the simple jurisdictional arrangement, then it has an empty winset in any complex jurisdictional arrangement covering the same set of policy dimensions, *providing it remains an element of the complex lattice.*

That some complex jurisdictional arrangements exclude the DDM follows from the fact that different parties may be median on the dimensions that are bundled together into a complex jurisdiction. Complexity requires that the *same* party possess jurisdiction over all the dimensions

243

in a portfolio, thus rendering the DDM allocation of portfolios infeasible in this event.[12]

Additional consequences flow from a consideration of complex jurisdictions, though we will refer to these only briefly. In particular, complex jurisdictional arrangements may *create* a strong party, a very strong party, or an empty-winset DDM, where they did not exist in the arrangement of simple jurisdictions. If the "right" simple-jurisdiction lattice points are eliminated as the lattice shrinks to its complex-jurisdiction version, then the contents of winsets can change in a manner that now supports one of these theoretical properties. (All points that some party cannot veto may be eliminated from the winset of that party's ideal, for example; or all points entirely may be eliminated from the winset of the DDM.) Consequently, under appropriate ceteris paribus provisos, complex jurisdictional arrangements will be associated with a greater frequency of our equilibrium concepts than will simple jurisdictional settings.[13]

Let us conclude this discussion, though promising the reader that we will take it up again in the next chapter when we discuss endogenous jurisdictions and administrative reorganization, with one last point. Jurisdictional complexity is effectively both an *administrative feature of governmental organization* and an *empirical feature of partisan preference correlations* across issues. As an administrative matter, jurisdictions may possess one or more than one issue dimension. But, even if the latter, the jurisdictional arrangement will be effectively simple if preferences across the bundled issues are correlated at a sufficiently high level. The existence of nominally multidimensional jurisdictions is a necessary, but not a sufficient, condition for effective complexity in our lattice of feasible cabinets.

CONCLUSIONS

In Part I of this volume, we made a number of assumptions in order to get our analysis of the making and breaking of governments off the ground. In this chapter we have relaxed some of them. In each case, the reader

[12]We know from the Kadane Theorem as applied to the (simple) lattice, that the DDM is the only point that can possess an empty winset (though it need not). But what happens if, as noted in the text, the DDM is not feasible under some specific set of complex jurisdictions? We have generated examples in which some non-DDM lattice point that survives the "shrinkage" process in going from simple to complex arrangements possesses an empty winset. From our experience in generating examples, we conjecture that the only such points for which it is conceivable that they possess empty winsets are those that are the "most adjacent" to the now vanished DDM. By "most adjacent" we mean that no other point that remains feasible lies "between" the putative empty-winset point and the now vanished DDM.

[13]In principle, and actually without too much practical difficulty, this implication may be verified by simulation techniques very much like those we have employed in previous chapters.

may well have thought at the time we initially made assumptions that we were oversimplifying, and have wondered how much of our analysis would hold if less restrictive assumptions were made. Of the three steps toward greater realism that we have made in this chapter, two, while didactically rather complicated, actually simplify our practical analytical task. The steps that make life simpler concern the existence of correlations in the positions of the various parties on different issue dimensions, and the fact that real cabinet portfolios have jurisdiction over more than one dimension of policy. In each case our analytical burden is lightened by a lowering of the "dimensionality" of the strategic environment of government formation – either by allowing us to consider fewer policy dimensions, or fewer cabinet jurisdictions.

The third step, allowing for policy preferences that make preferred policy on one dimension conditional on actual policy on some other dimension, undoubtedly makes life more complicated for us. Indeed, as we have seen, we cannot be sure that our main theoretical propositions hold in such circumstances. It must be said, however, that any spatial analysis of politics becomes very complicated under such assumptions, and our approach is not at any particular disadvantage in this regard.

Overall, however, the most important lesson from this chapter is that our basic approach can retain its essential character while being revised and extended to accommodate more realistic assumptions. In this sense, what we propose is not so much a single model of the making and breaking of governments, but a style of model that can be extended and adapted to particular circumstances.

12

Government formation, intraparty politics, and administrative reform

As is conventional, we bring this book to a close in the next two chapters by pointing out some directions for future research. The usual way to do this is to throw out a few general ideas in a relatively haphazard manner, some tough and not necessarily very tasty bones for graduate students to get their teeth into. However, we regard one of the great virtues of our approach – indeed its greatest virtue – to be the rich and varied menu of potential applications that it opens up for future research. We do not see these as the boring bits we could not be bothered to chew over ourselves. We see them as the exciting rewards that can be reaped as a result of developing an explicit and we hope realistic model of the government formation process. Accordingly, in this chapter we limit ourselves to three of the most promising potential applications of our approach, and take time to develop them in some detail.

The first application that we consider concerns the interaction of intraparty politics and government formation. We consider the general area of intraparty politics to be one of the most exciting and underdeveloped in the entire literature, since it generates the potential to provide some motivation for the actions of political parties, hitherto unrealistically seen by most theorists as anthropomorphic unitary actors. The second application concerns minority and surplus majority governments. The third and final application of this chapter focuses on administrative reform. Here we raise the prospect of endogenizing the assignment of issues to ministerial portfolios, thereby affecting the very way in which governments go about their business once installed in power. Obviously, each of these applications, developed exhaustively, would represent a major project in its own right. What follows here is the application of our model to a number of specific examples in order to demonstrate the potential of the portfolio allocation approach, and to show that a more systematic modeling exercise would be a very worthwhile endeavor.

GOVERNMENT FORMATION AND
INTRAPARTY POLITICS

Throughout all of the preceding analysis, we have heroically assumed that political parties approach the making and breaking of governments as if they are unitary actors. This assumption has been reviewed in the context of government formation theories by Laver and Schofield (1990). Their overall conclusion was that it is not too unrealistic in the modern European context, given the very high degree of party discipline that is observed among most political parties there. For the sake of clarity of exposition, therefore, we assume for most of this book that parties are unitary actors. Nonetheless, to treat parties as unitary actors in the government formation process is clearly a considerable oversimplification. The reader may recall that in Chapter 2 we promised "two bites" at the treatment of parties. The first bite – parties as unitary actors – has occupied our attention to this point. We now want to take that second bite, namely to begin to consider life within political parties. Furthermore, we believe our approach, unlike many others, is particularly suited to take account of the fact that most political parties are in practice characterized by internal divisions over both party policy and political strategy.

The reason why our approach can be easily adapted to take account of intraparty politics is that the basic actors with which we deal are not political parties, themselves, but important party politicians – cabinet ministers. Indeed it is fundamental to our approach that government ministers have considerable discretion to implement policy within their own jurisdiction. If they have this discretion vis-à-vis politicians from other parties, then they may also have it vis-à-vis politicians from their own party.[1] The argument we developed in support of the assumption of ministerial discretion may apply with equal force in either context. If we assume that parties are unitary actors, then this amounts within our approach to assuming that all ministerial candidates from the same party are forecast to implement the same policies in a particular jurisdiction if given the authority to do so. Given this discretion of ministers to implement their jurisdiction-specific policy preferences, this can only arise because all ministers from the same party have the same policy preferences, which seems rather implausible, or because parties are able to control the actions of their ministers. If we assume a diversity of views within the party, then a deeper consideration of intraparty politics is both appropriate and feasible.

[1]At the very least it is necessary to make explicit the mechanisms by which a party can control the actions of its ministers in their ministries.

Applications, extensions, and conclusions

Political careers and credible policy positions

The role of senior politicians in giving credibility to party policy obviously has very important consequences for the careers of these politicians. If a politician wishes to become a cabinet minister, then he or she must establish a credible policy position, one that is likely to be in demand from the party. It is at this point in our argument that we can finally turn to an issue that we have so far kept on the back burner – the difference between ministerial policy positions that are "sincere" expressions of personal tastes and those that are "strategic" responses to political exigencies.

Obviously, when a fledgling politician joins a political party, little is known about his or her true tastes in matters of public policy – these tastes are private information. If the politician speaks and behaves in a consistent manner, however, he or she may well become associated with a particular position on particular policy dimensions. This may be because the sincere tastes of the person concerned become progressively revealed over time. Or it may be because he or she becomes increasingly committed to particular strategic policy positions, with the political costs of deviating from this position going up the longer and more forcefully it has been advocated in public.

The costs to a politician of deviating from a policy position with which he or she has become publicly associated have to do with reputation and credibility. Credibility is a politician's main stock in trade; it is this which allows him or her to be the useful holder of a cabinet portfolio. If voters and/or party colleagues do not know what policy position a politician is likely to implement if given a free rein, then they will obviously be less disposed to give this person a free rein in the shape of a cabinet portfolio. Indeed, part of the essence of being a senior politician is the association with a set of policy positions believed by others to be either sincere or strategic positions with which the politician has become so inextricably associated that the reputational costs of deviating from them are very high. Otherwise, a politician has no role in underwriting the credibility of a particular party policy position by occupying the relevant portfolio.

The maturing process by which a new politician becomes a seasoned player in the government formation game might be seen as taking place in a sort of political quarantine, a place in the political arena in which he or she can be observed in action by those who are interested, while becoming ever more firmly associated with a particular policy stance. This may be achieved, for example, by a series of junior political appointments to jobs in which the aspiring senior politician cannot do too much damage, and during which he or she must engage in a series of observable actions that either reveal a sincere policy position, or force the person concerned to become irrevocably committed to an insincere position. Such junior

248

ministerial appointments are rather like the jobs given to aspiring Mafia soldiers when they are sent out to do their first piece of serious family business. The job is as much about revealing the perpetrator's inclinations and committing him to it as anything else. It does not really matter for our purposes whether the public expression of policy preference is sincere or not. What matters is that it is costly to turn back from this.

Thus even a politician whose private desires have to do only with getting into office for its own sake must become inextricably associated with a particular policy position in order to fulfill these objectives. At least, this will be true as long as some politicians and/or voters care about the policy consequences of the allocation of cabinet portfolios. Such people will see no point in allocating a portfolio to someone whose behavior in office cannot be predicted.

An important aspect of the process of building credibility within a political party is that, of its essence, this cannot be accomplished instantaneously. The establishment of a credible policy position involves making and keeping promises, and participating in a range of other actions that reveal, or at least commit the actor to, a particular position – something that clearly cannot be done overnight. From the perspective of the making and breaking of governments, the important point about this is that new credible policy positions, in the shape of new senior party politicians, cannot simply be conjured up in response to a particular bargaining situation. *For any particular government formation situation, therefore, the set of credible policy positions that can be underwritten by senior party politicians is fixed before the process starts.* Each party, in effect, has a "stable" of senior politicians, each with a particular reputation, from which it can select a set of ministers to underwrite its participation in cabinet.

Consequently, we treat a political party as a holding company for a cadre of senior politicians, each credibly associated with a particular policy position. These politicians are important resources for the party, since they allow the party to underwrite certain policy positions in government by making the appropriate ministerial appointment.[2] Any diversity in the policy positions associated with senior party politicians allows the party to change its overall policy profile by nominating a different politician as spokesperson for a particular area. Obviously, a party may well have an interest in changing its policy positions for all sorts of reasons to do with the larger electoral game and party competition in general. Of these, the reason that is of direct concern to us in this book is that, by credibly changing its policy position on some dimension, a party may

---

[2]For an empirical discussion of the relationships between cabinet ministers and party colleagues, see de Winter (1993).

advantageously affect its strategic prospects in government formation. This is the matter to which we now turn.

The intraparty politics of interparty competition over government formation

In order to explore the interaction between intraparty politics and interparty competition over government formation in a systematic manner, we need an explicit model of intraparty politics. Developing a rigorous and realistic model of intraparty politics is obviously a massive and daunting task, and something that lies quite outside the scope of this book. In the discussions that follow, therefore, we make some explicit but very basic assumptions concerning intraparty competition, and elaborate the effect of these within our model using a number of simple examples. We leave the development of a formal model of intraparty politics that could form the basis for a series of rigorous theoretical propositions to later work. Our purpose is thus to use our model of government formation to show that, in certain circumstances at least, intraparty politics can have a profound impact on the making and breaking of governments.

In the discussions that follow we assume a model of intraparty politics that makes the smallest possible step from the assumption that parties are unitary actors, since this enables us to make the most careful comparisons between our model predictions with and without the unitary actor assumption. We relax the unitary actor assumption very gently by allowing for the possibility that parties contain a group of ministerial-caliber politicians who do not share the same ideal point. Thus there is not a single policy position available to each party, but a set of positions, depending upon which senior party figures are nominated to which portfolios. The party is not a unitary actor, since there is diversity of policy preferences among its senior politicians. As far as decision making within the party is concerned, however, we still assume a very centralized regime in which all strategic decisions are taken either by a single autocratic leader or within a leadership faction, all members of which do share the same ideal point. Our analysis does not distinguish between these possibilities. Both have the consequence that all strategic decisions (particularly about government formation) are taken in terms of indifference curves centered on the ideal point of the autocratic leader or the one commonly shared by members of the leadership faction.

We analyze the impact of this diversity of party ideal points on three basic matters within a party characterized by a centralized decision-making regime. The first matter is the effect on the making and breaking of governments of having more than one credible policy position available to each party. The second is the effect on cabinet stability of changes

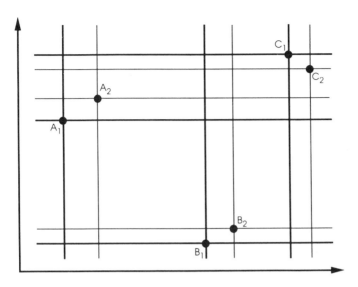

Figure 12.1. A hypothetical three-party system with two factions per party

in the leadership faction of some party. The third concerns the incentives arising out of the government formation process for parties and factions to split and fuse. This latter discussion may give us some insight into the strategic logic that might lead factions to band together into parties, and hence provide an endogenous, model-based interpretation of the logic of parliamentary parties.

The impact of factional diversity on cabinet stability

Figure 12.1 modifies the hypothetical two-dimensional system with three equally weighted parties that has been a running example throughout this book. Instead of three parties with unique ideal points, however, each party now has two factions, each faction having a distinctive ideal point. Parties A, B, and C are made up of factions A_1 and A_2, B_1 and B_2, and C_1 and C_2, respectively, and each faction has the ideal point shown by the black dot next to its name in Figure 12.1. In each case, the leadership faction is subscripted 1 and the nonleadership faction is subscripted 2.

The immediate effect of this is to increase the number of credible portfolio allocations from $3 \times 3 = 9$ to $6 \times 6 = 36$. (The intersections of the *heavy* black lines in Figure 12.1 show the nine credible portfolio allocations that would be available if parties consisted only of their leadership factions – the assumption hitherto made in this book. Intersections

251

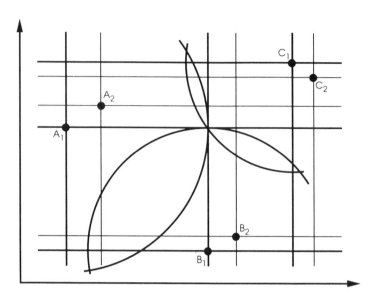

Figure 12.2. The winset of the dimension-by-dimension median (B_1A_1)

involving *lighter* black lines show the additional portfolio allocations generated by introducing a nonleadership faction into each party.) The situation shown in Figure 12.1 is quite different from one with six equally weighted parties, however. Since we have assumed that the leadership faction in each party makes all key strategic decisions, nonleadership factions effectively have no weight in the decisive structure. Thus indifference curves centered on nonleadership-faction ideal points play no part in determining winsets. The situation that arises is almost as if nonleadership factions are political parties with ideal points that generate credible portfolio allocations but control no legislative seats.[3]

This situation can be made clearer by considering Figure 12.2, which shows how the parties feel about the dimension-by-dimension median portfolio allocation B_1A_1. Note once more that we only consider indifference curves centered on the *leadership* faction of each party. Nonleadership factions, having no weight, cannot contribute to the definition of the areas of winsets.

If each party consisted only of its leadership faction, then Figure 12.2 shows that the DDM, B_1A_1, would have an empty winset – no points on what is by now our conventional lattice (i.e., at the intersection of heavy lines in the figure) lie within this winset. Given the existence of non-

[3]Vetoes have a different interpretation, as we shall shortly see when discussing strong parties.

leadership factions, however, we see that there are two credible portfolio allocations in $W(B_1A_1)$. These are A_2B_1 and A_2B_2. The important point to bear in mind here is that it is the very existence of the nonleadership factions in Party A and Party B that makes these credible points possible, *even though these "out" factions have no formal decision-making role whatsoever within their parties.* Our assumption of ministerial discretion is crucial in this context, since it implies that, should ministers from the nonleadership factions in either party be appointed to a portfolio for whatever reason, they will be able to pursue their own ideal points within their own jurisdictions. In other words, for many of the reasons we discussed in Chapter 2 that underpin ministerial discretion generally, we now assume that ministers also have discretion vis-à-vis their own party.

It is important to note that if we make the alternative assumption, that ministers have no discretion vis-à-vis their own party, then we are in effect making the unitary actor assumption, since all ministers from the same party can be made to function in their own departments as if they all had the same "official" party ideal point. The fact that they "really" have distinctive ideal points has no practical effect on the set of credible policy commitments in this case, since ministers from the nonleadership faction cannot use their distinctive ideal points to underwrite a distinctive policy position.

The upshot of this is that points A_2B_1 and A_2B_2 in Figure 12.2 cannot, for example, be made to go away by the leader of Party A banging the table and roaring that the A_2 faction is out of power within the party and will never be allowed to hold a portfolio. This threat can only be made credible by expelling the A_2 faction from Party A entirely (losing their votes and effectively creating a new party) or murdering all of its senior politicians (a strategy that is against the law in every parliamentary democracy of which we are aware). So long as the A_2 (or B_2) faction remains within Party A (or B), the fact remains that Party A (or B) *could* nominate an A_2 (or B_2) minister to the horizontal (or vertical) portfolio if it chose to do so – so that A_2B_1 and A_2B_2 remain credible policy commitments that have an impact on the making and breaking of governments. The very existence of cabinet-caliber politicians in nonleadership factions within their party opens up a range of possibilities otherwise infeasible under a unitary-actor conception of parties.

Some of the most striking effects of taking the factional structure of parties into account can be seen when we look at the impact of factions on the fortunes of strong parties. Figure 12.3 shows how Parties A and C feel about the ideal point of Party B. The intersections of the heavy lines, together with the heavy indifference curves, show that, if only the leadership factions existed for each party, Party B would be a strong party – B_1 can veto both B_1A_1 and B_1C_1, the only intersections of heavy lines in its

253

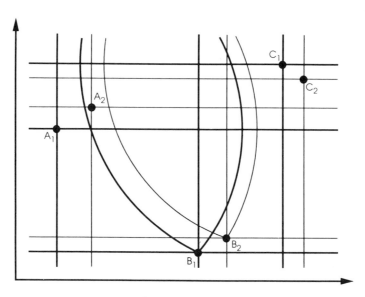

Figure 12.3. The winsets of (B_1B_1) and (B_2B_2)

winset created by the intersection of two heavy indifference curves. (Remember that the heavy lines and indifference curves show the situation when parties have only leadership factions.) Adding the nonleadership factions complicates this situation in a most interesting way.

First, we note that the addition of B_2 – the Party B nonleadership faction – puts new points into the winset of B_1. But we have assumed that the leadership faction of each party makes all important strategic decisions. These decisions include legislative voting – which is why indifference curves generating winsets remain centered on the ideal points of the leadership factions. They also include vetoing government participation – with the effect that the party leadership can veto the cabinet participation of both leadership and nonleadership factions, while the nonleadership faction can veto nothing, even its own participation in the cabinet. In effect, this amounts to an assumption that the party leader can instruct any party member to choose between leaving the party and taking a cabinet seat, even though the leader cannot control how the minister will behave in his or her department in the latter event. In the present example, the fact that the leader of Party B can veto the cabinet participation of leadership and nonleadership factions means that the addition of B_2 does not undermine Party B's position as a strong party.

Second, however, we note that the addition of A_2 – the Party A nonleadership faction – puts another set of potential cabinets into the

254

winset of B_1, this time points over which the leader of Party B has no control. These are A_2A_1, A_2A_2, A_2C_2, and A_2C_1. These potential cabinets *do*, therefore, undermine the position of Party B as a strong party. If Party B were a minority government with policies at B_1B_1, then the leader of Party A could undermine B's position by nominating the appropriate spokespersons to locate Party A's position at, say, A_2A_2.

Note in this particular example that Party B has a response, which is to move key cabinet appointments to the nonleadership faction, so as to shift party policy to B_2B_2. This restores the situation in which the only potential cabinets in the winset of the position of the Party B minority government (now located at the ideal of its nonleadership faction) are those that the leadership of Party B is also in a position to veto. The same effect can in this case be achieved by changing only one portfolio to make a smaller move, to B_1B_2, a position that the Party B leadership faction prefers to B_2B_2. After either possible response by Party B to the strategic move by Party A from A_1A_1 to A_2A_2, no other strategic move can destabilize the position of Party B as a strong party. Knowing this, the leadership of Party B can preempt A's move by awarding the vertical portfolio to the B_2 faction rather than holding on to this itself. We have thus found within our model a clear-cut specific example of a general rationale for the "in" faction of a party to strengthen its overall strategic position by awarding a cabinet portfolio to an "out" faction within the same party.

This example thus highlights a number of aspects of intraparty politics that our model has the potential to throw some light upon. As we have just seen, it first shows one possible reason for party leaders to include internal party opponents in the cabinet. These opponents may underwrite policy positions that forestall potential challenges to the government from the outside. Second, the example shows how developments within opposition parties can have an impact on government policy. In this case, the opening up of a policy rift within Party A between the leadership and nonleadership factions, creating the possibility of A_2A_2, forced the Party B government to respond with a cabinet reshuffle designed to change government policy a little. Third, we note that the leadership of Party B is able to respond precisely because it does not have total control over senior politicians in the nonleadership faction. If the party leadership were utterly autocratic and able to police what all party ministers did in their jurisdictions, then the only credible party policy position is the leadership faction's ideal point. In this event, Party B would not have been able to respond to the strategic move by Party A, and the government might well have fallen. *It is precisely the leader's lack of control over the nonleadership faction that establishes credible alternative policy positions within the party, and thereby gives the leader a viable response to Party A's "outside" move.* In general, a party with a leadership that admits no ideological diversity may find itself in a weaker strategic position than one that admits at least some diversity of ideal points among its senior politicians.

The impact of changes in leadership on government formation

We can also apply our model to the example elaborated in Figures 12.1–12.3 in order to explore the impact on government formation of shifts of leadership within parties. Thus far, we have assumed that the leadership factions are A_1, B_1, and C_1, but we can easily investigate the implications of changes of party leader between factions. In terms of our model, the implication of this change is that the party's weight in the legislature is moved from the ideal point of the old leadership faction to the ideal point of the new one – thus winsets in the legislature are calculated using indifference curves centered on the ideal policy of the new leadership faction. The old leadership faction still has an ideal point that affects government formation but now has no legislative weight.

In this example there are two ideal points to which the leadership of each of the three parties can be attached – a total of eight different configurations of leadership factions in all. Our original example configured the leadership structure in the party system as $A_1B_1C_1$. Alternative configurations, each of which can be investigated using WINSET, are $A_1B_1C_2$ (shifting the leadership of Party C to the C_2 faction) and, as a result of analogous leadership shifts, $A_1B_2C_1$, $A_1B_2C_2$, $A_2B_1C_1$, $A_2B_2C_1$, $A_2B_1C_2$, $A_2B_2C_2$.

In discussing this example, we noted that Party B was a strong party, but also noted that this position depended on the leadership of Party B not using its ideal point, B_1, as party policy, but instead using some other point that involves the participation of the nonleadership faction, B_2, in the cabinet. Figure 12.3 shows that this situation depends crucially on the preferences of Party C, whose leadership faction has an ideal point at C_1, and therefore prefers A_2 to B_1, but B_2 to A_2. If the leadership of Party C changed to C_2, then this situation would be transformed, since the C_2 faction prefers both B_1 and B_2 to A_2. This now allows the leadership of strong Party B to award all portfolios to its own faction and implement its ideal point B_1, provided it can win standoffs with the other parties. If Party B were a sitting minority government, in other words, its leadership might respond to the leadership change in Party C with a reshuffle that took portfolios away from its nonleadership faction, gave them to its leadership faction, and moved government policy to B_1B_1.

This example shows that we can extend our concept of a strong party to take account of factions within parties. Within parties, we can think of "strong factions" and nonstrong factions, where a strong faction is one that can control all cabinet portfolios allocated to the party, given the configuration of the party system. If there is no strong faction in the party, then in equilibrium portfolios must be allocated to different factions within the party. In the current example, when Party C is controlled by the C_1 faction, then strong Party B has no strong faction, because, even in a minority government, B's leadership is forced to cede cabinet portfolios to its nonleadership faction. When Party C is controlled by the C_2 faction, then strong Party B has a strong faction, since leadership faction B_1 can sustain a minority government without ceding portfolios to its nonleadership faction.

The impact of party splits and fusions on government formation

An analysis of the interaction between government formation and intraparty politics also gives us an interpretation of the incentives that parties may have to fuse into larger units, and that factions may have to split away from the parties to which they belong. This in turn gives us some endogenous rationale for the existence of political parties within legislatures. Once more, we can do no more in this context than to hint at the possibilities opened up by our approach, using a pencil-and-paper example to elaborate the basic ideas.

Imagine that, in the example set out in Figure 12.1, each of the six factions identified was an independent political party with one-sixth of the total weight. This means that we would be dealing not only with six ideal points, but also with six sets of indifference curves when determining winsets. Assume that one party may join another by giving its legislative weight to the other party and submitting to its party discipline. Unless they retire, die of natural causes, or are murdered, the senior politicians of both parties remain in business, and their ideal points remain as they were before. What changes is that, where before there were two one-faction parties there is now one two-faction party. The party leadership is controlled by one faction and all of the party's legislative weight is attached to the ideal point of this faction. Hence only one set of indifference curves, rather than two, is used by politicians of both factions to determine the winsets that underpin the making and breaking of governments. Will it ever be rational for one faction to cede its legislative weight and strategic autonomy to another faction in this way? A reanalysis of the example set out in Figures 12.1–12.3 shows that it can indeed be rational to do this in certain circumstances.

If each faction in Figures 12.1–12.3 is treated as an independent party

257

with one-sixth of the weight, then there is no strong party.[4] Consider now the situation that arises if there is a merger between one of the three pairs of adjacent parties, with the leadership of the merged party being given to one or the other faction. There are of course many other potential party mergers but, for the sake of clarity, we do not consider them here since the restricted set of mergers just mentioned allows us to make our main point. We can use WINSET to investigate the effects of each possible merger. When we do so we find that mergers of either the A or the C factions, if all other parties stay independent, do not make much of a strategic difference, but that a merger between the two B factions has a dramatic strategic effect. Whichever faction is given the leadership, Party B becomes a strong party as a result of the merger. This is because the two factions between them can now veto everything in the winset of both B_1 and B_2. If Party B can win standoffs, then there is a strong possibility that cabinet policy will be pulled toward both B_1 and B_2 as a result of the merger, an outcome preferred by both factions. We might thus expect such a merger to take place.

This is not the end of the story, however, though now things get a little complicated and we ask you once more to hold on to your hats! Consider the potential responses of the other parties to the merger of B_1 and B_2 and the consequent creation of a strong Party B. As it happens, there is no single other merger that undermines B's strong-party status. However, if the two A factions merge *and* the two C factions merge *and* Party C's leadership is controlled by C_1, then Party B remains a strong party but cannot implement B_1B_1 in equilibrium. For reasons we discussed in the previous section, it must cede portfolios to B_2. The other parties do not need to coordinate their action in order to achieve this. If the two A factions merge, then this creates an incentive for C_2 to join C_1 under C_1's leadership. Alternatively, if C_2 first joins C_1 under C_1's leadership, then the two A factions have an incentive to merge. Either way, they force Party B away from B_1B_1 to either B_2B_2 or B_1B_2, both of which parties prefer to B_1B_1. Anticipating this, the leadership of Party B may well set policy at B_2B_2 or B_1B_2 rather than B_1B_1, thereby removing the incentives for the other factions to merge.

A pencil-and-paper example such as this can be no more than suggestive. What it does show, however, is that there clearly are circumstances in which it is rational for one party to merge with another. Even if this means giving up strategic autonomy and putting its legislative weight behind a faction with which it disagrees over policy, the net result might nonetheless be to move forecast government policy toward the ideal point of the party giving up its autonomy.

[4]Our identification of Party B as a strong party depended on the party leadership's ability to veto the cabinet participation of both the B_1 and B_2 factions, a power that vanishes when each faction is independent.

Overall: intraparty politics and interparty competition

In the preceding discussions we have done no more than scratch the surface of what seems to us to be potentially some very fruitful avenues for further work. Unlike most other approaches to government formation, the portfolio allocation approach focuses on the role of senior party politicians, rather than on political parties seen as monolithic entities. If there is no diversity of taste within a political party, of course, then it might as well be a unitary actor. If there is some diversity of taste, but the party leadership is so totalitarian that, when party politicians are put in charge of government departments, any deviation from the official party line will be detected and corrected, then once more we in effect have a party that functions as a unitary actor as far as the outside world is concerned. But neither the assumption of homogenous preferences nor that of totalitarian control seems very plausible. We expect political preferences to differ, even within the same party. Our earlier arguments about policy initiation and implementation in government departments continue to imply that ministers will have considerable discretion to implement policies that they prefer. This discretion may well be as effective with regard to the minister's own party as it is vis-à-vis other parties. This implies that we should consider the impact of distinct policy positions within political parties as a first step in relaxing the unitary actor assumption, which is what we have done in the preceding discussions.

What we see is quite fascinating. First, we note that a party can gain useful strategic options from having senior politicians with diverse policy positions and the discretion to do something about these if they get into government. This situation provides the party leadership with the only really credible way to change the party's policy position, which it may want to do for a range of different strategic reasons. By changing ministerial nominees, the party can change the policies it is forecast to implement if it gets into office. This may, for example, allow a nonstrong party to take up a position that renders it strong in circumstances in which this could not be achieved if there were no policy position available to the party other than that of the party leader. We also see how changes in the leadership of an opposition party, by changing the basis of the indifference curves that determine the winsets that in turn determine the government's ability to win confidence votes, can create pressures leading to a cabinet reshuffle to generate a responsive change in government policy. Finally, we see situations in which there may be incentives for two hitherto independent parties to fuse, with one party ceding its strategic autonomy to the other, in the expectation of generating government policy outputs closer to its ideal point than would otherwise be the case.

We note in all of this that, when there is diversity of taste in a party that is not subject to perfect party discipline, then there are important strategic decisions to be made concerning the nomination of ministerial candidates. It then becomes important to know how such nominations are made. There is considerable variation in this, but it is quite common for either the party leader, or a party executive dominated by the leader, to play a central role in such nominations. Indeed, an important role for the party leader is very often to make strategic decisions about ministerial nominations. This in turn means that, within any coalition cabinet, party leaders will have an important strategic role over and above that of a minister.

Very often, of course, the prime minister is also a party leader, and his or her governmental and partisan roles may well interact synergistically.[5] In a single-party cabinet, in fact, it is typically the case that the prime minister is also leader of the only party in government, with the power to deploy all ministerial candidates. In such circumstances, it can be almost impossible to disentangle the governmental and partisan roles of the prime minister. Throughout this volume we have been silent on the distinctive roles of a prime minister. As we have just seen, however, we envision the prime minister to be the leader of one of the government parties, often a strategically advantaged government party, with the authority to exercise decisional powers – nomination of ministers from party ranks, vetoing of governmental participation, and so on – on behalf of the party.

Obviously, the arguments in this section have been based on pencil-and-paper examples. For a full-scale analysis of the interaction between intraparty politics and interparty competition over government formation, we need to specify and analyze a rigorous model. While time and space preclude us from doing this here, we hope that we have shown that the extension of our approach to take account of intraparty politics promises some very intriguing possibilities.

MINORITY, SURPLUS MAJORITY, AND DIVIDED GOVERNMENT

Ever since the publication in 1962 of William Riker's massively influential book, *The Theory of Political Coalitions*, the concept of the *minimal winning coalition* has dominated the government formation literature. A minimal winning coalition contains as many members as are necessary to win, given the operative decision rule, and no more. Thus when the decision rule is majority voting, as it often is in a legislature, a minimal

---

[5]For an empirical discussion of the role of prime ministers and prime ministerial staffs in cabinet government, see Müller, Philipp, and Gerlich (1993); Müller-Rommel (1993).

winning coalition is often referred to as a "bare majority" coalition. If a unanimity decision rule were employed, in contrast, there would be only one minimal winning coalition – the grand coalition of all actors. Associated with the concept of the minimal winning coalition, for obvious reasons, is the concept of a "surplus" coalition member – an actor whose participation in the coalition is not necessary for the coalition to win. If a surplus member leaves the coalition, then it is still winning, according to the decision rule (although as we shall shortly see the coalition may become nonviable for other reasons). In short, a minimal winning coalition contains no surplus member.

Riker's original formulation did not consider the possibility that coalition members were interested in policy as well as the spoils of office, and thus did not take into account the impact on coalition formation of potential policy disagreements between coalition members. However, the Size Principle was readily incorporated into explications of coalition formation that did take policy into account. These almost invariably predicted the smallest possible coalition, subject to some constraint derived from the policy compatibility of coalition members (see, e.g., Axelrod, 1970; de Swaan, 1973; Dodd, 1976).

Above all, however, until very recently theories of coalition government have not taken account of the institutional structure of government formation in parliamentary democracies. As we argued when developing our own model in the opening chapters of this book, this meant that such theories failed to distinguish between legislative and executive coalitions and thus modeled the making and breaking of governments as if parliamentary democracies were governed directly by their legislatures. One consequence of not making this distinction has been that the minimal winning criterion has been applied to government formation, not only to imply that governments will contain no surplus members, but also to imply that they will contain the minimal number of members needed to "win," given the decision rule (usually interpreted as majority voting).

In the case of a government containing "surplus" members, resources controlled by the winning coalition must be given to a member who is not essential to the government's winning status. In the case of a government containing fewer members than required by the decision rule (*minority government*), there must by definition be a majority in opposition that could pass the winning threshold at any time and distribute the spoils of office among its members, but does not do so. Each of these circumstances cannot be accounted for in an analysis of government formation that ignores the relationship between executive and legislative coalitions.

If minority and surplus-majority governments were rare in the real world, then this would not be a serious problem. But the facts are that both minority and surplus-majority governments are really rather com-

261

Applications, extensions, and conclusions

mon (Strom, 1990). Gallagher, Laver, and Mair (1995) classify the types of cabinet that have formed in 15 Western European parliamentary democracies from the end of World War II to 1 January 1993.[6] Among only legislatures in which one party did not win a legislative majority, only 35 percent of the cabinets that formed were minimal winning, 36 percent were minority administrations, and 29 percent contained surplus members. Dividing minority governments into single-party cabinets and coalitions, 12 percent of all cabinets were minority coalitions and 24 percent were single-party minority administrations.

Thus minority and surplus-majority governments are clearly not empirical exceptions – they are part of the mainstream of government formation in parliamentary democracies. And one of the very considerable comparative advantages of our approach is that it provides what we feel is a convincing theoretical account of both minority and surplus-majority cabinets. We begin with minority governments, the analysis of which flows directly from our concept of a strong party, and move on to look at surplus-majority governments.

Minority governments

A minority government is one in which the parties in the cabinet do not between them command a majority of legislative seats. How can such a government survive when it confronts what must by definition be a majority opposition in parliament? On the face of it, the very idea of a minority government seems both implausible and undemocratic. The key to understanding minority government in parliamentary democracies, however, once more lies in the relationship between the legislature and the executive.

In one sense, of course, every cabinet in a parliamentary government system can be seen as a majority administration, since it enjoys the support of a majority of the legislature. Every day that the government is not defeated in a legislative motion of no confidence, it implicitly wins a majority vote of confidence from the legislature. Given the tight party discipline to be found in most parliamentary democracies, this means that, when the parties in cabinet actually control a majority of legislators between them, they have a secure grip on government. The government can only be defeated in the legislature as a result of the withdrawal of one

[6]Switzerland is excluded because, technically, it is not a parliamentary system. The Swiss executive, once installed, cannot be removed by the legislature. Switzerland has been governed for almost all of the postwar era by "magic formula" coalitions that comprise almost all parties, and are thus surplus-majority governments. In addition, by convention, the position of chief executive rotates every year between the government parties so that, formally, there are very many governments in Switzerland, all lasting exactly one year (and almost all being surplus-majority governments). Special features of the Swiss case thus would seriously distort the overall empirical figures.

262

of the government parties or a collapse of party discipline. However, if the party or parties in cabinet do not control a legislative majority, then this does not necessarily mean that the legislature will throw out the government and replace it with something else. In order for this to happen, as we have seen when we set out to model the government formation process explicitly, some legislative majority must agree on an alternative government that it prefers to the incumbent administration. If politics were just about the spoils of office, then it is hard to see why a majority opposition would not always seize control when it had the opportunity to do so and distribute the spoils among its members. If, in contrast, politicians seek to implement distinctive policies, an assumption that is fundamental to our approach, then they will take into account the forecast policy position of any prospective government and compare this with the status quo. Our analysis has already shown that, taking portfolio allocations into account, it is quite possible for there to be *no alternative government with a forecast policy position that is preferred to the status quo by a legislative majority* (the status quo may have an empty winset). *This may be true whether or not the participants in the status quo cabinet control a legislative majority.*

Intuitively, this situation can arise if the status quo cabinet has a relatively central policy position, while the opposition to it is divided between parties at opposite ends of the policy spectrum. In such circumstances a minority cabinet can be quite stable, since the opposition parties cannot agree on anything that they prefer to it. They possess sufficient weight, but lack a shared purpose. Our model enables us to be much more systematic about this intuition.

Consider first the situation in which there is a very strong party, a party with an ideal point such that there is no alternative government preferred by a majority to one that gives the very strong party all portfolios. According to Propositions 4.1 and 4.2, combined into Implication 2 of Chapter 7, when there is a very strong party, the equilibrium in the government formation process is a cabinet in which all key portfolios are allocated to it. Another way of putting this is that the very strong party is in a position to form a minority government on its own. Implication 2 thus describes situations – when no party wins an overall majority but there is a very strong party – *in which our model explicitly forecasts the formation of a minority government and identifies which party will form it.*[7]

[7]We should pause here for a brief but important aside. As we saw in the previous chapter when discussing the effects of actors having correlated positions on different policy dimensions, it is neither practicable nor realistic to analyze government formation in a very high-dimensional space, with at least one dimension for every cabinet portfolio. We also saw that, given the high correlations between positions on different policy dimensions that we do observe in practice, there is not much to be lost, and quite a lot to be gained, from concentrating upon a limited number of key portfolios.

Applications, extensions, and conclusions

Far from treating minority governments as anomalous, our model contains an explicit account of this phenomenon. For one thing, minority governments will arise when there is a very strong party with no overall majority. Indeed, one intuitive way of understanding the bargaining power of a very strong party is that it is capable of forming an equilibrium minority government on its own, and thus does not need to take into account the views of other parties. The very strong party's ability to go it alone is its essential source of strength. We investigated this matter empirically in Chapter 8 when we evaluated Implication 2, which makes the same statement in formal terms. The results of this investigation were very encouraging, particularly since in this context the model-based empirical implication makes a very precise prediction, and thus has plenty of opportunity to get it wrong. Our model performed 14 times better than the null hypothesis, and was right for 70 percent of the time for which it could have been right during the postwar era, across the range of countries that we studied. There is thus no question at all about the strength of the empirical relationship between very strong parties and minority government.

Consider now a *merely* strong party – a party whose ideal point does not have an empty winset, although this winset does contain only portfolio allocations in which the strong party participates. Another way of putting this is that a merely strong party participates in every cabinet that is preferred by a legislative majority to a minority cabinet in which the strong party gets all portfolios, and thus has the ability to veto credible alternatives to this minority cabinet. We have also seen that the ability of a merely strong party to form a minority cabinet depends critically on its ability to win strategic standoffs with other parties. Without information on the bargaining resolve of particular strong parties, we cannot say whether a minority government is likely. Nonetheless, what we can say is that merely strong parties, if they can win standoffs, are in a strategic position to form single party minority governments in which they take all key portfolios. Once more our approach provides a clear logic for minority government. Evaluating this in empirical terms, however, requires systematic judgments about the ability of strong parties to win standoffs,

We thus expect government formation to be primarily concerned with the allocation of these key portfolios. This has the implication that our predictions of minority governments, strictly, are predictions that a party or coalition with less than a majority of seats will receive all *key* portfolios. We are silent on the allocation of other portfolios, though we conjecture that, since these relate to policy dimensions that are highly correlated to one or more key policy dimensions, they will be allocated to parties already receiving key portfolios. What is quite clear, however, is that, when there is a very strong party, our model implies that it will certainly get all key portfolios and is more likely to get every portfolio. Schofield's analysis of core parties in government formation, discussed in Chapter 5, could also be construed as identifying the core party as a potential *single-party* minority cabinet (although, as we saw, Schofield himself is silent on government participation as opposed to government policy).

264

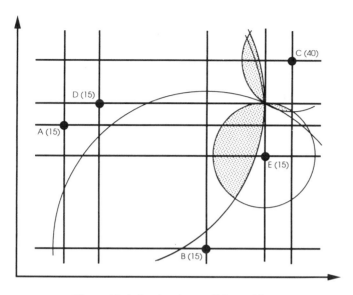

Figure 12.4. A minority coalition cabinet

information on which we do not at present have access, but which never-theless provides a fruitful avenue for future work.

Both very strong parties and merely strong parties are thus in a strategic position to form single-party minority governments in which they take all key portfolios. As we saw, two-thirds of all minority governments are indeed based on single-party cabinets, in which one party in a distin-guished bargaining position takes all key portfolios. One-third of all minor-ity governments, however, are coalitions. Our model also shows how mi-nority *coalitions* can form equilibrium governments. Consider the exam-ple in Figure 12.4. Five parties share 100 seats between them as indicated in the figure. The dimension-by-dimension median cabinet is ED, and the indifference curves through ED show that this cabinet has an empty lattice winset (the shaded area in the figure). If this cabinet were the status quo, for whatever reason, then Proposition 4.1 tells us that this cabinet would remain in equilibrium, despite controlling only a minority of legislative seats. There is no strong party in this example,[8] and thus no potential single-party minority cabinet is identified by our model. But a clear implica-tion of Proposition 4.1 is that ED is an equilibrium minority coalition.

Obviously, we once more have some way to go before we have a

[8]E is the only candidate for being a strong party (since EE is clearly preferred by both E and C to DD), but both BD and BC, in which E does not participate, are majority-preferred to EE.

rigorous and comprehensive model of minority government, and we intend to address this matter in future work. Nonetheless, the examples we have provided here make it clear that the portfolio allocation approach not only offers explicit and precise predictions about minority government in certain circumstances (when there is a very strong party, for instance), but also offers an explicit theoretical framework that can address the formation and stability of minority governments in quite a wide range of strategic situations.

Surplus majority governments

We have just seen that the requirement of majority support in the legislature does not rule out the possibility of an equilibrium government comprising parties that between them control only a minority of legislative seats. From the same logic it follows that controlling a majority of legislative seats is not always sufficient for an equilibrium government. Indeed, we make the even stronger claim that there are circumstances in which *surplus* coalition partners (at least in the conventional sense of this term in the literature) are required for a cabinet to be in equilibrium. This is because a party may contribute something other than legislative weight to an equilibrium cabinet. In particular, every party has senior politicians who can be given cabinet portfolios so as to underwrite a particular government policy position, *even though the party's seats are not needed for the government's majority.* This is a particular implication of a more general phenomenon – a party that is an essential member of no winning coalition (a "dummy" party) can nonetheless have a profound impact on government formation.

To get a sense of this consider the example in Figure 12.5. Imagine first that there were only three parties in the legislature – A, B, and C – and each party controlled 33 seats. In this situation, the set of portfolio allocations is shown by the intersections of the heavy black lines. The indifference curves of Parties A and C through BB show that Party B is a strong party – it participates in both BA and BC, the two points in the winset of BB. Now imagine that Party D is added to the system with only one seat. D is clearly a dummy party, in the sense that it contributes essential weight to no legislative majority. Another way of thinking of this is that we do not need to consider its indifference curves when constructing winsets – the addition of information about D's preferences never modifies a winset. Despite this, Party D is clearly not irrelevant to the government formation process, since its very presence renders Party B no longer strong – generating two portfolio allocations (DD and DA) that are in the winset of BB but in which B does not participate. The possibility of bringing a Party D minister into the cabinet undermines Party B's ability

266

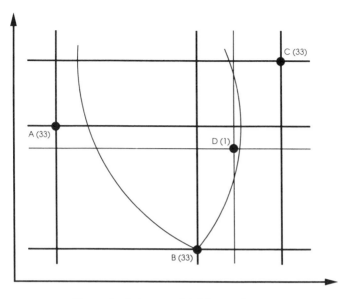

Figure 12.5. A powerful "dummy" party

to hold out for its ideal point and provides a stick for Parties A and C to beat B over the head with in a realistic attempt to get a government they both prefer to BB. Our approach thus implies that dummy parties may not be dummies at all, and we should give attention to all legislative parties, whatever their position in the decisive structure. Just because a party does not contribute to a government's majority does not mean that there is no role for it in government.

Our model allows us to extend this account of the role of dummy parties to the participation of surplus parties more generally in majority governments. As it happens, this can only happen when three or more dimensions of policy are important.[9] (In the example in Figure 12.5, both DD and DA are minority governments. Thus, while D is a dummy party, it is not surplus to some majority.) The logic of surplus parties only cuts in when there is at least a three-party coalition, at least two members of

[9]This is because, when only two dimensions of policy are important, there cannot be a surplus party according to our approach. In any legislature in which no party wins a majority and only two dimensions of policy are important, either both key portfolios will go to the same party, or to different parties. If they go to the same party, this obviously cannot be a surplus party. If they go to different parties, the only way in which one can be a surplus party is if one party has a legislative majority – a contradiction. If one party wins a legislative majority, then all other parties are by definition surplus parties. However, the majority party is, trivially according to our approach, very strong and will take all portfolios rather than allocate any to another party.

267

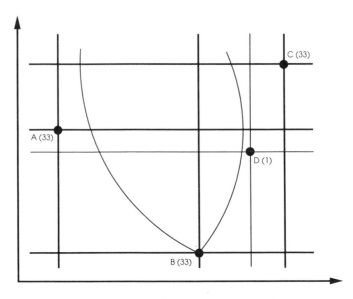

Figure 12.6. Party D is a "surplus" party needed by the government

which are needed for the government's majority, but one or more of which is not. How can this happen? We can't easily squash a three-dimensional example onto a two-dimensional page, but consider a modification of the example in Figure 12.5. A two-dimensional version of this is shown in Figure 12.6, which is identical to Figure 12.5 except that the position of Party D has been moved out of the winset of BB, rendering B a strong party.

Now imagine a third dimension leaping out of the page in your direction, on which Party A is the median party. The positions of the other parties mean that Party B remains a strong party; however, there are a number of points in its winset, some involving the participation of Party D. Proposition 4.2 tells us that the equilibrium government will be in the winset of BB. Depending on specific details, this could well be a government consisting of Parties A, B, and D. In this way, Party D may participate in an equilibrium government, despite its legislative seats being surplus to that government's majority. What Party D contributes to the government equilibrium is a policy position that generates lattice points in the winset of the strong party, which Proposition 4.2 tells us are potential equilibrium governments. While Party D is numerically surplus to requirements, its policy position makes it strategically essential to certain governments.

Once more, we can only hint at the possibilities opened up by our model in a limited discussion such as this. Clearly, we need a more systematic and explicit account of surplus majority government. But the preceding examples serve to show that such an account can in principle be provided within the framework of the portfolio allocation approach, which in no sense sees surplus majorities as pathological.

Divided government

The portfolio allocation approach, as we have just seen, throws light on phenomena regarded by some as anomalous, even pathological. In addition, as we now show, it highlights unexpected similarities in legislative–executive relations on opposite sides of the Atlantic. Divided government is a condition associated with the post-1945 United States, not a parliamentary government system of course. It involves one party controlling a majority in either or both legislative chambers, while the other major party controls the executive and, perhaps, a majority in one legislative chamber. At both the national level and in many states, as Fiorina (1991) points out, divided government has increasingly become the norm in the United States – the usual pattern is a Republican executive pitted against one or more legislative houses controlled by the Democrats. The election of 1992 which put the Democrats in control of the executive and both legislative branches at the national level, is regarded as an exception to the rule. This election notwithstanding, however, divided government is regarded as an important feature of the package of institutions that make America "exceptional" (Laver and Shepsle, 1991).

The portfolio allocation approach suggests otherwise. It does so by forcing us to focus explicitly on just what it means to describe a system of government as "divided." In the American context this means that some party controls the executive but lacks a legislative majority. But, as we have just seen, precisely this can also happen in a parliamentary democracy, *once we distinguish the executive from its legislative support coalition.* When the executive does not control a legislative majority in a parliamentary democracy, minority government is, in effect, divided government. There are two variants. The one most like the U.S. case entails a single-party executive that lacks a parliamentary majority – about one-quarter of all postwar Western European governments fall into this category. A second variant, occurring about half as often, involves minority coalition governments.

The sources of divided government differ on different sides of the Atlantic. In the United States, the source is *constitutional.* It derives from the fact that the connection between executive and legislative elections, and hence the partisan composition of the different branches of government, is quite deliberately attenuated by constitutional provisions relating to the constituencies used for elections, to their timing, and to the term lengths of executives and legislators. There is also a constitutionally

269

mandated separation of institutional powers. Given a particular election result, therefore, divided government in the United States is constitutionally determined.

The sources of divided government in European parliamentary democracies, in contrast, are *strategic* as well as constitutional. European constitutions tend to emphasize proportional representation (PR). Actual voting patterns under PR normally deny an overall legislative majority to any one party. Furthermore, while there is almost by definition no rigid separation of powers between legislature and executive in a parliamentary democracy, it is nonetheless the case that the institutions of executive decision making can be found away from the legislature, in government departments and the cabinet chamber. So, as in the United States, constitutional and institutional provisions create the possibility of divided government in Europe.

However, and quite unlike the situation in the United States, a given election result does not automatically create a situation of divided government in Europe. As we have seen, an election result may well create a situation in which the equilibrium executive does not control a legislative majority but, if such a government forms, this is the result of strategic choices made by legislators, not of "hard-wired" constitutional and/or institutional provisions. European legislators, in this sense, always choose strategically to have divided (minority) government, rather than having it forced upon them by a combination of the constitution and the electorate, as in the United States. But precisely because it is *not* hard-wired in Europe, divided government there is exposed to potentially destabilizing shocks (see Chapter 10). Thus, divided governments in Europe may come and go, whereas divided governments in America remain divided, at least until the next election.

Minority, surplus majority, and divided government

Taking our discussions of minority, surplus-majority, and divided government together, two general points emerge very clearly. The first is that modeling the government formation process in a way that takes explicit notice of the relationship between legislature and executive in parliamentary democracies allows us to account for phenomena that would otherwise be considered anomalous. Both minority and surplus-majority governments are common, and cannot be accounted for in a satisfactory way by theoretical accounts that elide the distinction between legislative and executive coalitions. The possibility of divided government, as well, is a product of this institutional differentiation. This seems to us to be evidence of the need to consider such a distinction in any model of government formation.

270

Government formation, intraparty politics, and reform

The second general point is that both surplus and minority governments are very hard to explain unless the policy positions of parties play a serious role in government formation. If parties are concerned only to get into office regardless of policy, then governments that are not minimal-winning appear anomalous. This seems to us to be evidence, notwithstanding some popular cynicism about politicians who would sell their very souls for a seat at the cabinet table, that policy is indeed important in the making and breaking of governments. Nothing else convincingly explains the prevalence of minority, surplus-majority, and divided governments.

ADMINISTRATIVE STRUCTURE AND REFORM

The final substantive topic to be treated in this chapter involves the administrative structure of parliamentary governments. As we observed in Chapter 11, our portfolio allocation approach has evolved from the conventional spatial model of Black and Downs. Its main innovation is the partitioning of an undifferentiated space of policy dimensions into a set of policy jurisdictions, each corresponding to a cabinet portfolio. This partition represents the administrative structure of government. It permits the exercise of jurisdiction-specific authority by a minister who can influence outputs on policy dimensions under the control of his or her portfolio. In most of this volume we treat these policy jurisdictions as unidimensional, in the sense either that each contains a single policy dimension or that preferences on a set of dimensions in some jurisdiction are so highly intercorrelated as to produce effective unidimensionality. Chapter 11 raised the possibility of complex jurisdictions containing a set of policy dimensions not highly correlated with one another, and established that many of our theoretical results continue to hold in such circumstances.

Whether portfolio jurisdictions are simple or complex, we have consistently taken the administrative structure to be fixed exogenously, before government formation begins. Indeed, we have implicitly assumed that this structure remains unchanged for all time, so that the rational foresight of actors about government formation revolves only around the assignment of portfolios to parties and not around the assignment of issues to portfolios. The assumption of an exogenously fixed partition of issues into policy jurisdictions is but a minor variation on conventions surrounding the standard spatial model (in which the issue space is taken as exogenously given), so that theoretical apologies are not required. Moreover, the administrative structure of the state changes only very occasionally in the real world. For both of these reasons, our assumption of exogenous portfolio definition will probably have raised few eyebrows among those readers who noticed it.

271

Nevertheless, a multidimensional issue space may in practice be partitioned into a set of portfolio jurisdictions in many different ways. Trade-related issues, for example, may be part of the jurisdiction of the finance portfolio or that of foreign affairs. Long-term economic planning may also fall into the jurisdiction of finance or, alternatively, be hived off into a separate Ministry of Economic Affairs. Issues relating to nuclear power could easily find their way into the jurisdictions of foreign affairs, defense, energy, or environment ministries. In short, there are "degrees of freedom" in structuring the administrative state. Some of this freedom is clearly exercised in the in-fighting over bureaucratic "turf" often witnessed in day-to-day politics. Jurisdiction over issues is claimed by one government department or another, with successful claims often constituting precedents for more-or-less permanent departmental property rights over the issue. But fights among civil servants are surely not the whole story since, as we shortly show, the particular allocation of issues to portfolio jurisdictions that is eventually adopted has considerable strategic impact on the making and breaking of governments.[10]

Once we abandon the notion that portfolios are defined exogenously, we are free to contemplate not only alternative jurisdictional arrangements, but also alternative rationales for these. Here we consider the possibility that the allocation of issues to portfolio jurisdictions is an intrinsic part of the government formation process. A considerable advantage of our model is that it allows us to explore this possibility. For any possible jurisdictional arrangement, we can use the model to deduce a cabinet equilibrium (if one exists) in the subsequent government formation game. Different jurisdictional arrangements may well generate different government equilibriums, and hence different eventual policy outputs. This in turn implies that policy-oriented politicians, exercising rational foresight, will have distinct instrumental preferences about jurisdictional arrangements and may well attempt to influence these jurisdictions, if this is possible, as part of the government formation process.

Imagine three parties, none of which controls a majority of legislative seats, whose positions on three policy dimensions are given in Table 12.1 (lower numbers indicate a more left-wing position and higher numbers a more right-wing one). In this illustration, party positions on the three issues are uncorrelated. If the issues comprise three unidimensional jurisdictions – the assumption for most of this book – then the DDM portfolio allocation is BAC, involving a grand coalition of all parties, and has an empty winset.

In addition to the partition of the three policy dimensions into three

[10]Jurisdictional arrangements for ministries share many of the features of committee jurisdictions in the U.S. Congress. The political infighting according to which the latter are determined and altered is described in a recent paper by King (1994).

Table 12.1. *Hypothetical positions of three parties on three policy dimensions*

	Position on dimension		
Party	X	Y	Z
Party A	1	2	3
Party B	2	3	1
Party C	3	1	2

Table 12.2. *Hypothetical positions of four parties on three policy dimensions*

	Position on policy dimension			
Party	Seats	Taxes	Social	Environmental
A (Lib)	20	9	2	9
B (Con)	40	8	9	8
C (SD)	20	4	5	5
D (Green)	20	3	3	3

simple jurisdictions, which we write [(X), (Y), (Z)], there are four complex jurisdictional arrangements. First, there is the "grand jurisdiction," in which all issues are under the jurisdiction of a single portfolio, [(X, Y, Z)]. In addition, there are three arrangements putting two dimensions under the jurisdiction of one portfolio, and the remaining dimension under the jurisdiction of another: [(X), (Y, Z)], [(Y), (X, Z)], and [(Z), (X, Y)]. In principle, each of these may be associated with different equilibrium cabinets. Hence policy-oriented parties will have preferences over different jurisdictional arrangements.

To see how this may actually transpire, consider the more elaborate hypothetical party system shown in Table 12.2. This has four parties and three salient policy dimensions, where A is a laissez-faire liberal party, B a conservative party, C a social democratic party, and D a green party.

273

Applications, extensions, and conclusions

We can now use WINSET to investigate cabinet equilibriums in this example under all possible jurisdictional arrangements.

Simple jurisdictions

If each policy is hived off into its own portfolio, then no party is strong and the DDM portfolio allocation, [(Tax), (Soc), (Env)] = [(B), (C), (B)], has an empty winset. From Proposition 4.1, BCB is a cabinet equilibrium in the government formation game with this jurisdictional structure.

Grand jurisdiction

If all policies are combined into a single jurisdiction, [(Tax, Soc, Env)], then, as noted in our discussion of complexity in Chapter 11, the only lattice points are AAA, BBB, CCC, and DDD – the party ideals. WINSET establishes that Party C is very strong; no majority prefers any other ideal point to it, so that CCC is the cabinet equilibrium association with this jurisdictional arrangement.

Other complex jurisdictions

The remaining complex jurisdictional arrangements are [(Tax, Soc), (Env)], [(Tax), (Soc, Env)], and [(Tax, Env), (Soc)]. In no case is there a strong party, but in each case there is an empty-winset equilibrium – [(CC), (B)], [(B), (CC)], and [(BB), (C)], respectively.[11]

Choosing a jurisdictional arrangement

The equilibrium cabinets associated with particular jurisdictional arrangements are each associated with a common-knowledge policy forecast, if one assumes each party implements its ideal point in jurisdictions over which it has control. Policy forecasts for this example are given in Table 12.3.

From our discussion in Chapter 11, we know that the lattice derived from the simple jurisdictional structure (Structure 1 in Table 12.3) has the full complement of lattice points. Since BCB has an empty winset in that structure, it will, according to Proposition 11.4, remain an empty-winset

---

[11]Note that the DDM portfolio allocation, BCB, is *not* a lattice point in a complex jurisdiction in which social policy is bundled together with either of the other policies. As we conjectured in Chapter 11, however, there are in fact empty-winset points in this example – in each case an "adjacent" point that survives the reduction in the number of lattice points. In the one case in which the simple-jurisdiction DDM survives the complexity transformation, [(Tax, Env), (Soc)], the DDM continues as the empty-winset point.

Table 12.3. *Policy forecasts for equilibrium cabinets under different jurisdictional arrangements*

			Policy forecast		
Jurisdiction Structure	t s e	Tax	Soc	Env
1. [(Tax), (Soc), (Env)]	BCB	8	5	8
2. [(Tax, Soc, Env)]	CCC	4	5	5
3. [(Tax, Soc), (Env)]	CCB	4	5	8
4. [(Tax), (Soc, Env)]	BCC	8	5	5
5. [(Tax, Env), (Soc)]	BCB	8	5	8

point in any jurisdictional structure in which it survives. That is, so long as neither tax nor environmental authority is bundled together with authority over social policy – and one or the other is indeed bundled together with social policy in Structures 2, 3, and 4 – then BCB will survive the shrinkage of the lattice and remain an empty-winset point, majority-preferred to all others. This means that, in expressing preferences over alternative jurisdictional structures, a legislative majority prefers either Structure 1 or Structure 5 to any other structure.

It is at least in principle possible to add a process of allocating policy dimensions to jurisdictions at the beginning government formation game set out in Figure 3.1. This in effect makes the choice of jurisdictional arrangement an endogenous aspect of government formation. Assuming no one party can veto the implementation of any given jurisdictional structure *as a whole* (as opposed to the allocation of particular portfolios to a party in particular jurisdictional structures, which our model assumes that party *can* veto), note that the policy forecast associated with either a simple jurisdictional structure or the complex structure packaging tax and environment policy authority together is majority-preferred to any other. Whichever of these two majority-preferred jurisdictional arrangements is in practice selected, the outcome is a government that implements the policy point BCB.[12]

[12]It is interesting to speculate on the relative virtues of Structures 1 and 5, each of which would produce the same empty-winset DDM policy, BCB. Though identical in terms of policy, they are quite different in terms of the number of seats around the cabinet table and, consequently, the impact on *intraparty* politics. A prospective Party B minister of taxes and environment would be loathe to partition that jurisdiction further, while an up-and-coming Party B politician might happily look forward to

Applications, extensions, and conclusions

We have done no more in this section than illustrate ways in which the administrative structure of a parliamentary democracy affects government formation and, given rational foresight and backward induction on the part of actors, how government formation affects the administrative structure of the state. It is clear that these things are intimately related in theory. In practice, too, squabbles over jurisdictional turf are constant features of political life. What we hope to have established, if only by way of some persuasive examples, is that partisan policy preferences may be at the root of these power struggles. The portfolio allocation approach, in principle at least, provides a useful analytical tool with which to investigate them.

CONCLUSIONS

Our main intention in this chapter has been to put our model through its paces in an attempt to see whether it could throw light on a number of interesting phenomena that are only beginning to be discussed in the literature on government formation. We have proceeded by analyzing specific examples rather than by developing explicit models of these phenomena. Our intention, as we stated at the outset, has been to whet the reader's appetite by demonstrating the potential of the portfolio allocation approach, rather than to have the last word on these matters. What we hope to have shown above all, however, whether we are dealing with intraparty politics, minority government, or administrative reform, is the potentially huge analytical payoff to be gained from having a systematic model of government formation in parliamentary democracies.

being minister of the environment. Who prevails under these circumstances depends on many things involving how party leaders handle intraparty rivalries of this sort. An alternative and perhaps more plausible sequence of events would have the jurisdictional structure settled *after* a government had been chosen. Whatever the status quo partition might have been, rational actors engaged in government selection could anticipate the subsequent administrative reforms that a newly installed government would impose. Thus, parties B and C in the preceding illustration, whatever the existing jurisdictions might be, could be expected to adjust policy responsibilities in order to enable equilibrium policies to be implemented.

276

13

Governments and parliaments

When we first began collaborating on a strategic spatial model of parliamentary government in 1988, we were struck by two patterns in the professional literature. In the United States, theories of political coalitions, close to the mainstream in the 1960s largely due to the impact of Riker's important book (Riker, 1962), had been relegated to a quiet tributary by the mid-1970s. The American modeling community had turned its attention to institutionally enriched models, with special emphasis given to the institutions of the U.S. legislature and executive. On the other side of the Atlantic, coalition theory was alive and well, principally as an empirical enterprise applied to European parliamentary democracies.[1] This apparent divergence in interest and emphasis stimulated us to think about how to apply institutional models of politics to the making and breaking of European coalition governments. It was our strong belief that there was nothing in principle distinctively "American" about such institutional models, despite the fact that in practice such models had been applied primarily to American institutions. The result is the present volume, an exercise in intellectual and geographical arbitrage.

Part I of this book lays out the institutional context of government formation in parliamentary democracies. In any parliamentary democracy, there is always an incumbent government – by which we mean a cabinet seen as an allocation of ministerial portfolios. The incumbent government remains in place until supplanted by some alternative. Parliamentary parties with policy preferences, bargaining reputations, a stable of senior politicians and a strategic weight determined by their proportion of legislative seats, continually assess and reassess the sitting cabinet. In effect they sit in the legislature as a permanent tribunal on the fate of

[1]Much of this work is reviewed in Laver and Schofield (1990). We should credit Schofield as one of the very few formal theorists who has maintained a consistent interest, over more than two decades, in theories of coalition formation and their empirical application.

the administration; they are continuously concerned with the making and breaking of governments. The equilibrium government generated as an outcome of this process must survive in a relentless stream of politically relevant events. Some of these, scheduled elections for example, are anticipated. Many of them are not. Such unanticipated events – deaths, scandals, unexpected upturns and downturns in the economy, international episodes – provide the shocks and surprises that give texture to domestic politics. Precisely because they cannot be foreseen, however, particular shocks cannot be taken into account by party politicians involved in government formation.[2] Politicians, and those of us who model their activities, must therefore focus on what is regular and anticipated.

In Part II we do just this. We formulate a strategic model of a government formation process that unfolds in continuous real time. In this game a sitting cabinet is constantly compared by legislative parties with the credible alternatives to it. In order to gain and retain office, a putative replacement for the status quo cabinet must obtain the consent of proposed members of the new cabinet, as well as the (explicit or implicit) approval of a parliamentary majority. If no such replacement can overcome these obstacles, then the incumbent cabinet remains in equilibrium. If on the other hand there is a successful replacement, then this new government is in turn subjected to continual reappraisal from the very moment it takes office. The making and breaking of governments is thus a continuous process. It is the essence of parliamentary democracy.

We have assumed throughout this book that the leaders of parliamentary parties are motivated by their policy preferences when they make strategic calculations, whether these have to do with proposing alternative cabinets, agreeing to serve in a proposed new cabinet, or voting to put an alternative cabinet into office. We assume that these policy preferences are commonly known to all relevant actors, so that they serve as a basis not only for each politician's individual decisions, but also as a basis for expectations in the political community as a whole about what every politician will do. Such expectations lie at the heart of our adaptation of the classical spatial model, in the form of predictions about what a particular party politician would do if given a particular seat at the cabinet table. Since there is a finite number of potential cabinet ministers, there is a finite number of potential cabinets. Tracing out the policy implications of each potential cabinet transforms a continuous space of theoretically conceivable policy positions into a discrete set of politically credible pol-

[2]Of course, sensible politicians and analysts know that political shocks will surely come. What they don't know is what those shocks will look like, and how they will affect politics. The possibility that some governments may be more susceptible than others to shocks in general can, however, be taken into account, using techniques we explore in Chapter 10.

icy forecasts, one for each possible allocation of cabinet portfolios. This is the feasible set from which parliamentary parties select a government. We show in this book that there are rather general circumstances in which the government formation process, confined to this feasible set, generates equilibrium cabinets. The propositions of Part II explore these circumstances and the resulting equilibriums.[3]

In Part III of the book we subject the propositions derived from our model to systematic empirical assessment. We tease out empirical implications from our propositions and evaluate these in terms of the experience of the formation of real governments in postwar Western Europe. We also formulate a multivariate model permitting us to employ a conventional statistical methodology for further assessment. All in all, the results of these empirical evaluations are most encouraging.

Part IV of the book elaborates a number of theoretical and methodological themes and applies our model to a variety of substantive topics. We first explore the stability of the equilibrium cabinets we identify in Part II. The simulation technology we employ for this purpose allows us to go beyond the mere identification of equilibrium cabinets to a characterization of their ability to withstand unanticipated shocks, the political lightning bolts to which any real government is continuously exposed. We then examine the effects on our theoretical propositions of relaxing certain restrictive assumptions. Thus, we consider the impact of policy preferences that are correlated across issues, of interdependent preferences, and of alternative ways of partitioning the issue space into ministerial jurisdictions. Finally, we use our model to investigate intraparty politics, minority and surplus-majority government, divided government, and the administrative structure of the state. While hardly comprehensive, these elaborations do, we hope, convey the potential richness of our approach.

In the remainder of this, the concluding chapter of the book, however, we put details of our model and its empirical assessment to one side so that we can focus more clearly on some larger issues. It befits a modeling approach such as ours to attend to fine-grained microfeatures of the phenomena under investigation. But we now want to stand back from these details and concentrate on more general matters.

THE LINK BETWEEN PARLIAMENT AND THE CABINET

Ours is the first formal theory we know of that distinguishes explicitly between the cabinet and its parliamentary support coalition, differentiat-

[3]The conventional multidimensional spatial model is plagued generically by disequilibrium, leaving the analyst tongue-tied in forecasting what will happen in any government formation situation. Our characterization of the government formation process provides a path around this embarrassing circumstance.

ing executive structures and responsibilities from their legislative counter-parts. This distinction arises in a parliamentary democracy because the government has very considerable agenda-setting power, on the one hand, and substantial implementation authority, on the other. It exercises each of these, however, at the pleasure of parliamentary majorities. At any time of its choosing, a parliamentary majority can rise up and strike the government dead.[4]

Consider first the cabinet's power to set the political agenda.[5] The relative advantage of the cabinet vis-à-vis parliament does of course vary from place to place and from time to time. The nature of such variation depends mostly on the ability of parliament to bring independent judgment to bear upon the government's proposals, as well as on the formal need for the government to acquire statutory authority from parliament for its activities.[6] This relationship, however, stacks the deck heavily in favor of the government. The government, after all, has a large and expert civil service at its disposal. Even in those cases in which parliament may muster some limited resources for detailed policy evaluation, the government's control of procedural levers (*en bloc* and *guillotine* procedures in the French Assembly, for example – see Huber, 1992) is sufficient to neutral-ize these. Finally, a parliament may even be put at a disadvantage as a result of the absolute power it has over the life and death of a government. This power provides parliament with a mighty big club, but it is one that can be used only sparingly. Its very size discourages its use.[7]

Our model characterizes the government's institutional advantages as if the cabinet effectively runs the country without needing parliamentary approval for each and every policy move. So long as it maintains the overall confidence of parliament, something it must take care to maintain at all times, the model assumes that the cabinet can maneuver in a more or less unfettered manner. A natural avenue for further work, of course, would relax this stricture, modeling agenda power in a more subtle and differentiated fashion. However this development might proceed, one thing is almost certain to remain clear. Whatever else it might be, *parliamentary democracy is not rule by legislature.*

[4] A majority can only do this if it can find an alternative with which to replace the incumbent government.

[5] On this aspect our approach resembles that of Romer and Rosenthal (1978) and Rosenthal (1990).

[6] It is a nearly universal requirement that a government obtain parliamentary ap-proval for its annual budget. Beyond this, however, there is considerable variation in the statutory activity of parliaments, with the U.S. Congress surely at the hyperactive extreme.

[7] All of these comments suggest, however, that governmental statutory power in parliamentary democracies is comparable to that of committees in the U.S. Congress armed with restrictive procedural rules.

This last sentiment is no more obvious than in the implementation of public policy. The government *formulates* policy ex ante, and *implements* it ex post. Parliamentary control over policy implementation, as with its control over policy formulation, is constrained by ministerial control over the administrative structure of the state, something, as we noted, in which senior civil servants also have a big stake. Parliamentary oversight undoubtedly arrests the most outrageous and scandalous ministerial and bureaucratic behavior, but its effect on the shape of government policy is nonetheless likely to be minimal.

The big point to make about policy implementation, however, is that, by distinguishing government from parliament, our model emphasizes the administrative side of cabinet government, a vital matter that is ignored by approaches that essentially model parliamentary democracies as being run by their parliaments. Spatial models that focus on equilibrium policies, and ignore the cabinet as the instrument of policy formulation and implementation, implicitly assume that implementation is nonproblematic, indeed almost mystical – that once parliament speaks, its will be done! Our approach, in contrast, identifies numerous "agency" relationships – between cabinet and parliament, minister and cabinet, civil service and minister – in which there can be many a slip 'twixt cup and lip.

Thus, one of the major themes of our argument concerns the theoretical importance of the structural division of labor in any parliamentary democracy. Undergraduate comparative government texts like to make a stark distinction between European-style fusion-of-power parliamentary systems and U.S.-style separation-of-powers congressional arrangements. Our discussion of the connection between cabinet and parliament suggests that, while such distinctions surely exist, they are less cut and dried than is often imagined.

DEPARTMENTALISM

The division of labor in both policy making and policy implementation extends beyond the relationship between legislature and executive to the cabinet and to the administrative structure of the state itself. The agenda and implementation power that the cabinet exercises vis-à-vis the parliament is in turn exercised vis-à-vis the cabinet by individual ministers and their civil servants. While it is surely true that cabinets typically make many thousands of formal decisions each year (Laver and Shepsle, 1994), for any particular decision the cabinet table is usually set, ex ante, by the minister and civil servants with jurisdiction over the issue. And cabinet decisions are implemented, ex post, by the same people.

One of the impressive regularities we have encountered is the manner in which policy formulation and implementation is divided and specialized in parliamentary democracies. The shape of the administrative state is remarkably stable within the same country over time and relatively invariant across countries at any one time. While this empirical regularity stimulates our theoretical instincts, its explanation extends beyond the scope of the present volume. The mere fact of it, however, stresses the importance of treating the cabinet agenda as a product of the activities of relatively autonomous and independent politicians, each with specialized responsibility for policy formulation and implementation in some particular field.

This is what we mean by *departmentalism*. Its pervasive influence on the practice of policy making in parliamentary democracy gives structure to our analytical framework. Our model emphasizes that the cabinet is not simply a *collection* of coalition partners, but instead is a *distribution* of specific powers over policy formulation and implementation among those partners. Thus, the very same set of parties in a cabinet comprise quite different effective governments if cabinet portfolios are reallocated between parties. In our running simple example of three parties and two jurisdictions (Figure 4.1), there are two possible cabinets involving Parties A and B. These cabinets involve identical coalition partners, but are forecast to implement very different policies, depending on which party gets which portfolio. In our terms, it is misleading to treat these two quite different cabinets as if they were effectively the same government. Even initially skeptical country specialists with whom we have discussed our model have readily agreed that swapping two key cabinet portfolios (e.g., finance and foreign affairs) between parties is likely to have an impact on effective government policy, despite the fact that the same parties are in government.

The simple fact of departmentalism forces both theoretical and descriptive work to come to terms with differentiated authority within the government. The doctrine of collective cabinet responsibility, the notion that all ministers must either publicly support what is decided in cabinet or resign their posts, in no way conflicts with the operation of a decision-making regime effectively based on departmentalism. *Collective cabinet responsibility does not specify what the cabinet is collectively responsible for,* which is the main concern of our approach. Much of what is important about substantive policy, as we have argued consistently, is determined departmentally, under the political control of the relevant cabinet minister. Significant substantive changes in cabinet policy typically necessitate replacing the minister in charge of the department concerned.

Our characterization of departmentalism is, like our formulation of cabinet dominance over parliament, necessarily an abstraction from a rich and complex reality. There are at least three amendments to it that might profitably be pursued, each of which somewhat mitigates the im-

Governments and parliaments

pact of departmentalism. The first takes account of the fact that the ministers of a government engage in policy making continuously in real time, rather than setting policy parameters in their respective jurisdictions once and for all. Even after a government has formed, policy making involves ongoing strategic interaction among cabinet ministers. This is important because, as some readers may have noticed, most of the lattice points we deal with allow for the prospect of joint gains from cooperation between the participants who underwrite them. In the BA government in Figure 4.1, for example, the point BA is not Pareto optimal for its participants. Both participants would simultaneously prefer cabinet policy to move in a direction southwest of BA, toward the line joining AA and BB. Such policies would be closer to the ideal points of both Party A and Party B.[8] This could be achieved by Party B cooperating with Party A by moving finance policy to the left, in a manner preferred by Party A, in exchange for Party A moving foreign policy down, in a manner preferred by Party B. Note that Party B is made worse off by the concession it makes to Party A on finance policy, while Party A is made worse off by the concession it makes to Party B on foreign policy. If each party can be sure that the other will honor its side of the exchange, however, really changing *and implementing* policy in the manner suggested, then the losses they suffer by making concessions in their own jurisdiction are more than compensated by the concessions they receive from the other party. The key question, therefore, concerns how, when we are dealing with what goes on inside government departments, government parties might become confident that their partners will actually honor their side of any bargains made. Game theorists have made considerable progress on understanding the emergence of cooperation between people who have a private incentive to renege on a bargain if they can get away with it, establishing that such cooperative concessions may be sustainable as equilibriums of this game.[9]

There are several complications, however, that suggest we should be very careful indeed about incorporating the possibility of cooperation in such circumstances into a model of the making and breaking of governments. If subsequent cooperation of the sort outlined in the previous paragraph can take place, then it can be anticipated at the time of government formation. By backward induction and common knowledge, all actors will *not* then forecast a BA government to implement policy at BA, but rather at the policy point reflecting the equilibrium of the subsequent

[8]The line connecting the ideal points of the participants is the A–B *contract curve,* the set of points from which no movement could make both parties better off. This is the set of Pareto optimal points for the coalition of Parties A and B.
[9]The classic citations in the political science literature are Taylor (1976) and Axelrod (1984).

283

cooperation between cabinet members that is anticipated to take place. It is essential, therefore, to be sure we understand precisely what the equilibrium consists of.

Before we can do this we must appreciate that any cooperation between A and B does not take place in a vacuum. If cooperation fails, then BA is the *reversion point* policy for the bargaining in the BA government. At the end of the day, if one party or the other refuses to concede, then each party can simply revert to running policy within its own jurisdictions as it sees fit. But this is not all a party can do. Party B, for instance, can threaten to leave the bargaining table and begin consulting with Party C about forming a new government. Again, however, we must be clear on precisely what this threat entails. In effect, it is a claim that a new government will be formed, say between B and C. Party B's threat to leave Party A out of the action is a threat to implement a different policy point, one made credible by forming a new government. But the policy of a BC government will depend on promises and threats similar to those we discussed in relation to a possible deal between A and B. In short, we have a bargaining game with endogenous threats. We have not systematically examined this formulation, but should it yield an equilibrium in which at least some cooperation of the sort described previously takes place, then governmental policy will look less "departmental" than our model suggests.[10]

There is a second qualification to our assumption of departmentalism, arising less from technical considerations like those of the last few paragraphs and more from a substantive omission in the specification of our model. Country specialists report that a constant complaint from cabinet ministers in nearly every parliamentary democracy is the way in which the finance ministry pokes its nose into other ministers' affairs (Laver and Shepsle, 1994). This happens because the minister of finance and his or her civil servants in practice serve a dual role, both as a *line ministry* with

---

[10]If we were to model the emergence of cooperation inside a government between cabinet ministers, we would need to redefine our lattice of feasible governments. There would still be a discrete set of possible portfolio allocations, each with a forecast policy output. Such policy forecasts, however, impounding as they do the prospect of subsequent cooperation (taking potential endogenous threats into account as well), will most probably differ from those of the original lattice, which uses information only about party ideals. We are reluctant to take this road. The lattice of feasible governments, as we construe it in this book, gives us very considerable analytical leverage, and opens up what seem to us (and we hope to the reader) to be plausible interpretations of a wide range of phenomena related to the making and breaking of governments. We take the plausibility of these interpretations to be in themselves a vindication of our approach. While it is ultimately a matter of taste in modeling that others might feel differently about, we do worry that, if we abandon our lattice and complicate our model to make it more and more realistic, we will compromise some of its more suggestive substantive applications. The model would simultaneously become more realistic and less useful.

284

jurisdictional responsibilities of their own and as a *fiscal watchdog*.[11] It is in this latter capacity that the folks from finance may undermine the departmentalism that we have described. Departmentalistic tendencies are subjected, often on a case-by-case, policy-by-policy basis, to the rough justice of fiscal prudence as interpreted by the Department of Finance. Policy implementation in line ministries, then, is surely the product of departmental dynamics, but it is also affected by interministerial bargaining, with the finance minister at the hub of these negotiations.

The third factor with a bearing on the effects of departmentalism on government decision making concerns the role of the prime minister, a matter we alluded to in Chapter 2. There we emphasized the role of the prime minister in dealing with contingencies unanticipated at the time of government formation. Here we emphasize the activities of the prime minister, analogous to those just described for the finance minister, in coordinating policy decisions that cross departmental lines. That is, on precisely those issues that are novel or that are not easily pigeon-holed into departmental jurisdictions, the prime minister may be a more consequential agenda setter.

We nonetheless believe that departmentalism, as we have qualified it, is one of the most salient features of policy making in a parliamentary democracy. Despite the possibility that the finance minister and the prime minister play an important role in setting the political agenda, that agenda must inevitably be constructed out of policy proposals that are generated departmentally. The consequent division and specialization of labor involved in doing the public's business thus has profound effects on government outputs, effects that can be thoroughly anticipated at the stage of government formation. In our view, it is just not possible to understand why particular governments form without taking account of the departmentalism that will so heavily constrain the way in which they subsequently make their decisions.

CENTRIPETAL TENDENCIES

One of the foundations of formal political theory is Black's Median Voter Theorem, which emphasizes *centripetal* forces in politics. Whether voting occurs explicitly, or whether parties throw their weight around implicitly when they bargain with one another, there is an intuitive sense that politics is compromise, that the rough "extremist" edges of potential public policies are smoothed down in the political process, and that pivotal or decisive actors tend to be moderates that lie between the extremes. Black's famous

---

[11]For an empirical discussion of the role of finance ministers in cabinet government, see Larsson (1993).

result gives logical force to this intuition. Unfortunately, his conclusion depends on the restrictive assumption that alternatives are effectively unidimensional.[12] For more than a quarter of a century, formal theorists have tried to extend this result to multidimensional settings but, while there have been some interesting developments along these lines, they have for the most part been very modest (summaries are found in Riker and Ordeshook, 1973, and Enelow and Hinich, 1984, 1990). Indeed, to the contrary, the general result plaguing theorists is the *absence* of equilibrium altogether in multidimensional settings.

Our multidimensional model was not formulated as an abstract effort to generalize Black's Theorem but rather as a substantive attempt to understand the making and breaking of governments in parliamentary democracies. It has, however, generated equilibriums in a specific (lattice-based) multidimensional decision-making setting where none exists in the conventional (continuous) multidimensional model. The most striking property of these equilibriums, furthermore, is their spatial centrality. This is revealed in its strongest form when the dimension-by-dimension median (DDM) cabinet has an empty winset. This is the multidimensional generalization of Black, par excellence.[13] Austen-Smith and Banks (1990) established that the DDM cabinet always has an empty winset in the three-party, two-dimensional case. Our simulations not only confirm their result, but establish further that empty-winset DDMs are quite common in higher dimensional multiparty cases as well. Finally, our multivariate probit estimations demonstrate that an empty-winset DDM constitutes a powerful empirical predictor of government participation. In short, our model provides one clear-cut generalization of Black's result, in the form of an equilibrium cabinet at the DDM, a result given theoretical, empirical, and simulation-based support.

If empty-winset DDMs are the purest examples of a centripetal tendency in government formation, then the existence of strong parties adds a further argument in favor of this. Recall that, when a strong party exists, the equilibrium of the government formation game is either the strong party's ideal or an element of the winset of that ideal (Proposition 4.2).[14] The reason this proposition implies a centrally located equilibrium

[12]We have seen that this might be because there is only one salient issue, or as a result of perfect interissue correlations in the positions of all actors.

[13]In the conventional spatial model, Kadane's Theorem implies that if there is any equilibrium at all, it will be this very same DDM. But, in order for the DDM to be an equilibrium in the conventional model, a very restrictive form of symmetry in the distribution of actor ideal points must be satisfied, something not required in our portfolio allocation approach.

[14]In Part II we did not establish general conditions for the existence of a strong party. Our simulation results, however, suggest that they are very common in lowish-

is that the strong party tends to occupy a central spatial position and that its winset is also very central, relative to the distribution of party ideals. If the winset of the DDM is empty, then a strong party must be median on at least one key policy dimension. Of course a very strong party is median on all dimensions – its ideal is located at the DDM. If the DDM has a nonempty winset, then a strong party may be median on no dimension (e.g., Party D in Figure 4.2), but nevertheless is, as far as we can determine, "in the middle of things" according to most intuitive standards.

These theoretical grounds for the expectation of spatially central equilibriums in government formation are given very substantial support in our multivariate statistical analysis (Chapter 9). The probit models, both for the cases in which a strong party exists and those in which it does not, provide a powerful endorsement for the argument that government formation in parliamentary democracies will tend strongly to favor parties with more central policy positions.

Our model-based arguments about the centripetal tendencies of government formation in no way undermine conclusions about the generic instability of majoritarian social choice in multidimensional contexts. It does suggest, however, that if actors cannot commit themselves in advance to honor promises and threats, then this, perhaps counterintuitively, reduces the probability of decision-making chaos and helps centrally located actors. This is because the inability to make such commitments creates a basis for commonly held expectations that cabinet ministers will ultimately do what they want when they have the effective power to do so, rather than what they might say they will do when making promises to other parties in order to get into the government. Indeed, if politicians could irrevocably commit themselves in advance to implementing any conceivable policy position, then any point in the continuous policy space becomes the potential subject of such a commitment and hence becomes a potential government policy position. If this were the case, then we would observe government formation beset by the generic instability implied by the McKelvey-Schofield chaos results. This highlights very clearly the novelty of our argument, which flows from our presumption that, once they get firmly ensconced in their departments, ministers possess a discretion, ex post, that they simply cannot disable while they are bargaining, ex ante, over government formation.

ONE FINAL THOUGHT

As this project (or at least this phase of it) concludes, we feel rather like golfers who have used every club in their bag. The government forma-

dimensional spaces, even in moderately large party systems. Their frequency declines with dimensionality and size of party system.

tion process is rich in theory and in practice. Intellectually and scientifically, it invites any number of different analyses – descriptive, theoretical, empirical, and experimental. The social science community clearly possesses the ability to construct such analyses – strong descriptive skills, well-developed theoretical tools, powerful statistical methodologies, and promising experimental (simulation) approaches, on all of which we have relied heavily. We believe the most pressing current need for those who want to understand the making and breaking of governments in parliamentary democracies, however, is for reliable and systematic information on matters as diverse as procedural rules, administrative structure, party preferences, and the intestinal fortitude of the actors in a potential showdown – indeed, on every matter that we need to consider before we can implement a rigorous model of government formation for a real case.

Theory and intuition can only take us so far without a systematic description of the real world that they set out to interpret. Theory and intuition also, of course, have a huge impact on how we describe the real world, telling us what to look at and what to ignore. While we have indeed engaged in some quite substantial empirical analysis in Chapters 6–9 of this book, it is fair to say that our main contribution thus far has been theoretical rather than empirical. We now feel we have reached the point, however, where the most effective way forward is to use our theoretical approach to structure a more thoroughgoing empirical investigation of the making and breaking of governments, an activity that we take to be at the political heart of parliamentary democracy.

References

Austen-Smith, David, and Jeffrey Banks. 1988. Elections, coalitions, and legislative outcomes. *American Political Science Review* 82: 405–422.

Austen-Smith, David, and Jeffrey Banks. 1990. Stable portfolio allocations. *American Political Science Review* 84: 891–906.

Axelrod, Robert. 1970. *Conflict of Interest.* Chicago: Markham.

Axelrod, Robert. 1984. *The Evolution of Cooperation.* New York: Basic Books.

Baron, David. 1991. A spatial bargaining theory of government formation in parliamentary systems. *American Political Science Review* 85: 137–165.

Baron, David, and John A. Ferejohn. 1989. Bargaining in legislatures. *American Political Science Review* 83: 1182–1206.

Black, Duncan. 1958. *The Theory of Committees and Elections.* Cambridge: Cambridge University Press.

Blondel, Jean, and Ferdinand Müller-Rommel, eds. 1993. *Governing Together: The Extent and Limits of Joint Decision Making in Western European Cabinets.* London: Macmillan.

Blondel, Jean, and Ferdinand Müller-Rommel. 1993. Introduction. In Jean Blondel and Ferdinand Müller-Rommel, eds. *Governing Together.* London: Macmillan. Pp. 1–22.

Brams, Steven, and William H. Riker. 1972. Models of coalition formation in voting bodies. In James F. Herndon and Joseph L. Bernd, eds. *Mathematical Applications in Political Science,* vol. 6. Charlottesville: University Press of Virginia. Pp. 79–124.

Browne, Eric, and Karen Feste. 1975. Qualitative dimensions of coalition payoffs: Evidence for European party governments 1945–70. *American Behavioral Scientist* 18: 530–556.

Browne, Eric, and Mark Franklin. 1973. Aspects of coalition payoffs in European parliamentary democracies. *American Political Science Review* 67: 453–469.

Browne, Eric, and John Frendreis. 1980. Allocating coalition payoffs by conventional norm: An assessment of the evidence for cabinet coalition situations. *American Journal of Political Science* 24: 753–768.

Browne, Eric C., John P. Frendreis, and Dennis W. Gleiber. 1984. An "events"

289

approach to the problem of cabinet stability. *Comparative Political Studies* 17: 167–197.

Browne, Eric C., John P. Frendreis, and Dennis W. Gleiber. 1986. The process of cabinet dissolution: An exponential model of duration and stability in western democracies. *American Journal of Political Science* 30: 628–650.

Browne, Eric C., John P. Frendreis, and Dennis W. Gleiber. 1988. Contending models of cabinet stability: A rejoinder. *American Political Science Review* 82: 930–941.

Budge, Ian, and Hans Keman. 1990. *Parties and Democracy: Coalition Formation and Functioning in Twenty States.* Oxford: Oxford University Press.

Budge, Ian, David Robertson, and Derek Hearl, eds. 1987. *Ideology, Strategy, and Party Change.* Cambridge: Cambridge University Press.

Burch, Martin. 1993. Organizing the flow of business in western European cabinets. In Jean Blondel and Ferdinand Müller-Rommel, eds. *Governing Together.* London: Macmillan. Pp. 99–130.

de Swaan, Abram. 1973. *Coalition Theories and Cabinet Formation.* Amsterdam: Elsevier.

Dodd, Lawrence C. 1976. *Coalitions in Parliamentary Government.* Princeton: Princeton University Press.

Downs, Anthony. 1957. *An Economic Theory of Democracy.* New York: Harper and Row.

Enelow, James M. and Melvin J. Hinich. 1984. *The Spatial Theory of Voting: An Introduction.* Cambridge: Cambridge University Press.

Enelow, James M. and Melvin J. Hinich. 1990. *Advances in the Spatial Theory of Voting.* Cambridge: Cambridge University Press.

Fiorina, Morris P. 1991. *Divided Government.* New York: Macmillan.

Friedman, Milton. 1953. *Essays in Positive Economics.* Chicago: University of Chicago Press.

Gallagher, Michael, Michael Laver, and Peter Mair. 1995. *Representative Government in Modern Europe.* New York: McGraw-Hill.

Gamson, William. 1961. A theory of coalition formation. *American Sociological Review* 26: 373–382.

Hotelling, Harold. 1929. Stability in competition. *Economic Journal* 30: 41–57.

Huber, John D. 1992. Restrictive legislative procedures in France and the United States. *American Political Science Review* 86: 675–688.

Kadane, Joseph B. 1972. On the division of the question. *Public Choice* 13: 47–54.

King, David C. 1994. The nature of congressional committee jurisdictions. *American Political Science Review* 88: 48–63.

King, Gary, James Alt, Nancy Elizabeth Burns, and Michael Laver. 1990. A unified model of cabinet dissolution in parliamentary democracies. *American Journal of Political Science* 34: 872–902.

Klingemann, Hans-Dieter, and Andrea Volkens. 1992. Coalition government in the Federal Republic of Germany: Does policy matter? In Michael Laver and Ian Budge, eds. *Party Policy and Government Coalitions.* London: Macmillan. Pp. 189–222.

References

Larsson, Torbjorn. 1993. The role and position of ministers of finance. In Jean Blondel and Ferdinand Müller-Rommel, eds. *Governing Together*. London: Macmillan. Pp. 207–222.

Laver, Michael. 1994. Party policy and cabinet portfolios in Ireland 1992: Results from an expert survey. *Irish Political Studies* 9: 157–164.

Laver, Michael, and Audrey Arkins. 1990. Coalition and Fianna Fáil. In Michael Gallagher and Richard Sinnott, eds. *How Ireland Voted 1989*. Galway: Centre for the Study of Irish Elections. Pp. 192–207.

Laver, Michael, and Ian Budge, eds. 1992. *Party Policy and Government Coalitions*. London: Macmillan.

Laver, Michael, and W. Ben Hunt. 1992. *Policy and Party Competition*. New York: Routledge.

Laver, Michael, and Norman Schofield. 1990. *Multiparty Government: The Politics of Coalition in Europe*. Oxford: Oxford University Press.

Laver, Michael, and Kenneth A. Shepsle. 1990a. Coalitions and cabinet government. *American Political Science Review* 84: 873–890.

Laver, Michael, and Kenneth A. Shepsle. 1990b. Government coalitions and intraparty politics. *British Journal of Political Science* 20: 489–507.

Laver, Michael, and Kenneth A. Shepsle. 1991. Divided government: America is not "exceptional." *Governance* 4: 250–269.

Laver, Michael, and Kenneth A. Shepsle. 1992. Election results and coalition possibilities in Ireland. *Irish Political Studies* 7: 57–72.

Laver, Michael, and Kenneth A. Shepsle. 1993. A theory of minority government in parliamentary democracy. In Fritz W. Scharpf, ed. *Games in Hierarchies and Networks*. Boulder, Colo.: Westview Press. Pp. 429–447.

Laver, Michael, and Kenneth A. Shepsle, eds. 1994. *Cabinet Ministers and Parliamentary Government*. Cambridge: Cambridge University Press.

Mackie, Thomas T., and Richard Rose. 1991. *The International Almanac of Electoral History* (rev. 3rd ed.). Washington, D.C.: CQ Press.

McKelvey, Richard D. 1976. Intransitivities in multidimensional voting models and some implications for agenda control. *Journal of Economic Theory* 12: 472–482.

McKelvey, Richard D., and Norman Schofield. 1986. Structural instability of the core. *Journal of Mathematical Economics* 15: 179–198.

McKelvey, Richard D., and Norman Schofield. 1987. Generalized symmetry conditions at a core point. *Econometrica* 55: 923–933.

Müller, Wolfgang C., Wilfred Philipp, and Peter Gerlich. 1993. Prime ministers and cabinet decision-making processes. In Jean Blondel and Ferdinand Müller-Rommel, eds. *Governing Together*. London: Macmillan. Pp. 223–258.

Müller-Rommel, Ferdinand. 1993. Ministers and the role of the prime ministerial staff. In Jean Blondel and Ferdinand Müller-Rommel, eds. *Governing Together*. London: Macmillan. Pp. 131–152.

Peleg, Bazalel. 1981. Coalition formation in simple games with dominant players. *International Journal of Game Theory* 1: 11–13.

Plott, Charles. 1967. A notion of equilibrium and its possibility under majority rule. *American Economic Review* 57: 787–806.

References

Riker, William H. 1962. *The Theory of Political Coalitions*. New Haven: Yale University Press.

Riker, William H., and Peter C. Ordeshook. 1973. *An Introduction to Positive Political Theory*. Englewood Cliffs, N.J.: Prentice-Hall.

Romer, Thomas, and Howard Rosenthal. 1978. Political resource allocation, controlled agendas, and the status quo. *Public Choice* 33: 27–44.

Rosenthal, Howard. 1990. The setter model. In James M. Enelow and Melvin J. Hinich, eds. *Advances in the Spatial Theory of Voting*. Cambridge: Cambridge University Press. Pp. 199–235.

Schofield, Norman. 1978. Instability of simple dynamic games. *Review of Economic Studies* 45: 575–594.

Schofield, Norman. 1986. Existence of a "structurally stable" equilibrium for a non-collegial voting rule. *Public Choice* 51: 267–284.

Schofield, Norman. 1987. Stability of coalition governments in Western Europe: 1945–1986. *European Journal of Political Economy* 3: 555–591.

Schofield, Norman. 1992. A theory of coalition government in a spatial model of voting. Political Economy Working Paper, Washington University, St. Louis.

Schofield, Norman. 1993. Political competition and multiparty coalition governments. *European Journal for Political Research* 23: 1–33.

Shepsle, Kenneth. 1979. Institutional arrangements and equilibrium in multidimensional voting models. *American Journal of Political Science* 23: 27–60.

Strom, Kaare. 1990. *Minority Government and Majority Rule*. Cambridge: Cambridge University Press.

Taylor, Michael. 1976. *Anarchy and Cooperation*. Cambridge: Cambridge University Press.

Taylor, Michael. 1987. *The Possibility of Cooperation*. Cambridge: Cambridge University Press.

Thiebault, Jean-Louis. 1993. The organisational structure of western European cabinets and its impact on decision-making. In Jean Blondel and Ferdinand Müller-Rommel, eds. *Governing Together*. London: Macmillan. Pp. 77–98.

van Deemen, A. M. A. 1989. Dominant players and minimum size coalitions. *European Journal of Political Research* 17: 313–332.

van Roozendaal, Peter. 1990. Centre parties and coalition formations: A game theoretic approach. *European Journal of Political Research* 18: 325–348.

van Roozendaal, Peter. 1992. The effect of dominant and central parties on cabinet composition and durability. *Legislative Studies Quarterly* 17: 5–36.

van Roozendaal, Peter. 1993. Cabinets in the Netherlands (1918–1990): The importance of "dominant" and "central" parties. *European Journal of Political Research* 23: 35–54.

Warwick, Paul. 1992a. Rising hazards: An underlying dynamic of parliamentary government. *American Journal of Political Science* 36: 857–876.

Warwick, Paul. 1992b. Economic trends and government survival in west European parliamentary democracies. *American Political Science Review* 86: 875–887.

Warwick, Paul, V. 1994. *Government Survival in Parliamentary Democracies*. Cambridge: Cambridge University Press.

References

Warwick, Paul, and Stephen Easton. 1992. The cabinet stability controversy: New perspectives on an old problem. *American Journal of Political Science* 36: 122–146.

Williamson, Oliver. 1985. *The Economic Institutions of Capitalism.* New York: Free Press.

Winter, Lieven de. 1993. The links between cabinets and parties and cabinet decision-making. In Jean Blondel and Ferdinand Müller-Rommel, eds. *Governing Together.* London: Macmillan. Pp. 153–178.

Woldendorp, Jaap, Hans Keman, and Ian Budge. 1993. Political data 1945–1990: Party government in 20 democracies. *European Journal of Political Research* 24: 1–120.

Index

administrative structure, exogenous, 271
    See also decisive structure
Alt, James, 7n4, 45
Arkins, Audrey, 145
Austen-Smith, David, 54, 112, 204, 286
Axelrod, Robert, 11n9, 156n12, 261,
    283n9

Banks, Jeffrey, 54, 112, 204, 286
bargaining
    advantages of coalition in, 186–187
    politicians' motivations in, 18–20
bargaining power
    factors influencing party's, 186–187
    of large parties, 186
    of very strong government, 264
Baron, David, 11, 12, 30n6, 57n15, 58,
    112
Black, Duncan, 9
Black's Median Voter Theorem, 9, 285–
    286
Blondel, Jean, 31, 32
Brams, Steven, 112
Browne, Eric, 12, 202n3
Budge, Ian, 12, 27, 129, 151n5, 236
Burch, Martin, 13, 32, 37, 38
Burns, Nancy E., 7n4, 45

cabinet
    See also cabinet in equilibrium; minority
        cabinet
    control of legislative agenda, 41
    as government, 28–30
    in government formation process, 43–46
    parties in minority government, 262–
        263
    perception of, 28–29
    retaining confidence of legislature, 48–49
    with strong party, 69–71

cabinet, caretaker
    with no-confidence vote, 56
    policy of, 46–48
    status quo of policy, 46–48, 50–51, 55
cabinet, status quo
    function of, 46–48, 50–51
    in government formation model, 147,
        162–166
    relation of legislature to, 55
    strategic equivalent of, 65–66
cabinet equilibrium theory, 17
cabinet in equilibrium
    See also cabinet stability
    attractive and retentive forms, 61–62
    concept of, 61
    DDM cabinet, 66–69
    destabilizing shocks, 196–197
    at dimension-by-dimension median, 215
    effect of decisions on, 39
    effect of identity of cabinet in winset,
        198–199
    government formation in Germany,
        125–139
    in government formation model, 147
    moving from unidimensional to complex
        jurisdictions, 241
    simulation of destabilizing shocks, 200–
        203
    strong party representation in, 73–74
cabinet ministers
    as agents of their party, 24–25, 33
    discretion of, 32–33
    as heads of government departments,
        30–32
    responsibility of, 36–39
    veto power, 50–51
cabinet portfolios
    See also key portfolios; portfolio alloca-
        tion

295

Index

Index

Index

301